Stop, Look, Listen
Celebrating Shabbos Through a Spiritual Lens

MAGGID

Nehemia Polen

STOP
LOOK
LISTEN

CELEBRATING SHABBOS
THROUGH A SPIRITUAL LENS

Maggid Books

Stop, Look, Listen
Celebrating Shabbos Through a Spiritual Lens

First Edition, 2022

Maggid Books
An imprint of Koren Publishers Jerusalem Ltd.

POB 8531, New Milford, CT 06776-8531, USA
& POB 4044, Jerusalem 9104001, Israel
www.maggidbooks.com

Cover photo: "Smeared Sky Sunset" by Matt
Molloy (@MattMolloyPhoto)

The publication of this book was made possible
through the generous support of *The Jewish Book Trust*.

ISBN 978-1-59264-570-1, *hardcover*

Printed and bound in the United States

CONGREGATION AHABAT SHOLOM

151 Ocean Street, Lynn MA 01902

From its founding in 1901 until its closing 120 years later,

CONGREGATION AHABAT SHOLOM
LYNN, MASSACHUSETTS

was the place where generations of people nourished their spiritual lives, found friendship, and held closely to each other in times of joy and in times of need – and where Kiddush after Shabbos services was simply unsurpassed.

To honor the legacy of this beloved Shul, to remember the dear rabbis and rebbetzins, leaders, members, and friends who gave so much to create and sustain this worthy, holy congregation – our support of 'Stop, Look, and Listen' is proudly dedicated.

May the warm memories of Ahabat Sholom remain in our hearts, be passed on l'dor v'dor, and continually inspire all who seek and all who cherish love of peace.

The Carlebach Shul
in dedication

Some years ago, in response to requests made by visitors to The Carlebach
Shul to provide direction on how to enhance their Shabbat experience, the
Board of Trustees undertook a project to develop materials which could
accompany our unique and uplifting Carlebach davening. Although Carlebach
melodies are known throughout the globe, the many Torah teachings
emanating from our humble abode have not been so readily available.

With the goal of unlocking some of the deeper teachings pertaining to
Shabbat, we turned to Rabbi Nehemia Polen, a brilliant Judaic scholar
who, together with his wife Lauri, has spent many a Shabbat as scholar
in residence with us, sharing his uncommon and captivating observations
with the Chevra. Nehemia is a "destination speaker" whose insights and
commentaries are so integrated into Torah and Rabbinic texts that one
wonders how one may interpret the text in any superior fashion.

We would like to thank the following organizations and
individuals for enabling this great undertaking:

The Covenant Foundation for supporting our mission

Rabbi Naftali Citron, our Rabbi and community leader

Leon and Karen Sutton, tireless laborers on behalf of our
community, who co-sponsored this work in memory of their parents,
Murad and Adele Sutton and Sam and Toby Ehrlich

Shy and Tami Yellin, pillars of our community, who co-sponsored
this work in memory of their parents, Leonard and Florence
Yellin and Rabbi Dr. Samuel and Miriam Stern, to whom they
are eternally grateful for their example, love, and vision

**Ilan and Debbie Richland, Oren and Mira Richland, Chana and
Jeremy Kanzen, Rifka Meyer, Sora and Rafe Ibgy**, co-sponsors, in
honor of their parents, Faye Richland (a former long-time member
of The Carlebach Shul during the lifetime of Reb Shlomo),
Dr. Paul and Beverly Weber, and Simcha and Shifra Richland

Liron and Talia David, long-time members of The Carlebach Shul, who
co-sponsored this work in honor of their parents, Rafi and Julie David z"l
and Moussa and Shulamit Soleimani, whose love and respect for Shabbat,
along with their values and warmth, have always been a guiding light.
Liron and Talia follow in their footsteps as they raise their children with
deep respect and appreciation for the Almighty, family, and community.

Libby Dreisinger and Barbara Meyer, early enablers of this project

For my parents

Rabbi David S. Polen ע״ה
and Nettie (Keller) Polen ע״ה

and Lauri's parents

Reb Noah Wolff עמו״ש
and Marilyn (Rudin) Wolff עמו״ש

who inspired us to cherish Shabbos

Contents

Prelude

From its earliest days, The Carlebach Shul has been blessed with a beautiful tradition. The Shul is known not just for its spirited Shabbos davening, which has become quite popular, but for the whole Shabbos experience – Friday night dinners, *Seuda Shelishit,* Havdala, and *melaveh malka.* These shared Shabbosim bring the teachings of the Baal Shem Tov and the Maggid, along with their students and their students' students, to life. The Shul on W. 79th St. feels like an extension of Mezibuz or Berditchev.

Over the years, we have hosted many wonderful guest rabbis and teachers. One of these teachers, Rabbi Dr. Nehemia Polen, stands out for his exceptional ability to conjure up the hasidic masters in an articulate way, drawing from the deep wells of the teachings of the Baal Shem Tov, the Rebbe of Chernobyl, the Sefas Emes, and the Piaseczner Rebbe. This book is about more than sharing ideas. It is about helping people share Shabbos with each other. The ideas in this book will taste better with gefilte fish and chicken soup (or their vegan alternatives).

We would like to thank the Covenant Foundation for their generous grant, allowing us to share our Shabbos experience with others. The mission of the Covenant Foundation is to uphold the verse in

Isaiah (59:21): "This is My covenant with you.... The words which I have put into your mouth shall not depart from you, not from your children, not from your children's children henceforth and forever." We would also like to thank Nehemia for his outstanding scholarship and his warmth. As a professor of Jewish studies and a rabbi who is passionate about his students and who loves Torah, he is uniquely able to marry a rigorous academic approach with a warm, inviting, and uplifting teaching style.

We hope that in this work you will be able to appreciate not just Nehemia's scholarship and depth, but also the spirit of the Baal Shem Tov and his followers and the vibrancy they brought into Judaism.

Rabbi Naftali Citron
October 11, 2021
The Carlebach Shul

Preface

My father was a heavy smoker. If my childhood memories are accurate, his habit exceeded a pack a day. He was not proud of this fact, but there was, so he said, nothing he could do about it. He had started in his teens, during a period when, as he recalled, smoking not only had positive social cachet but also the endorsement of many medical professionals. Advertisements featuring physicians would tout smoking as a healthy practice: "Reach for a Lucky Strike instead of a sweet."

On Shabbos, my father didn't smoke. This was not surprising, since our family was *shomer Shabbos* (Sabbath observant), as we called it. What was remarkable, however, was the fact that my father did not feel the urge to smoke on Shabbos. With the welcoming of Shabbos came a release from the incessant desire to light up another cigarette. Shabbos freed my father from enslavement to tobacco. I recall him once expressing dread of the moment when, just after Havdala (the liturgy of bringing Shabbos to a close on Saturday evening after nightfall), the ache for nicotine would reappear. What was it about our family's Shabbos observance that supplanted, if only for a day, his intense physiological need and psychological dependency?

It is the experience of Shabbos in my childhood home that motivates me, in part, to write this book.

There are many books that present Shabbos as an opportunity for celebration, for sanctifying time, for deepening family ties, and, of course, for rest and relaxation, a necessary respite from the weekly grind. Each of these perspectives captures an aspect of the day's significance. Together, they highlight beneficial outcomes of Shabbos observance, but they do not reach the core of Shabbos – Shabbos's sheer *palpability,* heft and presence, felt so strongly and so tangibly that addictions are pushed aside, making room for air in body, love in heart, grace in spirit, light in soul. To be touched by Shabbos's richly vibrant and animate personality is to be transformed, liberated. How does this come about?

I recall the sounds of my father's review of the weekly Torah reading every Friday afternoon. He had been chanting Torah since his bar mitzva many decades earlier, and he knew the entire Torah nearly by heart, but discipline and reverence led him to review the following day's synagogue reading. This was sacred preparation, and the fact that he used an old, tattered *Tikkun* (Bible specially designed for cantillation practice) only added to the sense of noble vocation. Friday also brought the smells of my mother's cooking and, close to sunset, the sight of her candle-lighting with tenderness and devotion, beseeching the Almighty for blessing upon her household.

A particularly strong memory is that of our family coming home after Shabbos morning services. One could feel the joy of arrival when my parents returned to their modest residence, offering refuge from the noise of street traffic and the frenzy of weekday life. My father would open the door and pronounce in a hearty Yiddish, "*Gut Shabbos!*" But who was he saying "Good Sabbath" to? The house was empty! It dawned on me that he was addressing the house itself – the house as person, as living being with agency and presence, having achieved that status by my parents' work of preparation that culminated at sunset on Friday but was in fact unfolding all week long.

Shabbos's presence is invited and made palpable by purposeful cultivation. It exists in space as much as in time, and it involves a thousand preparatory thoughts and acts that transpire before the onset of the day. If life is an overgrown forest whose tangled branches tear at our skin as we race to traverse it, Shabbos is a graceful clearing that makes room for breath and blessing.[1]

This is a truth that my parents learned from *their* parents. Both sets of grandparents came from Russia in the early years of the twentieth century, my father's parents to the Lower East Side of Manhattan and my mother's parents to Providence, Rhode Island. Family lore emphasized the struggle to remain *shomer Shabbos* in the face of strong economic and social headwinds. My parents lived Shabbos and passed it on to me and my brothers, imparting it as sacred practice, the legacy that is the most precious part of our family heritage.

When I met Lauri, the woman who would become my wife, I was delighted to discover that her family traditions were very similar to mine, especially with respect to Shabbos observance. Her fondest childhood memories involve walking to synagogue as a family and singing *zemirot* (hymns serenading the day) at the Shabbos table. She appreciated that her parents presented Shabbos not as a day of restrictions, but rather as a time of uninterrupted togetherness. To this day, Lauri recalls the long walk from home to synagogue as a time to be close, to converse, or to luxuriate in trusting, loving silence. Her father's work involved hundreds of miles of driving weekly. He did not need to verbalize his commitment to surrender the car for a day; it impressed itself silently and effortlessly.

Lauri and I both came of age at the height of America's love affair with the automobile. The mid-twentieth century American auto was a work of art on wheels, exuding stylish elegance and panache. The parallel decision of our respective families to forgo on Shabbos the appeal of this icon of modernity – signifying effortless mobility, empowerment, social status, and independence – was a clear statement that spiritual values reigned supreme in our households.

But there was another marvel of engineering that for a while threatened to impair our experience of Shabbos – television. My parents were early adopters of this technological wonder, which, like all such advances throughout history, was promoted as not just a scientific

---

1. The phrase "graceful clearing" is from Wendell Berry, *The Country of Marriage* (New York: Harcourt Brace Jovanovich, 1973), 7.

breakthrough but as an agent of cultural and even moral progress. Educational programs would elevate the level of learning in every household. News would be accurate and more informative because it would be conveyed in pictures as well as words; everyone knows that one picture is worth a thousand words, and furthermore, pictures don't lie. American families would now be able to view Shakespeare in the comfort of their homes! And so on.

It did not take long for powerful economic forces to take control and for astute observers to recognize that programming, in a race to the bottom, had quickly become a "vast wasteland."[2] But by then it was effectively too late. The TV set dominated our small family room that we called "the den," and I was in the thrall of situation comedies and action shows that in retrospect can only be called truly insipid.

What about Shabbos? Saturday morning was prime time for cartoons, and the urge to watch them seemed irresistible to one young boy in Boston, Massachusetts. For a while, we settled on the following arrangement: The TV would not be turned off Friday afternoon, but the controls would not be touched on Shabbos. This meant that I could select one channel among the three available. My choice was made with care and due diligence, maximizing access to the programs I most wanted to see. Of course, this inevitably had an impact on Shabbos morning. Arrival time at services kept slipping later and later, and sacred benedictions were sidelined by the likes of *Bugs Bunny and Friends*.

I don't recall how long Saturday morning cartoons lasted at our house (possibly as long as several years), but eventually they came to an end. It may not have been verbalized in quite this way at the time, but it became clear that this arrangement did not conform to the spirit of Shabbos. The Shabbos home – meant to be a refuge from invasions of all kinds, especially commercial encroachments and shallow distractions – needed to be safeguarded and returned to its state of quietude and equilibrium. What is remarkable is that Lauri's family in Gary, Indiana, went through essentially the same trajectory – first

---

2. The phrase was made famous by Newton Minnow, then chairman of the Federal Communications Commission, in a speech delivered in 1961 to the National Association of Broadcasters.

leaving the television on during Shabbos, and then realizing that (as Lauri's father put it) "the television needs to rest, too."

I mention our parallel experiences to indicate that the hegemony of brightly shining novel devices is not inevitable; it can be resisted and even rolled back by the soft power of Shabbos. Our two families – separated by nearly a thousand miles and entirely unknown to each other at the time – went through matching lines of development, first allowing and then subduing the brash interloper.

This supremacy of Shabbos – so urgently needed to tame our own era's new devices with their siren song of connectivity and unlimited content – depends on truly inviting Shabbos to take up residence in our homes, our hearts, and our neighborhoods.

These considerations lead to the following questions: What is the core of Shabbos experience? How can it be cultivated, sustained, enhanced? What is the most effective way to introduce Shabbos to those not familiar with it? What is the best way to explain Shabbos to newcomers, as well as to those who have grown up with it, who consider themselves veterans but may be in danger of lapsing into habit and taking Shabbos for granted? How can we immerse ourselves in the sublime delight that this day offers in a way that totally surpasses the beckoning immediacy of flickering screens? These are some of the questions that this book seeks to explore.

A lexical note: I speak of "Shabbos," rather than "Shabbat" or "Sabbath." This is the way I heard the word pronounced as I was growing up. It is the way my parents and grandparents spoke as they honored the day in an American environment that was generally resistant or actively hostile to it. My grandparents brought Shabbos as their most precious possession from the Old World of Eastern Europe, and they saw themselves as carrying forward the heritage of untold generations before them. The alternate forms are equally authentic, to be sure. But since one of my goals is to present Shabbos as a family legacy and to invite readers into that legacy, it is important for me to refer to the day in the way that seems most natural, that comes to me honestly and without affectation.

Introduction

S habbos is the generative kernel at the center of the Jewish spiritual universe.

A parable:

Rabbi Jacob Kranz (1741–1804), known as the Maggid (preacher) of Dubno, told the following story in a sermon about Shabbos:

> A poor man was trudging along the road on foot, carrying a heavy duffel bag on his shoulder. Suddenly, he was overtaken by a large, well-appointed carriage, drawn by a team of handsome horses. Carriages such as this would usually pass him by, leaving him in the dust or even splattering him with mud. But this time, the carriage stopped. A nobleman called out from the window, "Would you like a ride?" The poor man gratefully accepted the offer, boosted himself up, and took a seat. At first, the nobleman, engrossed in his papers, did not glance at his passenger, but eventually he looked up and noticed that the poor man was still holding the bag, his shoulder bent from the weight. The nobleman said, "Why are you still carrying your load? Why didn't you take it off and place it in the cargo space?"

The poor man replied, "I was so grateful for your kindness in stopping to give me a lift, I didn't have the audacity to ask you to carry my baggage as well!"

The nobleman smiled and said, "But don't you realize that even with your duffel on your shoulder, I am carrying your baggage anyway?"[1]

This parable holds several layers of meaning that call for careful unpacking. First of all, Shabbos is about stopping. The poor man is given respite from his exhausting trek by the grace of the wealthy nobleman who stops to offer entry into his carriage. Perhaps it is weariness that does not allow the poor man to realize that he can put down his load. Force of habit keeps the duffel bag on his shoulder until specifically prodded. He must be awakened to the realization of his new situation in the carriage – a place of buoyant grace and kindness – and this does not happen at once. It takes new awareness, and most of all trust in the goodness of his benefactor, to release the weight on his shoulder.

As a preacher, the Dubno Maggid's style was to explicate the moral of his parable, not only by placing it in the context of scriptural verses, but also by making the story's meaning explicit in the lives of his listeners.

The Maggid explains that God carries all creatures, as the verse states, "I created you and I shall carry you" (Is. 46:4). Every human being is freighted with burdens, especially the burden of earning a living. For the Eastern European Jews whom the Dubno Maggid was addressing, that burden was often crushing. The point of the parable was to frame Shabbos as an exercise in trust. Shabbos meant not only ceasing from work but also – what was much more difficult – ceasing to think about work, halting the endless internal ruminations about customers, markets, supplies, regulations, accounts payable, taxes, making enough profit to survive and feed one's family. Many workers lived day to day, never far from the threat of actual starvation and destitution. Ceasing from work one day a week took genuine courage and commitment. The Maggid knew his people; although they might be physically in the synagogue,

---

1. *Mishlei Yaakov*, ed. Moshe Nisbaum (Jerusalem 5749/1989 [1875]), 158–59.

their minds were still consumed by work-related worries. Deeper trust required putting down the duffel bag in the carriage provided by God – the carriage called Shabbos.

This lesson is as timely today as it was in the late-eighteenth century. Not all of us have the same kind of economic pressures as Jewish laborers in the old country, though we should not dismiss job worries even in our own day. But new types of burdens have appeared, mostly due to technological innovations that promise convenience and connectivity but have tethered and tangled us in a way unprecedented in history. The burden now is fear of missing out – what some have archly tagged with the acronym FOMO. The latest email, text, update, newsfeed, blogpost, tweet – the urgent swirl of audible pings and visual flags demanding our attention has become an irresistible burden. More than ever, we need to realize that the carriage has pulled up at our side, that a domain of safety and repose beckons, and that we can put down the burden of boundless distraction, so that we can enter the realm of the sacred and reencounter the world, each other, and our own selves.

THE NATURE OF THIS BOOK

There are many kinds of books about Shabbos. Perhaps the most common type addresses the laws of the day, giving procedural instructions in line with the halakha. The writing tends to get technical very quickly; I know of one such effort that attempts a comprehensive presentation in four densely packed volumes. There are works that give a pragmatic rationale for Shabbos observance as a time to refresh and recharge, noting that rest and time off from work are necessary for optimal human functioning, especially in our 24/7 world. Some books provide a poetic evocation of the sublime spirit of the day, while others introduce the reader to the world of Kabbala and its symbolism in order to lay the groundwork for a mystical understanding of Shabbos as the time for cosmic restoration and unification. Other books suggest engaging family activities, while others offer instructions for ḥalla-baking and cooking traditional Shabbos foods.

The theological significance of Shabbos is emphasized by some writers; this perspective is rooted in the Torah itself, which emphasizes that observance testifies to God's creation of heaven and earth in six days (see Ex. 20:11, 31:17). The theological rationale was developed with great sophistication by Rabbi Samson Raphael Hirsch (1808–1888), who argued that desisting from *melakha*, "work" as defined by the Mishna and Talmud, is a proclamation of God as Creator of all things, an assertion of human subordination to God, and an affirmation of the creation account in Genesis 1. Hirsch's rationale, which frames *melakha* as creative manipulation and mastery of the physical world, has enjoyed much popularity and is often quoted in expositions of the laws of Shabbos.

A new genre has appeared recently, in which the author describes his or her experiment with the Shabbos lifestyle, reporting on the experience as a tourist with literary talent might do after a visit to a foreign country. This genre might be called the "Shabbos travel memoir," as it combines elements of personal discovery, exotic experience, and pratfalls and mishaps, along with lessons learned and (perhaps) wisdom gained. The exemplars I have seen tend to be tentative and ambivalent, mixing admiration for Shabbos-keeping with doubts about feasibility in the modern world.

Given all the halakhic manuals, theological treatises, how-to guides, and other works endeavoring to explain and motivate Shabbos observance on utilitarian or religious grounds, the reader may fairly ask what I hope to add to an already crowded landscape.

Before responding to this question, I want to focus on one book that deserves special mention, Abraham Joshua Heschel's *The Sabbath: Its Meaning for Modern Man*. The book was first published in 1951, near the beginning of the post-war American boom, a time when spiritual aspirations were largely eclipsed by a focus on technological innovation and the striving for material success and economic growth. In this milieu, *The Sabbath* appeared with its powerful statement of the supremacy of spirit. A landmark of expository eloquence, it helped countless individuals grasp the mood of the day.

Heschel's book is a love poem to Shabbos, highlighting its role in the sanctification of time. Indeed, he places the elemental reality of time and its potential for sanctity at the very center of Judaism's message. The seventh day, Heschel teaches, is an eruption of eternity into time.

The aphoristic gems that give the book its sparkle and energy succeed in conveying the day's sublimity and transcendence. *The Sabbath* may have been the first work to introduce to the English reader the majestic poetry, evocative mystique, and luminous glow of this most enchanting and sublime day, explaining why the relationship between Shabbos and the community of Shabbos observers is a romance, a passionate love story.

Yet all this magic is accomplished with little specific information on what Shabbos observance entails. The "Palace in Time" of which Heschel speaks is so inviting, but just how is the palace constructed? While *The Sabbath* remains an enduring classic that deserves a place in any English-language reading list of recommended books on Shabbos, its message must be augmented and its focus expanded. Shabbos needs to be anchored in specific practices, objects, and spaces, realizing holiness in place and material bodies – especially human bodies and the objects they lovingly hold – and thereby transforming ordinary time into sacred space-time.[2]

Sacred space and sacred time come to us dovetailed, jointly braided in the fabric of being. They are affiliated, mutually reinforcing dimensions of sacred reality. By giving due attention to both sacred space and sacred time and underscoring their tight interconnection, one sets the stage for an appreciation of Shabbos that has room for embodiment, material objects, locatedness, and the formation of social communities of physical proximity.

A robust religious phenomenology must bring into the conversation the earliest identifiable work of Jewish mysticism, *Sefer Yetzira*.[3] A key teaching of *Sefer Yetzira* is that reality is composed of three fundamental

---

2. See the observations of Marcia Falk, *The Book of Blessings* (Boston: Beacon Press, 1999), 42–44. I thank my daughter Adina Polen for alerting me to this text. For similar views based on classic rabbinic sources, see David Kraemer, "The Sabbath as a Sanctuary in Space," in *Tiferet LeYisrael: Jubilee Volume in Honor of Israel Francus,* ed. Joel Roth, Menahem Schmelzer, and Yaacov Francus (New York: Jewish Theological Seminary, 2010), 79–91.

3. Precise dating of this work is debated and varies widely, but I consider the third or fourth century of the Common Era the most plausible dating for the core text, which circulated orally for centuries before being committed to writing. In the Geonic and medieval periods, *Sefer Yetzira* became a foundational work for a variety of esoteric trends in Judaism: philosophical mysticism, magical-shamanic mysticism, and, in particular, the luxuriant symbolic world of the Kabbala, as developed most richly in the Zohar.

axes: *Olam/Shana/Nefesh* – Space/Time/Person. Features found in any one of these axes map isomorphically onto the other axes, and the three must always be taken holistically, forming an indivisible relational lattice.[4]

A discussion of Shabbos must include the most central of places, the home. It is the home where Shabbos is welcomed and celebrated, enacted, and made tangible – where Heschel's "palace in time" becomes a luminous residence in space and in human hearts. Furthermore, the network of Shabbos-keeping homes creates a Shabbos community. In community, individuals express their social nature and practice ethical virtues, especially the virtues of hospitality, generosity, and listening. These communal practices enable Shabbos-observers to avoid the hazard of Heschel's admonitory words that "through my ownership of space, I am a rival of all other beings."[5] When a cluster of householders greets Shabbos in concert, those homes become a cradle of welcoming relationships. Shabbos neighborhoods have a beckoning pull and a firm center.

How-to guides, theological tracts, halakhic manuals, utilitarian rationales, and metaphysical poetics all have a role in presenting Shabbos, but there is a pressing need for another approach. *Stop, Look, Listen: Celebrating Shabbos Through a Spiritual Lens* takes the view that holding space is essential for Shabbos, but rather than a display of territoriality, this is a gracious beckoning. By keeping Shabbos, we construct *invitational* space.

WHAT IS SPIRITUAL PRACTICE?

Since this book will focus on spiritual practice in relation to Shabbos, it is important to clarify what I mean by this term. There are many situations in life when we may feel spiritual, but transforming vague and fleeting sentiments into full-fledged and robust spiritual practice requires focus, intentionality, and long-term commitment. When we devotedly engage in a suite of actions that remove calcification and sharpen awareness, foster deeper ethical sensibility, open our eyes to more noble horizons,

---

4. This point is made by Rabbi Re'em HaKohen in his illuminating essay, "*Makom* [Place]" (Otniel, 5775/2015), 12–13. My thanks to Avinoam Stillman for pointing me to and providing me with a copy of this work.
5. *The Sabbath* (Cleveland and New York: Meridian Books, 1963), 99.

and free our feet from the web of earthbound entanglements and our hearts from gauzy illusions, then we are in the blessed domain of spiritual practice.

Prior to entering the practice space, it is important to set one's intention. This means having an idea – not overly specific but not entirely inchoate either – of what one seeks to achieve, the goal one hopes to reach, and how this particular engagement will transform one's being. Setting intention establishes a safe harbor against distraction and a compass to give direction and propel the spirit forward.

Spiritual practice is greatly enhanced when a supportive community sustains it. This can be a community in time as well as in space. The practitioner is in dialogue with masters who helped show the way, who formulated guidelines and gave suggestions, and whose achievements are treasured – mentors who may have lived in one's own day or perhaps thousands of years ago.

Furthermore, there is dialogue with generations yet to come, who will look to you for guidance, example, and inspiration. The spiritual practitioner is always asking: What can I leave for the benefit of others who will one day inhabit this space and embrace this practice?

Spiritual practices work best in ensemble, as elements in a palette of multi-hued actions and dispositions. For example, later in this book we will explore *niggun* – sacred melody – as a core spiritual practice in Hasidism, but *niggun* fulfills this role most effectively when it is one element of a coherent panoramic system, embracing prayer, study, contemplation, dance, quietude and silence, as well as other facets of a vibrant devotional life. The entire ensemble focuses intently on internal states – sensations, perceptions, emotions, cognitive spaces – all marshaled in the service of higher aspiration, uncovering deeper levels of soul. Mindful intentionality must precede the practices, assuring that they rise beyond mere aesthetic uplift, emotional stimulation, and self-cultivation.

This is what it means to say that Shabbos is spiritual practice. Shabbos is an integrated suite of intentions and actions that transform the practitioner in positive, noble, and sublime ways, moving the individual beyond self-absorption toward an expansive, exhilarating domain of transcendence and higher purpose.

Shabbos is *embodied* spiritual practice. Shabbos's dispositions and spiritual states are grounded in and flower from choices made by the practitioner before Shabbos begins, choices relating to where and how to locate the embodied self. Further choices are called for as Shabbos proceeds, in a coordinated itinerary that fuses action and intention, body and spirit.

The spiritual practice of Shabbos is anchored in a tradition that imparts depth, wisdom, capaciousness, transgenerational experience, resilience, dynamism, and momentum. Jewish tradition, beginning with the Bible, provides the vocabulary and the syntax for the language of Shabbos as spiritual practice. Reverence for the traditional framework is essential for entry into the practice, yet each faithful practitioner leaves a personal stamp on the practice and on the tradition itself.

The fact that Shabbos is not a modern strategy designed to relieve contemporary problems ("Too much time on the internet? There's an app for that!") but an ancient institution – arguably the most ancient, universally accepted cultural time-marker based on spiritual values – gives Shabbos enormous depth, resonance, and power. Shabbos is not a contrivance, not a scheme dreamed up adventitiously, but a sacred interval, a devotional cadence that has been with humans longer than the reach of human memory.[6]

Shabbos, like all spiritual practices, is cumulative, asymptotic. Practices are never fulfilled perfectly; one is always aiming for closer and closer approaches to the goal. They demand focus, seriousness of purpose, accountability, and the willingness to start anew. Whether a particular effort has reached its aim, fallen far short, or something in

---

6. The fact that calendrical institutions lose legitimacy when they are contrived to advance political and economic agendas is noted in I Kings 12:33, where Jeroboam is critiqued for celebrating a holiday on the fifteenth day of the eighth month, "the month he had contrived of his own mind." Jeroboam, the secessionist Northern king, is seen by the biblical author as illegitimately attempting to simulate the festival of Sukkot/Tabernacles a month later than the fifteenth day of the seventh month mandated by Leviticus 23:34. The warning against calendrical contrivance has been disastrously disregarded by schemers over the centuries, especially during the French and Russian revolutions, both of which saw attempts to create new calendars uncoupled from biblical models; lacking ancient gravitas, they quickly collapsed and were rolled back unceremoniously.

between, we return with fresh energy and commitment. Both neophyte and veteran practitioners are always learning, always growing, always on the path. The nominal end is not a terminus, but rather sets the stage for the next encounter.

In his memoir, *Practicing*, Glenn Kurtz vividly describes the joys and struggles of a guitarist aspiring to a career as a world-class virtuoso. Kurtz is candid about the challenges he faced and the setbacks he suffered as he realized that he would never achieve the mastery or fame of a Segovia. Abandoning the goal of a professional performance career, Kurtz came to embrace practice as an act of love. He writes, "Practicing music – practicing anything we really love – we are always at the limit of words, striving for something just beyond our ability to express."[7] "Practice gives direction to your longing."[8] Kurtz quotes the cellist Pablo Casals, who, each day for eighty years, began his day by playing two preludes and fugues of Bach. As Casals says, "Each day it is something new, fantastic, and unbelievable."[9]

Kurtz evokes the discipline of practice as a narrative that lifts up and weaves the strands of one's life in struggle, joy, faith, and longing, "absorbing what is within you and making it productive. Because when you truly believe your story of practicing, it has the power to turn routine into a route, to resolve your discordant voices, and to transform... disappointment into the very reason you continue."[10]

This wisdom applies to Shabbos. One approaches the perfection of Shabbos every week but never reaches it. Every Shabbos is unique and different, with its own sublime texture and taste, and therefore always leaves room for the tantalizing attraction of the Shabbos to come.

Seeing Shabbos through a spiritual lens charts a different path alongside presentations that frame Shabbos as religious obligation, theological affirmation, utilitarian boon, or metaphysical poetics. Shabbos is a concrete commitment that is life-affirming, joyous, and intensely pleasurable, but also demanding. To receive Shabbos's blessings most

---

7. Glenn Kurtz, *Practicing: A Musician's Return to Music* (New York: Vintage Books, 2007), 7.
8. Ibid., 15.
9. Pablo Casals, *Joys and Sorrows* (New York: Simon and Schuster, 1970), 17; citation from Kurtz, *Practicing*, 6.
10. Kurtz, *Practicing*, 19.

fully, one must be truly open to them, ready to embrace them and ready for the stretch that the embrace entails.

Many introductory tracts elide the fact that Shabbos takes effort. As the Torah says, we "make Shabbos" (Ex. 31:16). Active focus is required to reach the sublime state of Shabbos, and one must be given guidance and mentoring. Merely reading about Shabbos is not enough; one must direct effort to make it happen. The deeper the commitment, the more profound the life-changing outcome. Touristic excursions into Shabbos territory are unlikely to lead to lasting transformation.

Every spiritual practice invites the practitioner to make a commitment. Articulating Shabbos practice with clarity enables one to fully grasp what the commitment entails. That is my aim in this book. The practice of Shabbos is multi-stage, flowering and ripening over a full day, understood in the Jewish sacred calendar as extending from sundown Friday to nightfall Saturday.[11] During the course of this twenty-five hour period, you are in one place. By holding that place, you dive more deeply into your own life and those of your loved ones. You ennoble and refresh the habits of your heart; you inhabit the inner recesses of your soul.

THE THREE STAGES OF SHABBOS

Shabbos has its own flow, a sequential arc of posture, perception, and awareness. The sequence unfolds in three stages that choreograph mood and ambience in sync with the path of the sun – sunset-sunrise-gradual fading of sunlight and bringing the day to closure.

---

11. From antiquity, commentators have discussed the literal meaning of the phrase "And there was evening and there was morning" (Gen. 1:5, 8, 13, 19, 23, 31); see Nahum Sarna, *The JPS Torah Commentary: Genesis* (Philadelphia: The Jewish Publication Society, 5749/1989), 8, on Genesis 1:5. Sarna cites Rashbam, who interprets the phrase to mean that the day begins with the dawn. But there is strong biblical warrant for taking the liturgical day as extending from evening to evening, as mandated regarding the "Shabbos" of Yom Kippur (Lev. 23:32). Adele Berlin and Marc Brettler point to Psalms 55:18, which speaks of pleading to God "evening, morning, and noon," suggesting that "the liturgical day began at or after sunset, as in post-biblical Jewish practice." See Adele Berlin and Marc Zvi Brettler, *The Jewish Study Bible*, second edition (Oxford and New York: Oxford University Press, 2014), 1328. Of course, as Sarna notes, in the Jewish religious calendar, "the Sabbath and festivals commence at sunset and terminate at the start of the following night" (p. 8).

I have adopted the rubrics **Stop, Look, Listen** for these stages. I remember these terms fondly from my childhood as essential features of road-safety education, and they remain important today not only for children but for adults as well, as we endeavor to traverse the path of life with care and wisdom. This triad is more than a catchy mnemonic, however. The sequence follows the three modalities of Shabbos as they emerge from biblical and rabbinic texts, as well as from the legacy of our people's practice over millennia.

The key move of Friday evening is **Stop**. Friday's sunset beckons us to the zone of safety that God has provided, inviting us to put down our burdens (as in the parable of the Dubno Maggid) and enter into Shabbos. **Stop** involves committing to a locale, settling into place, and completely letting go of the world of work, which includes any endeavor whose focus is earning a living, buying and selling, business decision making, finance, or investments. **Stop** means setting aside all communication devices, all enablers of vehicular mobility, and financial instruments of any kind. This act is the most significant commitment you can make to your neighborhood, your family, and yourself. It is a profound affirmation that anchors you in the *here* and the *now*, but also locates you in Shabbos's infinitely rich past and luminous future.

First light of dawn and morning sunrise bring the opportunity to **Look** at the world with fresh eyes, eyes bathed in grace and gazing with benevolence. Then, late Shabbos afternoon, as the natural light of the sun slowly fades, there is the opportunity to **Listen** with greater presence and acuity – to ambient sounds, to the voice of loved ones and wisdom teachers, to the whispers of one's own heart, to the silence of the infinite.

The three stages are cumulative, growing in amplitude and richness in a coordinated fashion, executed in unbroken sequence. Their power emerges from presence and commitment that are not just uninterrupted but also uninterruptable. The ability to **Look** in the morning depends crucially on having come to a full **Stop** the night before, and the sweet stillness of **Listen** on Shabbos afternoon is the result of having spent a full day in the ambit of Shabbos's tranquil domain.

The interaction goes in both directions. My **Stop** on Friday night is informed and influenced by my awareness that I will rise in the morning in the same location with fresh eyes and see the world anew. Furthermore,

I will be spending the next twenty-four hours with people who have made the same situated commitment I have, and my goal is to be able to **Listen** to them more deeply, with greater attentiveness and sensitivity, and therefore come to know them and myself better.

Stop, Look, Listen is a schema, a heuristic that I hope will be helpful to the reader in introducing the three stages of Shabbos, but like all schematizations, it is not meant to be taken too rigidly. Each stage interacts with, is informed by, and is infused with the other two. Their power and effect rise together or not at all.[12]

I suspect that some introductions to Shabbos elide the step of commitment to a disciplined practice because they do not want to presume to offer directives. I, too, do not want to appear overly prescriptive, but I owe it to the reader to articulate the practice with clarity and conviction as it has come down to me from my parents and as (so I hope) my grasp has deepened through study, reflection, learning from teachers, and proximity to virtuosi.

SHABBOS AS LOCALIST PRACTICE

Many books on Shabbos avoid discussing the key step of committing to one location for a full day. Perhaps it is because this immersive resolve flies in the face of the human infatuation – especially in the modern age – with mobility, with change, with the illusion of absolute erasure of limits or encumbrances of any kind, with denial of embeddedness. We feel it is our right to move about effortlessly, unimpeded by constraints, in particular the constraints imposed by inhabiting a physical body, located in one place at any one time. The poet Robert Frost expressed this well: "What comes over a man, is it soul or mind/That to no limits and bounds he can stay confined?"[13]

Expositors of Shabbos often rhapsodize about the infinite, about how the spirit of the holy day soars above all mundane boundaries. They speak the truth. But there is another side to the story that provides an essential

---

12. This is also true of the *sefirot*, the ten divine manifestations of the Kabbala. It is a complete misunderstanding to take them as static representations of divinity; all kabbalists understand them as dynamic constellations interacting and shaping each other in an ever-fluid cosmic divine dance.
13. Robert Frost, "There Are Roughly Zones."

counterpoint to the discourse of infinity, one that emphasizes limits and the boundedness that comes with embodiment. Shabbos has a strong localist emphasis, in principle and in practice. The Bible's first introduction to the special character of the seventh day in Genesis emphasizes God's calling a halt to the process of creation, manifesting awareness of conclusion and the sense of an ending. Over the millennia, the Garden of Eden story (Gen. 2–3) has been taken literally, metaphorically, or allegorically, but one thing is clear – the narrative voice wishes readers to enter the Garden in their mind's eye as a *place*, carefully located at the head of four named rivers. While Genesis 1 invites humans to dominate and range over "the whole earth" (Gen. 1:26), in Genesis 2, God *emplaces* the first human in the Garden (2:15). I would actually translate the Hebrew word *vayaniḥehu* as "installed" or "ensconced." This Hebrew word shares the same root as one of the classic descriptors of Shabbos – *menuḥa*, typically translated as "rest," but which, as we will see in a later chapter, is better rendered "equipoise" or "tranquility." It is also worth noting that the first time the word *"sham"* (there) is found in the Bible is in Genesis 2:8: "The LORD God planted a garden eastward, in Eden, and *there* placed the person God had formed." Gertrude Stein's famously cutting remark about her birthplace, "There's no there there," finds its anticipatory reversal in the Garden of Eden narrative – this is where the very idea of *there* comes from. Exile from the Garden means not just estrangement but displacement. In this reading, the yearning for Eden is fundamental to human existence, a constitutive core of the human psyche.

The pain of displacement is underscored in Genesis with the fate of Cain (4:12), and the punishment of exile is a central concern of the entire Bible. But Shabbos is a kind of return to Eden, and this involves not just entering a time apart, but returning to the locatedness and emplacement of the Garden. With confidence and conviction, we can reply to the first question God poses to human beings: "Where are you?" (3:9).[14]

An essential aspect of human nature is revealed by observing that the urgency of knowing one's position is even greater than the urgency

---

14. It is worth noting that while nowadays the word "nostalgia" is generally employed rather dismissively to describe overwrought romantic longings for an idealized past, the term was once a rigorous medical diagnosis; nostalgia was a disease of displacement. Insofar as Shabbos effects a return to Eden, it is the antidote to this condition.

of knowing the date and time. Consider: A person waking from a coma first says, "Where am I?" and only then, "What day is it?"[15]

In the book of Exodus, God enjoins the people not to leave their place on the Shabbos (Ex. 16:29). When we look to the prophets, the emphasis on boundedness and location is even more pronounced. Isaiah makes it clear that the essence of honoring Shabbos is restraint in all aspects of life. He particularly underscores setting limits to travel, as well as refraining from business activities and workaday conversation:

> If you restrain, because of Shabbos, your feet; refrain from pursuing your affairs on My holy day; if you proclaim Shabbos as delight, God's holy day as honored, and you honor it by not engaging in your own ways, not attending to your own affairs, nor speaking of material matters... (Is. 58:13)

Isaiah's concern with setting limits extends to the moral dimension as well. This explains the relationship between the verse just quoted and the verses that precede it in that seminal chapter, which is read in the synagogue as the *haftara* (prophetic selection) for Yom Kippur, the holiest day of the year. The earlier verses condemn superficial acts of piety and stress vigorous pursuit of justice and active intervention on behalf of the poor and vulnerable:

> To share your bread with the hungry, and bring the homeless into your house; when you see the naked, you should cover him, and hide not yourself from those most close to you. (Is. 58:8)

When such juxtapositions are noted in the Hebrew Bible, it is generally said that Judaism makes no distinction between moral and ritual demands and that both are essential for the religious path. While this is correct, the deeper truth indicated by our Isaiah passage is that the

---

15. Edward Tuck, pioneering entrepreneur in Global Positioning System (GPS) technology, writing in the prospectus for Magellan Navigation, Inc. (1986), as cited by Greg Milner, *Pinpoint: How GPS Is Changing Technology, Culture, and Our Minds* (New York and London: W. W. Norton, 2016), 89.

Shabbos rules are not to be seen even provisionally as merely ritual enactments; they are ethical from their very inception.

The prophet asserts that when we observe boundaries, when we settle in to one place and refrain from overreach on Shabbos, we are granted genuine expansiveness and a buoyant freedom:

> Then you shall delight yourself in the LORD; and I will mount you upon the heights of the earth, and nourish you with the heritage of Jacob your father, for the mouth of the LORD has spoken. (Is. 58:14)

Isaiah assures us that local is not narrow.

Shabbos is about *the recognition of human limits, acceptance of individual boundedness.* Respect for boundaries is the essence of Shabbos – boundaries of the self, the body, and the human ego. Awareness of the humanity and dignity of others is therefore at the very core of Shabbos observance. Setting limits to one's sense of personal entitlement, self-empowerment, and self-importance is part and parcel of being within Shabbos. Bringing the poor into one's house and one's heart is the true enactment of *teḥum Shabbos* – the rabbinic term for Shabbos boundary-awareness.

Creating a Shabbos atmosphere is an important element in welcoming the day. Nothing beats the aroma of *ḥalla* baking in a kitchen oven to suffuse an entire house with joy and delight in both body and spirit. Setting the table with white tablecloth and best dinnerware invokes a luxuriant mood of sublime expectancy and noble occasion. But we should not introduce Shabbos with detailed suggestions for ambience while omitting the key practice of settling into place and coming to a complete stop for a full day. By way of analogy, consider a tract on hatha yoga that gives advice on attire, incense, lighting, background music, ideal room temperature, décor, and the like, but never explains that yoga involves situating oneself on or astride a mat, executing postures that may stretch the limits of one's comfort zone in order to cultivate deeper states of bodily and mental awareness. Even beginners must know that when the feet are securely in place and in proper alignment, one inhabits one's physical and spiritual place with equipoise. Much the same can be said for the spiritual practice of Shabbos. Ambience deserves attention, but nothing is more important than committing to one specific place and the inhabitation of self and connectedness with others that follows.

Young people who have attended a Shabbos-observing summer camp often attest to the enchantment and transformative power of Jewish camping, in large measure because campers experience the fullness of Shabbos, week after week, perhaps for the first time in their lives. They participate in the alternation of sunset-sunrise-nightfall with the accompanying rites and celebrations, they live the rhythm of **Stop, Look, Listen**, and most of all, they tacitly learn the power of joining with a like-minded cohort, a convivial community that embraces them with the bonds of sweet celebration and shared sacred space.

Adults may have a similar experience on a retreat that includes Shabbos. Such retreats are destination events, where participants travel to a set location and commit to a structured program in a group setting. This assures that, like summer campers, they are available to each other and to a central noble focus in a manner that would not be possible with the manifold distractions of their regular lives.

But in truth, every Shabbos is a destination event, even for city dwellers. The fact that one orders one's life to ensure arrival at a particular place by sunset on Friday, and that others who share the same commitment are doing so as well, means that a Shabbos society is being formed, that sacred space is arising, that a convivial community is awaiting.

Choice is indispensable for religious life in our day. Religious cultures reliant on coercion or compulsion never turn out well. Thank God, we live in a time when we can choose our practices. But choice works best when it is informed choice, and this calls for a full-throated articulation of a practice as seen by an enthusiast. Each and every Shabbos observance – every liturgical word intoned, every song sung, every special meal prepared and enjoyed, every synagogue service celebrated – is of infinite worth and fulfills the Decalogue mandate of "Remember the Shabbos day to sanctify it" (Ex. 20:8). That said, it is my deep conviction and personal experience that something new and unexpected emerges when individuals traverse the trajectory of **Stop, Look, Listen** for a full sunset-through-nightfall period. An emergent property of sacred embodied space is constructed.

One's being undergoes a phase transition that is not fully explainable or predictable from the individual elements. This is especially true when the trajectory is experienced in community, in concert with a like-minded collectivity. One encounters a higher order of being, a dispensation that can justifiably be called paradisic.

By advancing **Stop, Look, Listen** as the heart of Shabbos, as the armature around which everything else is wound, it is my hope that a new paradigm for understanding Shabbos will emerge, opening to a practice that is not only celebratory but also transformative. While this emergent surplus of meaning is ultimately inexpressible, it is the aim of this book to point to it and surround it by an envelope of specific movements and postures. There are no guarantees, least of all in the spiritual life, but the first step in realizing a goal, preceding even the realization that the goal is attainable, is the awareness that the goal exists.

The emphasis on spiritual practice leads to a fresh approach to biblical sources for Shabbos. Many expositions look to the account of the building of the Tabernacle (Ex. 25–40) as a model for the types of world-constructing activities that must be avoided on Shabbos, the day when such interventions must cease. The Tabernacle is a microcosm of the world, and in rabbinic analysis, the account of its construction becomes a template for rigorous definition and classification of *melakha*, "work" as a legal category, leading to the development of the list of thirty-nine rubrics of *melakha* listed in Mishna Shabbat (ch. 7). The talmudic discussion aims for consistent and logical definition, and the list of thirty-nine categories reflects the rabbinic impulse for articulating clear taxonomic groups. Furthermore, it examines the role of intention (*maḥashava*) and the interplay between intention and action (*melekhet maḥashevet*). These are all important topics when we seek to place the concept of Shabbos "work" on firm conceptual footing and subject it to scholarly analysis. But this project of tight classification may not be the best point of entry when we are interested in Shabbos as spiritual practice. Indeed, in the biblical account of events during the first few months after the exodus from Egypt, Shabbos is introduced to the Israelites early in the narrative, well before the Tabernacle account, even before the Revelation at Sinai and the Decalogue (Ex. 19–20).

Shabbos is introduced precisely one month after the exodus, when the supply of matza that the freed slaves took from Egypt ran out and people were given manna, described as "bread from heaven" (Ex. 16). The narrative informs us that the children of Israel ate manna for the entire forty years of their wilderness trek. They frequently balked at this diet, and the narrative makes much of their resistance and recalcitrance. But a close reading makes clear that a central aim of this episode is the introduction not just of manna but also of Shabbos. The manna did not fall on Shabbos; a double portion mysteriously appeared on Friday, and the people were told to prepare it, by baking and cooking, for the holy day to follow. In addition to preparation, the people were asked to settle in and stay in place on Shabbos. These elements – preparation beforehand and settling in and remaining in place on the holy day – are the core practices of Shabbos, then and now. Every other element of Shabbos observance and celebration is built on this foundation, and we shall examine Exodus 16 carefully to attempt to learn its lessons well.

This book also turns to the world of Hasidism for guidance. The great hasidic masters, beginning with the Baal Shem Tov, were wisdom teachers who assisted their followers in pathways of spiritual advancement. They showed how to apply the mystical symbolism of the Zohar and other kabbalistic texts to the human psyche, so that it could guide practitioners in a more vibrant and meaningful life of prayer, contemplation, and devotion. In particular, hasidic masters gave powerful guidance in awareness and presence, in coming more deeply into the self so that one can be of service to others and to God. By showing the path to a rich inner life, they advanced the project of Judaism by drawing upon resources going back to the Bible itself.

The hasidic emphasis on presence and mindfulness is relevant in all times and places, but, as we shall see, it speaks with special resonance on Shabbos. Furthermore, Hasidism provides a rich treasury of sacred melodies, tales, Torah discourses, and contemplative techniques that enhance and deepen Shabbos observance and celebration.

SUMMARY OF OUR GOALS

The following are some of the goals of this book on Shabbos:

- Articulating Shabbos as full-day uninterrupted practice – **Stop, Look, Listen** – in phases linked to the natural cycle of solar movement: setting – rising – setting
- Foregrounding place (including home, neighborhood, and community) in Shabbos observance
- Offering fresh readings of core biblical passages relevant to Shabbos, such as the creation narrative in Genesis and the manna story in Exodus
- Applying hasidic wisdom for experiencing Shabbos as the ultimate immersive rite, leading to full *presence*
- Explaining how Shabbos forms a field of force, a gradient of holiness transforming every aspect of life in blessed ways, reversing estrangement, achieving locatedness, and restoring access to one's inner being
- Showing how Shabbos fosters a gift-exchange relationship with God – each partner in the relationship achieving attentiveness and awareness. On Shabbos, God is felt as palpable, sensate Presence.
- Showing how Shabbos-consciousness percolates into the week, transforming and elevating mundane time, safeguarding the virtuous dispositions realized on Shabbos
- Finally, while Shabbos proclaims a much-needed technological interregnum, a respite from the corrosive effects of social media and commercialized surveillance, Shabbos's deepest blessings are not utilitarian but in the realm of the sacred. Shabbos is cessation that is *directed*, a vector of intentionality focused on divinity, aimed and lovingly handed up to God as offering. Shabbos enables us to feel ḥibbat hakodesh – the sweet, precious embrace of the sacred. A textured landscape of indescribable beauty, Shabbos is the greatest, most noble gift we can give to the world, to our communities, to ourselves, and to God.

Chapter 1

How to Think About Shabbos

THE ORIGINS OF THE SEVEN-DAY WEEK

The near-universal prevalence of the seven-day week – from a secular perspective, an arbitrary convention – is traceable to the Hebrew Bible and Judaism.

Regarding the biblical origin of Shabbos, Nahum Sarna writes, "The biblical institution of the weekly Sabbath is unparalleled in the ancient world. In fact, the concept of a seven-day week is unique to Israel."[1]

---

1. Nahum Sarna, *The JPS Torah Commentary: Genesis* (Philadelphia: The Jewish Publication Society, 5749/1989), 14. In the same vein, Baruch Levine writes that "the Sabbath is an original Israelite institution." Levine dismisses the supposed identification of the seven-day cycle with Mesopotamian markings of the phases of the moon, insisting that "the biblical Sabbath has nothing to do with the lunar cycle" and is a uniquely Israelite innovation. See Baruch Levine, *The JPS Torah Commentary: Leviticus* (Philadelphia: The Jewish Publication Society, 5749/1989), 237. Similarly, Carol Meyers, after noting the wide range of historical theories that have been suggested to account for the origins of the biblical Sabbath, dismisses them all as implausible and suggests that "the Sabbath actually originated among the Israelites." See Carol Meyers, *Exodus: New Cambridge Bible Commentary* (New York: Cambridge University Press, 2005), 133.

The classical world did not know of the seven-day week until it was adopted from Judaism and then mediated by Christianity. University of Chicago historian and Librarian of Congress Daniel J. Boorstin writes:

> Why a *seven*-day week? The ancient Greeks, it seems, had no week. Romans lived by an eight-day week.... The Roman change from eight to seven seems not to have been accomplished by any official act. By the early-third century A.D., Romans were living with a seven-day week.
>
> There must have been some popular new ideas afloat. One of these was the idea of the Sabbath, which appears to have come to Rome through the Jews.[2]

Robert Goldenberg provides more detail. Citing Josephus, he notes "a long series of Roman laws...in which the right of the Jews to observe the Sabbath without disturbance was recognized and protected." Goldenberg concludes his essay as follows:

> The Christian week in its final form is the product of...the ancient Hebrew notion of the Sabbath, eventually revived by the Church but transformed into something new, the practical need of the Church for a recurring day set aside for liturgical gathering, and the distinction acquired by a certain day during the last decades of imperial solar monotheism. The week which thus emerged from the Jewish Sabbath was carried by the Church to the far corners of the earth, and eventually became the legacy of the entire world.[3]

Struggling Against Headwinds

During much of the history of Christendom, seventh-day Shabbos was often treated with contempt; Jews faithful to Shabbos were frequently beset by legal restrictions. In modern times, the extractive capitalism of

---

2. Daniel J. Boorstin, *The Discoverers* (New York: Vintage Books, 1985), 13.
3. Robert Goldenberg, "The Jewish Sabbath in the Roman World up to the Time of Constantine the Great," in *Rise and Decline of the Roman World*, ed. Wolfgang Haase (Berlin: De Gruyter, 1979), 446.

the United States brought a different, but no less intense, challenge. Factory owners desiring to maximize profit were largely unsympathetic to the religious needs of workers. Immigrant laborers who crowded the tenements of the Lower East Side, desperate to eke out a livelihood, would seek work in the sweatshops. Many wanted to keep Shabbos but would be told, "If you don't show up on Saturday, don't come in on Monday."[4]

The struggle of Shabbos observers to remain true to their ancestral practice benefited our society at large. According to *The Atlantic*:

> In 1908, a New England mill became the first American factory to institute the five-day week. It did so to accommodate Jewish workers, whose observance of a Saturday sabbath forced them to make up their work on Sundays, offending some in the Christian majority. The mill granted these Jewish workers a two-day weekend, and other factories followed this example.[5]

By the 1950s, post-war economic prosperity and contracts negotiated by powerful unions made the two-day weekend standard in many industries.

---

4. See Jonathan Sarna, *American Judaism: A History* (New Haven and London: Yale University Press, 2004), 159–65. Sarna recounts the early struggles of Harry Fischel (1865–1948), who later in life became a successful businessman and prominent Jewish communal leader. In his early years as a new immigrant, he found work but was dismayed at the requirement that he come in on Saturday or lose his job. At the end of his first week, he was about to succumb, but as he prepared to go to the office on Shabbos after attending early-morning services, he experienced what he described as a "mysterious manifestation of the divine power" that enabled him to resist what he considered "the greatest temptation he had ever known." As Sarna recounts, "Fischel lost his job but subsequently prospered – good fortune that he credited to his lifelong 'principle' of Sabbath-observance" (p. 163).

5. Philip Sopher, "Where the Five-Day Workweek Came From," *The Atlantic* (August 21, 2014). See also Benjamin Kline Hunnicutt, "The Jewish Sabbath Movement in the Early Twentieth Century," *American Jewish History* 69, no. 2 (December 1979): 196–225. Hunnicutt describes how in the early decades of the twentieth century, rabbinic leaders joined forces with the labor movement in demanding a five-day workweek. In addition to the straightforward argument that a shorter workweek provided stressed and overburdened factory workers with necessary leisure, the rabbis argued that the Jewish Sabbath countered modern materialism and the "gospel of consumption," clearing time for higher pursuits and transcendent values.

For second- and third-generation American Jews, the economic pressures may have been less acute, but cultural trends – including the rise of suburbia, near-universal ownership of automobiles and the romanticization of mobility, individualism, and freedom, and the ascendancy of consumerism, with weekends dedicated to shopping at the mall – all conspired to weaken traditional Shabbos observance. Our own time is characterized by cultural amnesia. Many young Jews do not know of Shabbos in the biblical sense – as cessation, as full stop, as committing to one particular place – even as an outmoded vestige of a distant past. They have simply never heard of it. When introduced, it comes as a revelation.

"DAY OF REST"?

The most common framing of Shabbos is as a "day of rest." Yet Shabbos-keepers may not have too much time for rest on Shabbos. They are actively engaged in study, prayer, sacred meals, sharing insights and stories, singing, hosting and visiting family and friends, taking in the world with open heart, noticing how the sun orchestrates the cycle of dark-light-dark, and in general inviting themselves and their companions to touch the deepest places in their individual and collective souls.

Rather than sedentary relaxation, Shabbos calls for maximum alertness and focused awareness. This is the time to ponder what really matters in one's life and how to increase the scope and clarity of one's vision.

Whatever Shabbos is, it has little to do with "rest" as conventionally understood. Foregrounding Shabbos's utilitarian function as a boon for our overscheduled, increasingly fast-paced lives is appealing and points to something genuine, but it overlooks the deeper truth that the "rest" we achieve is a gentle clearing of space that opens the heart to blessing and holiness aiming for the sublime. Shabbos is the most dynamic and vibrant, non-sedate day of the week.

Astute cultural observers point to the tyranny of technology and the need to decouple from electronic devices that tout convenience but mostly entangle us in an endless web of distractions. Indeed, one virtue of Shabbos in our time is the proclamation of a technological interregnum, a domain of freedom and a refuge from the mere simulation of connectedness. Shabbos is a time of genuine availability to ourselves and others, a shelter of compassionate spirit. Yet here too we must not place the pragmatic motivation first and foremost. As a spiritual practice, we should think of Shabbos as a gift from God to us and an offering from ourselves to God. Overemphasis on utilitarian considerations tends to undermine the power of the practice. The inner freedom achieved by keeping Shabbos is a blessing to us; it is unseemly and likely counterproductive to claim worldly benefit as the primary reason for observance.[6]

What, then, is Shabbos? It is the day when core Jewish spiritual practices such as *niggun* (sacred melody), prayer, study, storytelling, and interpersonal sharing find their most robust expression and when core spiritual dispositions – such as joy, respect, and loving-kindness – are most fully realized. It is the time best suited to practice desirable ethical traits and to bring those traits, dispositions, and practices to higher levels and make them available for the rest of the week and the entirety of one's life. The practices and dispositions should not be considered in isolation but in concert, as a coherent, cohesive suite whose goal is to impart meaning, propulsive direction, and noble aspiration for the individual and the community. The habits of heart, mind, and spirit fostered by Shabbos percolate everywhere.

---

6. Emmanuel Levinas points to this in his essay "Desacralization and Disenchantment," in *Nine Talmudic Readings*, trans. Annette Aronowicz (Bloomington and Indianapolis: Indiana University Press, 1990), 136–60. He elucidates the talmudic passage in Sanhedrin 67a–68a, a complex discussion combining legal analysis with dramatic narrative that, *inter alia*, explores the structural relationship between Shabbos on the one hand and magic or sorcery on the other. In Levinas's understanding, "sorcery" means "the sacred degenerating into the prestige of technique." As he goes on to say, there is an expression of technique that is rational, at the service of human ends, and this may devolve into "a technique that is the source of illusion, a technique which allows the production and sale of [material goods]: the technique displayed by the beneficiaries of stock exchange speculations." Further on in the essay, Levinas warns against a de facto erasure of Shabbos by "the magic of spiritualization, of interiorization," by claiming that since Shabbos is "made for man," it follows that concrete acts of service responding to divinely instituted sacred time are not necessary. Levinas suggests that exclusive emphasis on interiority without commitment to law leads to "an interior magic with infinite resources [wherein] all is allowed in the inner life, all is allowed, including crime" (p. 149).

Shabbos is the core devotional practice of Judaism, the reverential offering to God of the most precious thing humans possess: presence.

The practices and the dispositions are intimately connected. The practices include both the *don'ts* – that is, the things we abstain from, surrender, and hand back to God – and the *do's* – the specific actions we engage in. The dispositions include joy, equanimity, generosity, hospitality, thirst for wisdom, trust, tranquility, acceptance, gentleness, receptivity to grace and beauty, appreciation of community, embrace of human diversity and difference, non-judgmentalism, assuming good intentions, buoyant and serene hope, and peace. In sum: love of God, people, and Torah. This is a long list! But every one of these (and more) is to be found in our sacred sources, exemplified in the lives of noble spirits (some famous, some hardly known), and captured in stories that are told about great masters.

This book attempts to clarify how Shabbos fosters and cultivates these dispositions. We shall see how Shabbos opens our hearts and enables the dispositions to flower more fully, robustly, effectively, blessedly, and enduringly.

Some readers will be familiar with a list of activities to be avoided, the *don'ts*. The list is long, and for some it is daunting. Some people perceive the prohibitions as prohibitively difficult, a barrier to Shabbos observance. One way to respond is by focusing on the *do's* – highlighting activities that are immediately accessible, enjoyable, even fun. This is an especially attractive way to introduce Shabbos to families, and precedent can be found for it in tradition. But an exclusive emphasis on immediately gratifying and entertaining activities risks turning Shabbos into a day of amusement, rather than a time to explore heights of spirit and treasuries of wisdom in heart and home. The goal should be mindful awareness, not diversion. And the deeper truth is that without the *don'ts* that frame and guard the container of blessing and holiness – Heschel's "Palace in Time" – the foundations of the palace would quickly erode.

This book takes a dual approach to Shabbos. The *do's* are indeed highlighted, here inflected through a hasidic lens. At the same time, the activities are buttressed by a foundation that upholds them, anchoring and embedding them. The first step is **Stop.**

REDISCOVERING OUR FEET

One of the gifts of Shabbos is the invitation to rediscover our feet. On Shabbos, we set aside the enablers of propelled mobility: vehicle keys; wallet or purse stuffed with license, cash, and cards; electronic communication devices.

E. M. Forster, in his dystopian novella *The Machine Stops* (1928), anticipated much of our current technological situation, imagining a voice-controlled virtual assistant ("the Machine") that responds to verbal commands and affords effortless mobility. The inhabitants of this world are seduced by the Machine's convenience and seeming empowerment. But the hero foresees the corrosive effects of total dependency on an apparently omniscient and omnipotent contrivance whose inner workings are opaque and entirely hidden from end users. Among many other observations, the hero of *The Machine Stops* says:

> You know that we have lost the sense of space. We say "space is annihilated," but we have annihilated not space, but the sense thereof. We have lost a part of ourselves.... "Near" is a place to which I can get quickly on my feet, not a place to which the train or the air-ship will take me quickly. "Far" is a place to which I cannot get quickly on my feet.[7]

The famous literary critic, medievalist, and theologian C. S. Lewis (1898–1963) considered it a blessing that when he was a boy, his father had no car. He writes:

> The deadly power of rushing about wherever I pleased had not been given me. I measure distances by the standard of man, man walking on his two feet, not by the standard of the internal combustion engine. I had not been allowed to deflower the very idea of distance; in return I possessed "infinite riches" in what would have been to motorists "a little room." The truest and most

---

7. I was introduced to Forster by an anthology that I received for my bar mitzva, *The Armchair Science Reader*, ed. Isabel S. Gordon and Sophie Sorkin (New York: Simon and Schuster, 1959), 774–75.

horrible claim made for modern transport is that it "annihilates space." It does. It annihilates one of the most glorious gifts we have been given.[8]

As a religious person, Lewis realizes that space is a gift, and when vehicles enable the "annihilation of space," the seeming ability to be anywhere quickly devolves into the sense that one is nowhere. If distance has been erased, so has embodied proximity – physical closeness and the "infinite riches" of genuine relationship.

Forster and Lewis recognize the inflated sense of power and psychic decoherence that result from technologically propelled mobility. Neither author can offer a clear remedy to the corrosive effects of the automobile. Forster's commitments were humanistic. Lewis, for his part, famously became a convert to a robust Christian faith, about which he wrote with great eloquence and conviction, but he could not plausibly counsel renouncing the automobile.

Similar sentiments about vehicular mobility were expressed by a Jewish thinker who lived in England during this period, Rabbi Yehezkel Abramsky (1886–1976). One of the greatest rabbinic authorities of the age, Abramsky served for many years as head of the London Rabbinical Court. In the preface to the Shabbat volume of his classic commentary on Tosefta (the companion corpus to the Mishnah), *Ḥazon Yeḥezkel,* published in 1934, he writes in a manner remarkably reminiscent of Forster and Lewis. He urges his readers not to squander Shabbos's opportunity for release from burden and worry. To lose such an opportunity would be like

> a person traveling in an automobile far from home, engulfed in the pace of his forward momentum, unaware that the engine's power will soon be exhausted, that the fuel is running out, until the car stops suddenly in the middle of nowhere and there is no one to call on for assistance.[9]

---

8. C. S. Lewis, *Surprised by Joy* (London: Geoffrey Bles, 1955), 156–57.
9. Yehezkel Abramsky, *Tosefta im Perush Ḥazon Yeḥezkel, Seder Mo'ed, Shabbat* (published by the author's sons, Jerusalem, 5766/2006), unnumbered pages at the beginning of the volume, "The Shabbos." The quotes are my translation from the Hebrew.

All three writers could remember a time before the widespread adoption of motor vehicles, and they were sensitive to the displacement, ersatz power, and hubris to which automobile drivers are prone. Abramsky, however, has Shabbos as his heritage and recognizes how Shabbos offers an antidote to the auto's corrosive effects. Master talmudist and halakhist that he was, Abramsky writes with the eloquence of a poet and the soaring spirit of a mystic:

> On Shabbos, repose and holiness are interdependent. In order to be infused with Shabbos's holiness, one must completely and absolutely exit the burden of enslavement to workaday material concerns. Only by throwing off the weight of worries about real or imagined needs can one realize the prophetic promise, "Arise and shine, for your light has come" (Is. 60:1).
>
> A spirit of repose and tranquility suffuses the world on the Shabbos day, and this is sensed by the Shabbos observer in the hidden recesses of the heart. To become aware of the hidden interiority of Shabbos demands the most subtle delicacy; one's perceptions must be attuned to the sacred and removed from corporeal attachment. On this day of serenity and spaciousness, you are able to attain an elevated state, a sublime centeredness; you are set to receive the *neshama yetera*, the "supplemental spirit."[10]

It is after this rapturous passage on the enchantment of Shabbos (only part of which is translated here) that Abramsky speaks of the effects of automobiles. His preface in its entirety is not an exercise in nostalgia for a simpler era, and certainly not a futile wish to renounce cars, but an eminently achievable vision of coming into tranquility on the holy seventh day, only one aspect of which is putting aside the car keys. Shabbos affords opportunity for balance, for holding firm to human embodiment and emplacement, while not renouncing the inevitable march of technology with all its intended and unintended consequences. By bringing repose, Shabbos restores spatial intelligence and inner balance.

---

10. Ibid.

Because Abramsky has personally known the "elevated spirit that results from pondering ultimate concerns, First and Last Things" on Shabbos, he is able to surrender the auto for a day without deprivation. Arrival and settling in before sunset on Friday is not a suppression of freedom; it is the very essence of liberation. Sublime fulfillment, ethereal whispers, elevation to a higher dispensation – these interior gifts are utterly palpable and transform us. Who needs to drive when you have already arrived?

Once every week, Shabbos provides an opportunity to rediscover our embodied selves and the blessing of being in one place at one time. Shabbos invites us to commit to our feet and the range that they afford us. We are encouraged to walk slowly, taking the time to proceed with awareness and deliberation. This is very different from succumbing to viscous drag or heavy-footed fatigue. It is a conscious choice to relax one's pace. Moving with measured step averts turbulence; it opens eyes, heart, and mind. When our feet propel us at a non-frenetic pace, they open apertures and leave room for serendipitous encounter.[11]

---

11. The main talmudic source for modestly paced walking on Shabbos is Shabbat 113b, which asserts that overly large strides "diminish the light of the eyes by one part in five hundred." Notably, Rashi on this passage (s.v. *mahu lifso'a pesia gassa*) labels giant striding as a violation of Isaiah 58:13, "If you restrain your foot because of Shabbos, from pursuing your affairs on My holy day; if you call Shabbos 'delight,' the LORD's holy day 'honored'; and you honor it by not making your way [with haste], nor look to your affairs, nor strike bargains." Rashi takes the Hebrew phrase *me'asot derekhekha* not metaphorically (making one's way in the world), but quite literally. Giant strides are an indication that the individual is vested in personal ambition and private goals. Isaiah evidently understood that when you move quickly, you are likely to break things, and unlike some voices in our contemporary culture, he did not consider that a virtue.

The fact that Shabbos affords the opportunity to slow down is frequently celebrated in the *zemirot*, the special Shabbos hymns. See *Kol Mekadesh Shevi'i KaRa'ui Lo* (line "*Pose'im bo pesia ketana*"): "On Shabbos, we take small steps;" *Koren Siddur with Introduction, Translation and Commentary by Rabbi Jonathan Sacks, Nusaḥ Sefarad* (Jerusalem: Koren Publishers, 2012), 431; *Mah Yedidut* (line "*Hilukhakh tehei benaḥat*"): "Your walk should be calm"; *Koren Siddur*, 435. All citations from the *Koren Siddur* are from this edition.

Rabbi Yaakov Leiner (second generation master in the Izbica lineage), writing from a hasidic perspective, understands "taking big steps" to mean attempting to gain access to a realization beyond one's level, "for everyone has a boundary, a

On Shabbos, we walk freely, lightly, unencumbered by shopping bag on arm and by wallet in pocket. We are not weighed down by tokens of a regime of commercial transaction, regulation, and control. Because our gait is slow and measured, we tread with gentle confidence and expansiveness, aware of surroundings in their most noble and beatific aspects.

SHABBOS PREVAILS, SHABBOS FLOURISHES

Jane Jacobs, in her now-classic book *The Death and Life of Great American Cities*, celebrates the virtues of walkable neighborhoods and the vitality of city life that they foster. The humble sidewalk is for Jacobs an essential feature of livable communities. Jacobs became famous for her struggles against the urban renewal movement of the last century, and especially for her successful campaign to save Greenwich Village from a plan that would have permanently scarred it by building an "expressway" through its heart. Her nemesis in this battle, as in many others, was the influential New York power broker Robert Moses.[12] In the foreword to the Modern Library Edition of *Death and Life*, Jacobs wrote that "we can speak of foot people and car people," and that her book was instantly understood by foot people and sneered at by car people. Jacobs berated the so-called experts who "did not respect what foot people knew and valued." She rued the fact that foot people were dismissed as "old-fashioned and selfish – troublesome sand in the wheels of progress."[13]

My views obviously have much in common with those of Jacobs. I celebrate local focus, walkable neighborhoods, and the vibrant quality of life they foster. Yet I feel that Jacobs draws the contrast between

---

domain of operation in this world that one's mind can safely absorb. If the person attempts to go beyond that level, one's mental stability suffers (*matrid et daato me'od*). This removes a five-hundredth of one's eyesight.... By reciting Kiddush on Friday evening [acknowledging the orderliness and sacred origin of the world and one's place in it] ... the eyesight is restored." Rabbi Yaakov Leiner, *Seder Haggada shel Pesaḥ im Sefer HaZemanim* ([Lublin: Steinmeser/Hirshenhorn, 1903] Brooklyn, NY: M. J. Lainer, 1990), 15.

12. See Robert Caro, *The Power Broker: Robert Moses and the Fall of New York* (New York: Knopf, 1974).

13. Jane Jacobs, *The Death and Life of Great American Cities* (New York: Modern Library, 2011), xxii.

foot people and car people too sharply. The two types need not be in stark opposition. There is a lacuna in *The Death and Life of Great American Cities*: surprisingly for a book on the urban life of Manhattan in the early and mid-twentieth century, there is almost no discussion of the role of religion in general or Judaism in particular. Jacobs's descriptions would have benefited from reference to the synagogues, religious schools, kosher restaurants and creameries, bookstores specializing in sacred tomes and ritual objects such as tefillin, mezuzas, and menoras, and other markers of the rich Jewish life of the Lower East Side and elsewhere on Manhattan Island, but these are strangely absent. Shabbos – especially Shabbos's role in creating community and shared sacred place – is given no role in her presentation.

By contrast, Robert Caro – author of the landmark study of Robert Moses, New York's "power broker" – took care to interview many of the people whose lives were crushed when they were evicted from their homes to make way for expressways. Caro captures the closeness that pervaded the old neighborhoods and that was never recovered when the residents were forced to move and relocate. One person reminisced about the synagogue and the rabbi, the *Kaddish* that was said when his father had died and that he expected to be said in the same synagogue, with the same rabbi, when he would die. But now it was all gone, not to be reestablished where the displaced residents had scattered. Community was gone and proximity to synagogue was gone, which meant that the foundation of Shabbos observance had been stripped away, bulldozed from bedrock.

Yet despite upheaval, pockets of Shabbos communities survived and even flourished. In this way of framing the narrative of the shape and character of American cities in the last century, there was a hidden force that resisted strong crosswinds and that at least in some cases made for a localist outcome: Shabbos.

Shabbos enables one to transcend the polarity drawn by Jacobs between "foot people" and "car people." We may be car people during the six days of the week, but as long as we are foot people on Shabbos, every aspect of our lives is shaped by Shabbos awareness. When we surrender motorized vehicles one day every week, our patterns of residence as well as our internal, mental maps are sculpted by Shabbos.

TAMING THE TECHNOLOGY BEAST

We have become aware of the dark side of technology's breezy maxim to "move fast and break things." Shabbos invites us to move slowly and savor things. We freely set aside electronic devices that promise convenience but deliver entrapment.

There have always been pressing challenges to Shabbos observance. Exodus 34:21 enjoins: "Six days you shall work, and on the seventh day you shall desist; you shall desist [from work even] during plowing season and during harvest time." In an agricultural society, plowing and harvest season are times of great urgency, offering a limited window for essential work to be done before weather conditions change, possibly ruining the crop. Yet, the Torah says, Shabbos overrides these considerations. In our day, there is a new challenge to Shabbos – the allure of intrusive technology.

There is a midrash about the threat of powerful technologies, among the first of which was the refinement of metal for use in sharp instruments: "When iron was created, the trees began to tremble. God said to them, 'Why do you tremble? Let none of you provide wood for the handle, and no tree will ever be harmed.'"[14] This is a wonderful metaphor: it is not the new technology itself that is hurtful, but the way we give it dominion over us, the way we become willing facilitators to our own subjugation. We may rail against the pervasive intrusions of digital technologies in every aspect of our personal, social, and political lives, but it is we who have allowed them entry into the most intimate places. We are all complicit. Shabbos pushes back, providing a consistent, recurring clearing of space and a proclamation of freedom. This is one reason why Shabbos is called a "remembrance of the exodus from Egypt."

It is futile to attempt to completely halt the development of technology. As the *midrash* cited above suggests, we are all involved in the embrace of what appears to be the irresistible cutting edge, and eagerness to adopt innovation is simply a feature of our human psyche. Yet communities of Shabbos-keepers naturally avoid the most destructive effects of the technological reshaping of society. Shabbos-friendly neighborhoods encourage walking; they are vicinities where distances are not

---

14. Genesis Rabba 5:9 on Genesis 1:11.

so large as to make the motor vehicle indispensable. And the patterns of residency that are shaped by Shabbos inevitably hold for weekdays as well. The urban landscape is more congenial to pedestrians and to face-to-face contact because of Shabbos.

The presence of Shabbos in our family life limits the power that communication devices can have over us. Knowing that one day a week we will be freed from electronic entanglements, we are open to a more expansive view of the world, at once more localist and more universal. Shabbos exerts a beneficial influence on what we read, on how we read, the way we relate to friends, the amount of time we have available to reflect, to listen, to ponder, to nuance, to share. The effects of intimacy-inhibiting devices are mitigated on Shabbos, and this opens up blessed possibilities at all times. Shabbos tames technology – every day of the week.

By disengaging from electronics, we reverse the compression of time so corrosive to genuine relationship. Shabbos permits us to live in spacious, expansive time, not in a static eternity but in a mindfully unfolding landscape that welcomes broadly smiling human faces.

SHABBOS: THE SMILING FACE OF TIME

The weekly cycle plays a central role in our sense of temporal location, our social situatedness, our very being in the world. Without the consistency and regularity of the week, we would be disoriented and adrift in a world devoid of temporal markers.

The sociologist Pitirim Sorokin wrote that "if there were neither the names of the days nor weeks, we would be liable to be lost in an endless series of days – as gray as fog – and confuse one day with another." Sorokin is quoted by another sociologist, Israeli-born Eviatar Zerubavel, in his book *The Seven-Day Circle: The History and Meaning of the Week*. In this informative and entertaining book, Zerubavel is concerned to show that the week is a cultural construct, a social convention. Nothing in astronomy requires the seven-day cycle that we call a week. But without that universally acknowledged and anticipated, structured rhythmic interval, days would not have identity; one would be hard-pressed to differentiate the quality and character of one day from the next.[15]

---

15. Zerubavel, *The Seven-Day Circle* (Chicago: University of Chicago Press, 1989), 136.

The creation story in Genesis culminates with God establishing the fundamental, universal rhythm, the beat of days:
One-two-three-four-five-six-STOP!
One-two-three-four-five-six-STOP!
One-two-three-four-five-six-STOP!
By "blessing" and "hallowing" the day (Gen. 2:3), God in effect invites creation to join in this foundational rhythm, to pick up the beat and carry it forward. God punctuates time and invites us to do so as well. We would do well to think of the musical "rest" in a score. String players in an orchestra lift their bows and pause to provide the sonic syntax that elicits meaning from the sequence of notes. The biblical day of rest/cessation does exactly the same.

The Bible deploys a wide range of metaphors for God – king, father, mother, shepherd, kinsman-redeemer, rock, shield, warrior, eagle. The Talmud and Midrash provide many more. To this rich array, another one suggests itself to me: God as divine conductor, wielding not a sword but a baton, beating out time for the cosmos, inviting all beings to join in the musical rhythm and the associated choreography of the dance.

This suggestion yields *rest* as a musical instruction, a mark in the cosmic score calling for a pause. We can hear the invitation at the end of Genesis's creation story as follows:
One-two-three-four-five-six-REST!
One-two-three-four-five-six-REST!
One-two-three-four-five-six-REST!

Restoring Lost Time

Many biblical passages highlight the fleeting nature of time and the transitory nature of human life. This reality is captured in verses such as I Chronicles 29:15: "For we are strangers before You, and sojourners, as all our fathers were; our days on the earth are as a shadow, and there is no abiding." And Psalms 39:6: "You have made my days like hand-breadths." Compare Job 7:6: "My days are swifter than a weaver's shuttle." With painful accuracy, Job says (8:9): "For we are but of yesterday, and know nothing, because our days upon earth are a shadow." This follows standard translations, but the Hebrew is actually starker and more forceful: *Ki temol anakhnu* – "We are yesterday!" As we get older, days pass more swiftly, and, even worse, we are perceived by others as belonging to a time gone by. Sooner or later, we see in the eyes of both strangers and friends that we are viewed as relics of the past, to be treated with respect (if we are fortunate) but kept as holdovers from a distant age, like antique vehicles that are preserved and polished but only driven on ceremonial occasions.

How are we to respond to this existential ache at the core of human existence?

Let us turn to Psalm 90:

(1) A Prayer of Moses the man of God.
Lord, You have been our dwelling-place in all generations...
(12) So teach us to number our days,
That we may get us a heart of wisdom...
(14) O satisfy us in the morning with Your mercy;
That we may rejoice and be glad all our days...
(16) Let Your work appear unto Your servants,
And Your Glory upon their children.
(17) And let the graciousness of the Lord our God be upon us;
Establish the work of our hands for us;
Yes – establish the work of our hands!

God is our dwelling place and refuge. God is the place we have in the world, and that refuge gives substance to time as well as to space. God shows us how to number our days. Tracking the Hebrew of verse 12 more accurately, we ask God to give us *daat* – awareness, alertness, discernment, and perception – to be able to count our days, and thereby to become worthy of receiving the "heart of wisdom." Nothing can stop the passage of time, but when we take refuge with God, in God, then time takes shape; we are able to count our days and make our days count. Finding meaning in time and finding one's secure place are intimately related in this psalm.

Advances in technology, such as electrical illumination, as well as other aspects of modernity, effectively erase night, eroding the rhythms of the sacred; they have dulled the punctuation, blurred the syntax, and confounded the rhythmic dance of time. Psalms 90:5 asserts that the rushing stream of life can be overwhelming, putting us to sleep in the middle of the rapids. The way to wake up and avoid drowning is to enter God's time with the divine dance of "One-two-three-four-five-six-REST!"

Without Shabbos, there would be no Tuesday, and the rhythm of human life would be lost. Sacred time redeems personal time from vanishing. Shabbos creates the week. The week gives time a human face – and when time has a face, the days smile at us and we smile back.

Shabbos punctuates time's flow, giving us the gift of coherence and structure. It is the cessation that allows us to live in the imprint of the work that has already been done.

HOSPITALITY AND ARRIVING IN PLACE

Collective commitment to Shabbos – especially its call to *be in place* – motivates the practice of hospitality. The hasidic master Rabbi Simcha Bunem of Pshiskhe (Przysucha Poland, 1765–1827) taught that "Shabbos is a gracious hostess."[16] By this he meant that the Shabbos prayers always make room for liturgical special guests, such as Festivals, Rosh HaShana, and Yom Kippur. But the insight is surely meant quite literally as well. The Shabbos community is a community of hospitality that secures space and then opens that space to guests in generosity.

When speaking with old friends or meeting new ones, Shabbos-keepers often conclude a conversation by saying, "Come for Shabbos!" This is not a mere tagline or lightly uttered slogan. It is a deeply felt offer to share a spiritual experience in a social way, like a dinner party, but with a gravitas that goes beyond sociability, rising to nobility and sublime aspiration – which is another way of saying holiness. Shabbos is the time to get together without haste, to allow souls to unfold and unburden themselves at their own pace. If the guest lives beyond comfortable walking distance, "Come for Shabbos!" is an invitation to be hosted by a focused family and intentional community for an overnight stay. The members of a Shabbos-keeping community live within walking distance of each other; a radius of ambulatory intimacy defines their neighborhood. Shabbos community becomes a space of inclusion, not exclusion. Those in community are in a deeply relational proximity; they are close to each other, but not cloistered.

---

16. See Yehudah Menahem Baum, *HaRebbi R. Bunem miPshiskhe* (Bnei Brak: Torat Simcha Institute, 1997), vol. 2, 472.

Shabbos hospitality is relational, not transactional; it brings out the best in both guests and hosts. The hosting family is motivated to tap the most gracious places of their selves – their *ruaḥ nediva*, "spirit of generosity," as the *zemer Menuḥa VeSimḥa* puts it.[17] And the guests are motivated to express gratitude, to savor the ambience and be respectfully sensitive to the customs and practices of the hosting family.

Shabbos creates an extraterritorial domain outside the impulse for possession and accumulation, beyond the world of commodity transaction.

THE CONVIVIAL PASSION OF SHABBOS COMMUNITY

When we welcome guests into our homes as part of the community of Shabbos-keepers, we participate in an ancient practice that is ongoing, vibrant, and blessed. The hosting is really being accomplished by Shabbos. Our children benefit by meeting people of diverse backgrounds and experiences, and they learn the art of graciousness. There is mutual trust and an undercurrent of reciprocity. We know that during the course of a lifetime of Shabbos-keeping, we will receive as well as give hospitality (often with different people, as the favor of hospitality is generally paid forward, not back).

Committing to a place creates the possibility for true conviviality, knowing that others have made the same commitment as you have made to this place at this time. This, in turn, facilitates non-commodified hospitality; we invite others not only to meals but to stay for the full cycle of sunset-sunrise-sunset, with the understanding that both guests and hosts are sheltering under the canopy of peace provided by Shabbos.

Shabbos is embeddedness that creates expansiveness – the choice of one place that opens to spaciousness. Shabbos is holiness that does not isolate. It is the capstone of the week, but it does not encapsulate; it breathes a boundless horizon of welcome.

A Shabbos community is a network of filiation, a neighborhood with lines of connection lifted up and held by Shabbos. We all know that our modern secular society is beset by loneliness and craves community. But you cannot conjure community merely by wishing it into

---

17. See *Koren Siddur*, 433.

being; lecturing people to stop bowling alone is not likely to be very effective. By contrast, Shabbos communities have an organic natural feel, created not by force of will but though a relational lattice of blessing and holiness that the participants enter gratefully and enthusiastically. The philosopher Michael Polanyi wrote:

> The riches of mental companionship between two equals can be released only if they share a convivial passion for others greater than themselves, within a like-minded community – the partners must belong to each other by participating in a reverence for a common superior knowledge.[18]

The members of the Shabbos-keeping community have chosen to live within walking distance of each other in order to celebrate Shabbos together, placing hospitality and holy aspiration at the center of their personal, family, and communal lives. They are in what Polanyi calls a "like-minded community," whose members belong to each other in a reverence for a "common superior knowledge," in this case an embodied knowledge-practice of great antiquity and infinite worth. They testify to the holiness of space as well as time; their community has meaning, moral force, and blessed possibility. The members of a Shabbos community know even in repose that they are tending God's garden.

Shabbos as Trust Practice

Entering into Shabbos is an act of trust. It means trusting that I am exactly in the place that I most want to be now and that all the people I most desire to be with are within my perimeter of perambulation. It means trusting my own preparations, that I have done everything I need to do and now have everything I will require for the next twenty-five hours.

---

18. Michael Polanyi, *Personal Knowledge: Towards a Post-Critical Philosophy* (Chicago: University of Chicago Press, 1974), 378, 380. Like many twentieth-century Hungarian Jews, Polanyi grew up with little overt knowledge of his Jewish heritage (his family tree included illustrious rabbinic figures), but I see his post-critical approach to knowledge, values, and human aspirations to be profoundly religious and rooted in Judaic thinking. I return to Polanyi's ideas in the last chapter.

This sense of trust evokes a deep sense of being-in-place, of entering completely into my here, my now, home, family, friends, body, and soul.

It takes trust to bring weekday activities to a halt, to have faith that one's surroundings, for the next twenty-five hours, will not only remain stable but will also benefit from the Shabbos that is being honored and hallowed. The gnawing sense of unease that accompanies modern life is countered by staying true to the day of cessation. Holy desisting is the most effective move one can make to enter the peace that one wishes to channel for the world as a whole.

In the culture we inhabit, it takes trust to power down, to disengage from the market economy, from the political circus, from inner frenzy, from the conceit that constant accessibility is essential for societal functioning. One must trust that every worthwhile opportunity will still be available when secular time returns. Nothing will fall apart and everyday life will resume intact. This disengagement is an unfastening from bondage, a dropping of the illusion that one is the director of the conditions of one's life. Trusting in this way is a surrender – not a despairing, aimless surrender, but a yielding that is itself a vital course of action, a movement of one's being upward and inward. There is pleasure and joy in this yielding. One feels a lightness that is buoyant, expansive, and gently caressing.

Achieving trust in Shabbos calls for advance planning. Your trust is not foolhardy, without foundation; it is based on the knowledge that you have endeavored to anticipate contingencies as far as possible. You trust that your arrangements are adequate, sufficient for the zone of intimacy that you are about to establish and maintain – with God, with Shabbos, with loving family and friends, and with your own inner self.

Chapter 2

Shabbos in Scripture

Shabbos is blessed with a vast treasury of practices, lore, liturgy, and custom, reflecting millennia of the Jewish love affair with Shabbos, but it all begins in Scripture. We will explore Shabbos spirit by encountering the main biblical passages relating to the holy seventh day in a new way, aiming to give fresh meaning to familiar verses and suggesting more precisely nuanced translations of key terms.

We will first look at the creation account in Genesis, concluding with the establishment of the rhythmic seven-day cycle and the conferral of identity on the seventh day. Next, we turn to the manna chapter in Exodus, which is primarily about the gift of Shabbos. The manna teaches the need for preparation on the sixth day and staying-in-place on the seventh day. The seventh day is named Shabbos in the manna chapter, for the first time in Scripture, and the recently freed slaves are called "The House of Israel," also for the first time. Shabbos and Israel-as-household have risen together. They are a pair with a common destiny, a dyad of mutual recognition, and once they are established, the Israelites are ready to enter into a sacred covenant with God, summarized in the Decalogue (Ten Commandments), where Shabbos plays a pivotal role.

Then we turn to the prophets, beginning with Isaiah, who emphasizes "restraining the feet" from travel, complete cessation of business activity, and the elevation of all action and conversation to a sublime register of nobility, interpersonal sensitivity, and social inclusiveness. Isaiah's prophetic voice invites us to proclaim Shabbos *oneg* (delight). This call has been heard throughout the ages; the sheer delight of Shabbos remains its salient characteristic to our own day.

Our study of Shabbos in Scripture reverses a common perception of Shabbos as a day that enforces suppression of weekday enablements. In truth, Shabbos is the day of expansive liberation, not only for Shabbos itself, but for weekdays, endowing them with dignity and elevated stature. Shabbos raises weekday projects and activities to the realm of artistic creation and accomplishment.

Our investigation of Shabbos in Scripture reminds us that Shabbos's Edenic ambience was present from its very inception. Recent expositions of Shabbos have tended to emphasize the day's mystical aspects, and it is certainly true that kabbalistic poetics and hasidic practices have added new dimensions to Shabbos's expansive possibilities and enhanced Shabbos's immersive power. But much as this book draws on Hasidism for insight and inspiration, it begins with a careful reading of the biblical texts. Kabbala and Hasidism amplify the classic sources, but it is a mistake to think that their work is alchemy, turning base materials into gold. The gold was always there; Shabbos was always soaring, sublime, and spacious. When consulting mystical texts for their depth and resonant tonalities, it is important to remember that Shabbos's spiritual dimension was not the discovery of thirteenth-century kabbalists in Provence and Spain, nor of eighteenth-century Hasidim in Russia and Poland. Clearly evident throughout Scripture, Shabbos's shimmering, captivating buoyancy sparkles through every verse of the many biblical passages that address the holy seventh day.

SECTION ONE: CREATION AS WORK OF ART, CESSATION AS CREATIVE CONFIDENCE (GEN. 1:31–2:3)

The first biblical reference to the special character of the seventh day appears at the end of the creation narrative in Genesis, called by Jon

Levenson "the great cosmogony that is the overture to the Bible."[1] The cadence of the text – solemn, rhythmic, sonorous – has been leading up to this moment. As Nahum Sarna writes, on the seventh day "all the creativity of the preceding days achieves fulfillment."[2] Here is a standard translation of Genesis 2:1–3, as found in the still commonly used Jewish Publication Society 1917 version:

> And the heaven and the earth were finished, and all the host of them. And on the seventh day God finished His work which He had made; and He rested on the seventh day from all His work which He had made. And God blessed the seventh day, and hallowed it; because that in it He rested from all His work which God in creating had made.

In truth, the Hebrew root SH-B-T in Genesis 2:2–3 does not mean "rest," but rather "ceased" or "desisted," and recent translations have indeed substituted the word "ceased" for "rested." But this is not the only Hebrew word in this passage where conventional translations mislead by suggesting an imprecise, vague, or overly broad semantic field. Greater clarity and precision in translating the other key words of the passage will assist us in grasping how the Bible wants us to perceive Shabbos.

In particular, *vayekhulu/vayekhal* (translated by both old and new JPS as "finished") and *melakhto* (JPS: "His work") need to be revisited. Further, although "blessed" for *vayevarekh* and "hallowed" for *vayekadesh* are adequate translations, the deeper resonances of these central terms in the constellation of biblical theology must be explored and amplified. This is not a fussy obsession with correct translation, but rather a desire for conceptual clarity on key terms whose sense emerges from a careful reading of the biblical texts and that are central to our understanding of the seventh day and its relationship to the other days of the week.

---

1. Jon D. Levenson, *Creation and the Persistence of Evil: The Jewish Drama of Divine Omnipotence* (Princeton: Princeton University Press, 1988), 98.
2. Nahum Sarna, *JPS Torah Commentary: Genesis* (Philadelphia: Jewish Publication Society, 5749/1989), 14.

VAYEKHULU / VAYEKHAL

With reference to the creation of heaven and the earth, the Hebrew word *vayekhulu* is generally translated "were finished." This is fine as long we realize that the passage is not referring to an objective end, a conclusion that occurs with deterministic inevitability. When you are performing a task such as washing dishes or mowing a lawn, at some point, the work is done; the task is finished. This is obvious and inescapable. There is simply no more to do – no more dishes in the sink, no more grass to be cut. Now you can stop. You can say, "I'm finished," and no one can argue with you. Similarly, a well-defined arithmetic calculation, such as long division or extracting the square root of a perfect-square integer, is executed and simply halts.

That is not the sense of *vayekhulu*. The project of creation was not a set of operations that, like an algorithmic mathematical procedure, came to an ineluctable halt, or, like a chemical reaction whose initial components were consumed and the energy exhausted, slowed down and finally ceased. The word *vayekhulu* is meant to convey an ending based on choice and decision. If we are to render it in English by the word "finished," we should have in mind thoughtfulness, intentionality, craft, responsibility assumed, and pride taken. To say *vayekhulu* is not to assert a bare fact; it is to make an evaluative assessment. In this way, *vayekhulu* follows from the prior verse, "And God saw all that God had made and behold (*vehineh*), it was very good" (Gen. 1:31). This is a judgment of aptness, appropriateness, aesthetic satisfaction. The parts fit together into a harmonious whole. An aesthetic judgment is never conditioned by a set of rigid rules or ineluctably predetermined. It is because God saw that what God had made was "very good" that *vayekhulu* could be stated.[3]

---

3. "Very good" should not be confused with "perfect." There is no assertion of perfection in the creation narrative. Philosophical claims of perfection are foreign to the spirit of the Bible and are explicitly ruled out by the early Midrash. See Genesis Rabba 11:6 on Genesis 2:3: "Whatever was created during the six days of creation needs further work.... Even human beings need work!" The Midrash commentary attributed to Rashi (not from his hand but nevertheless an early and authoritative source, likely from Rashi's circle) adds:

> All the works of creation were precious in God's eyes, as it is written, "God saw all that God had made and behold, it was very good." Nevertheless, everything needs further improvement.... See Genesis 2:3: "That God had made *laasot*" – "for further improvement." This phrase shows you that everything requires further work.

This sense is captured by the translations that render Genesis 2:1 as, "*Thus*, the heavens and the earth were completed," rather than, "And" (1917 JPS), or, as some recent versions do, leave out the connective entirely.[4] The adverbial "thus" links the "completion" of 2:1 to the appraisal "very good" in 1:31; the completion is a direct consequence of the aesthetic approval.

This reading is supported by a comment of Rabbi Barukh Ha-Levi Epstein (1860–1941) in his work *Torah Temima*. Rabbi Epstein cites a talmudic passage:

> Whoever prays on the eve of Shabbos and recites, "Thus [the heaven and the earth] were finished," Scripture considers him as though he became a partner with the blessed Holy One in the creation, for it is said, *Vayekhulu* ("and they were finished"), but the word can be read *Vayekalu* ("and *they* finished").[5]

As Rashi explains, the plural pronoun "they" in the verse refers to God and the person who is praising God. By proclaiming the project of world-creation as having reached a satisfying conclusion, the human being joins with God, whose own creative activity was effected by verbal declaration and brought to closure with an assessment of satisfaction. The person can join with God because creation is an expressive endeavor, a result of declamation and decision. Ten divine utterances brought the world into existence, and the recitation of Genesis 2:1–3 is a performative rite of closure, a reenactment of the original creation capstone that expresses the pleasure of fulfillment.[6]

Rabbi Epstein further suggests that the Hebrew *tzevaam* in Genesis 2:1, usually rendered "their host" or, more recently, "their vast array," should be connected to *tzevi*, a biblical word that carries the sense of "beauty, honor, splendor, full stature." He refers to Isaiah 28:5: "On that day, the LORD *Tzeva'ot* will become a crown of beauty (*tzevi*)

---

4. Such as new JPS and *Jewish Study Bible*.
5. Shabbat 119b.
6. I am amplifying Rashi's words with the aggadic commentary of Maharsha (Rabbi Shmuel Eliezer Eideles, 1555–1631), as suggested by Epstein.

and a diadem of glory for the remnant of His people." Following Rabbi Epstein's lead, we might translate *tzevaam* as "their arrayed splendor."[7] This has the advantage of curbing an overemphasis on the metaphor of military formations and supports the sense of the passage as primarily aesthetic. Heaven and earth and their contents rose to full stature. They are splendidly ordered, arranged for beauty and magnificence. When one ritually confirms that assessment through verbal declaration (as in the recitation of Kiddush), he or she partners with God in world-creation, which is to say the perception and disclosure of meaning, delight, and worthiness in existence.

In this light, let us examine the word *vehineh*, "and behold," in verse 31. As Rabbi Samson Raphael Hirsch notes in his Torah commentary, *hineh* "always introduces us to something we have not yet seen: 'See there!'"[8] As with every statement in the Torah referencing God, this passage has a strong anthropomorphic element; readers are invited to feel God's own delighted surprise at the beauty of the creation in its totality. The voice of Scripture wishes us to see the world as God saw it, so to speak, in its totality for the first time – not just the parts created in days one through six, but the whole. Hirsch writes: "God saw the whole of what God had created, saw how everything fitted together harmoniously..."[9] Similarly, Umberto Cassuto writes:

> While the prior days have "it was good" with reference to a specific detail, now God saw "all" that God had made – the creation in its totality – and saw that not only the separate parts were good, but that each one of them fitted congenially with all the other

---

7. Rabbi Yaakov Zvi Meklenburg (1785–1865) makes much the same point in his *HaKetav VehaKabbala*, commenting on Exodus 38:8. Meklenburg cites Jeremiah 3:19: *Ve'eten lakh eretz ḥemda, naḥalat tzevi, tzive'ot goyim*, "I gave you a desirable land – the fairest heritage of all the nations." In this verse, the wordplay *tzevi-tzive'ot* is unmistakable; indeed, the King James Bible translates, "[I gave you] a pleasant land, a goodly heritage of the hosts of nations." Meklenburg suggests that the name *Tzeva'ot* as applied to God is meant to connote beauty and honor.

8. *The Pentateuch: Volume I Genesis*, trans. and explained by Rabbi Samson Raphael Hirsch, rendered into English by Isaac Levy (second edition; Gateshead: Judaica Press, 1989), 38.

9. Ibid.

parts; so the totality was not just good but "very good." By analogy, imagine an artist finishing a work, stepping back to consider the piece in its entirety, taking delight in the result, noting with satisfaction the elegant coherence of parts and whole.[10]

Readers with a philosophical mindset will be prone to thinking that God could not be surprised, of course. God could not be delightfully startled by the beauty of the creation in its totality. The philosopher will sternly remind us that God knows everything, even before it happens. However, this feeling of rising awareness is exactly what the biblical text wants to impart – the sense of an artist who has not fully anticipated the splendor of what has been accomplished, what has emerged when the project came to fruition. We as readers are meant to enter into the experience of beholding the creation in its full glory for the first time and being left breathless by what we see. The element of unanticipated emergence, of being caught unawares by a sight, is what is conveyed by the formula *vayar... vehineh* ("And God saw... and behold").[11]

Genesis 1:31 conveys the voice of admiration. It invites us to form a picture in our mind, anticipating by millennia a certain iconic photo of the whole earth.

On December 24, 1968, astronauts aboard the Apollo 8 mission took the first color photograph of the earth rising over the moon, from a distance farther than any humans had ever been. The

---

10. Umberto Cassuto, *A Commentary on the Book of Genesis* (fourth edition; Jerusalem: Hebrew University Magnes Press, 1965) [Hebrew], 37 (translation mine).

11. This formula appears (with slight variations) no fewer than twenty-five times in another context, the chapters of the Torah discussing various surface anomalies (*tzaraat*) that have appeared on a person's skin, on garments, or on the walls of a house (Lev. 13–14). The priest is called in, often after a seven-day waiting period, to view the phenomenon and note its progression or disappearance. Time and again, the Torah says, "the priest sees (*veraah hakohen*)...and behold (*vehinei*)..." In each instance, the priest does not know ahead of time what will confront him; frequently, the condition has cleared up and the priest – presumably with delight – is called upon to declare, "Pure!" This precise pattern is what we find in Genesis 1:31, but with God in the role of priest and with the delight due not to a restoration of healthy appearance, but rather the espying of a dazzling beauty that surpasses the merely "good" of the previous days of creation.

astronauts were "dazzled by the luminescent blue sphere, whorled by a white cloud cover."[12] The photograph caused a sensation, inspiring wonder and amazement, a feeling of shared human destiny and a call for heightened responsibility for the earth and its fate.[13] After fifty years, the sight is still arresting. Together with a subsequent photograph taken four years later from Apollo 17, it is said to be among the "most reproduced photographs in human history."[14] But students of the Bible need not have waited for moon missions to get a feeling for the wonder of seeing the world from a distance, of contemplating the scope of its vastness and beauty. This is precisely what Genesis chapter 1 does. To read Genesis 1:1–2:3 – and especially to hear it read liturgically, sonorously, sequentially, in its austere grandeur (as is done on the holiday of Simḥat Torah, the annual celebration of completing the Five Books of Moses and beginning anew) – is to obtain a verbal sketch of the world sculpted into regions of land and sea, dominated by darkness and light, and compassed by sun, moon, and stars, much as in the iconic photos taken by the astronauts.

Like those photos, the Genesis depiction has very little detail, but details are not the point. The panoramic view of the biblical narrator is meant to evoke a perspective on creation from the point of view of its Creator; we the listeners, by being invited to adopt that vantage point, are elevated into something more than mere earthlings. We are allowed to perceive the world's "exquisite rarity and value," and it dawns on us that we "live on a marvel to behold."[15] Genesis goes beyond even the most dramatic photos taken from the frigid isolation of outer space; it invites us to see the world as inherently meaningful, redolent with significance, and pregnant with purpose – a purpose and meaning that are all the more enchanting because they are never made fully explicit.

---

12. The description is from a retrospective account published on the fiftieth anniversary of this event. See Ted Widmer, "What Did Plato Think the Earth Looked Like?" *New York Times International Edition*, December 27, 2018, 9.

13. See Matthew Myer Boulton and Joseph Heithaus, "We Are All Riders on This Planet," *New York Times International Edition*, December 27, 2018, 9.

14. Ibid.

15. Ibid.

The *vayekhulu* moment is the divine Artist's coming to awareness, the supernal Maker's standing back and noticing that this is an opus, a work of art, and it is "very good" – an elegant and satisfying accomplishment that reflects the Maker, not in any directly iconic manner, but more subtly. By analogy with a human maker, the opus is worthy of the artist's signature.

As we read these verses of Torah, we might hear them as encouragements for human action, invitations to adopt certain postures, attitudes, and modes of being in the world. We are invited into a life of service, a life such that we will have the creative confidence to bring our week to closure because we find satisfaction in what we have accomplished, because we too wish to find that what we have done in the preceding six days is a work of art. We can exit the maker-train not because the train has reached the end of the line but because, taking satisfaction in what we have accomplished in six days, we are ready to release it as a signed work that represents us with grace and elegance and is worthy of our signature.

MELAKHA: "WORK" OR CREATIVE ACTIVITY?

Having established that *vayekhal* indicates a deliberative decision – finished in the artistic sense – the next key word to focus on is *melakha,* translated nearly universally in this passage as "work."

Here is JPS 1917 again, with the English translation of *melakha* in bold:

> And the heaven and the earth were finished, and all the host of them. And on the seventh day God finished His **work** which He had made; and He rested on the seventh day from all His **work** which He had made. And God blessed the seventh day, and hallowed it; because that in it He rested from all His **work** which God in creating had made.

New JPS and *The Jewish Study Bible* modify and update this translation – as we saw, "rested" is now "ceased" – but the three-fold deployment of "work" for *melakha* remains. We need to find a better translation for *melakha* – better in the sense of more precise, more aligned with the biblical context, and less likely to lead a reader astray with unintended associations and confusing implications. This is crucial for our exposition, since, while not naming the day explicitly, our Genesis passage is the foundation for the entire subsequent conceptual and ritual development of Shabbos.

The *Oxford English Dictionary* devotes no less than twenty-eight columns to the word "work," and a large and salient proportion of the definitions relate to actions involving effort, exertion, labor, and toil.[16] In Genesis 2:1–3, however, bodily exertion is not relevant to *melakha*. Interpreters ancient and modern have recognized that these verses do not mean that creation involved toil and effort on the part of God. Even readers living in a pre-philosophical world did not think that God broke into a sweat as a result of the "work" of creation; there was no depletion of energy or exhaustion of creative impulse. That being so, it might not be wise to translate *melakha* with a word whose main connotation is drudgery and fatigue. We ought to deploy another English word for *melakha*.

The word *melakha* occurs three times in various forms in Genesis 2:1–3, and the same word root makes multiple appearances in the book of Exodus, especially in the account of the construction of the Tabernacle – a total of twenty-two times.[17] *Melakha* is what the Decalogue asks us to engage in during the week and desist from on Shabbos (Ex. 20:9–10; Deut. 5:13–14).

The multiple occurrences of the term *melakha* at the beginning of Genesis and in the latter part of Exodus are one example of a pattern of terminological and conceptual correspondences that link these two scriptural sections. They are meant to be read as one, and they mutually inform each other. The creation narrative (Gen. 1:1–2:3), on the one hand, and the Tabernacle instructions (Ex. 25:1–31:11) and implementation (35:4–40:38), on the other hand, are two bookends, designed to be understood as parallel units, coupled descriptions that together describe

---

16. I consulted *The Compact Edition of the Oxford English Dictionary*, Complete Text Reproduced Micrographically (Oxford: Oxford University Press, 1971), vol. 2, s.v. "work."
17. See Exodus 31:3, 5; 35:21, 24, 29, 31, 35 (twice); 36:1, 2, 3, 4 (twice), 5, 6, 7 (twice), 8; 38:2 (twice); 39:43; 40:33.

divine and human making of sacred domains. The significance of these two descriptions emerges when they are read in tandem. Together they suggest that the world as a whole is a sacred macrocosm (Genesis) and that the Tabernacle is a sacred microcosm (Exodus), each space representing the other on a different scale. As Jon Levenson observes, the Sanctuary is depicted "as a world, that is, an ordered, supportive and obedient environment," while the world is depicted "as a sanctuary, a place in which the reign of God is visible and unchallenged, and His holiness is palpable, unthreatened, and pervasive."[18] To be sure, this way of looking at the world does not focus on its current aspect, which is often messy and chaotic, but on its ideal state – the way it once was and yet could be.[19]

The verbal correspondences linking Genesis and Exodus were pointed out in a classic rabbinic text, *Midrash Tanḥuma*:

> Regarding the seventh day, Scripture writes: "The heaven and the earth came to closure (*vayekhulu*)" (Gen. 2:1).
> Of the Tabernacle, it is written: "Thus came to closure (*vatekhel*) all the work of the Tabernacle" (Ex. 39:32).
>
> Of the creation of the world, it is written: "And God blessed" (Gen. 2:3).
> Of the Tabernacle, it is written: "Moses blessed them" (Ex. 39:43).
>
> Of the creation of the world, it is written: "God brought to closure" (Gen. 2:2).
> Of the Tabernacle, it is written: "On the day Moses brought to closure" (Num. 7:1).
>
> Of the creation [Shabbos], it is written: "And God hallowed (*vayekadesh*) it" (Gen. 2:3).

---

18. Levenson, *Creation and the Persistence of Evil: The Jewish Drama of Divine Omnipotence* (Princeton: Princeton University Press, 1988), 86.
19. Levenson puts this as "the world viewed *sub specie creationis*," protologically – which is to say, the world in its original pristine state.

Of the Tabernacle: "[Moses] anointed it and hallowed (*vayekadesh*) it" (Num. 7:1; cf. Lev. 8:10).[20]

The attentive reader of Scripture cannot help but notice this web of correspondences and draw the conclusion that the world and the Sanctuary are bonded to each other, meant to reflect each other; they reciprocally shine light upon the other's significance and role in a life of sacred purpose.

Establishing this correspondence is important, because it suggests that whatever *melakha* means in the Tabernacle account, it means in the creation account as well.

It is not difficult to find other terminological parallels between the Tabernacle passages and Genesis 1:1–2:3. These include *ruaḥ Elohim*, the "spirit of God," that hovered over the face of the waters at the beginning (Gen. 1:2); this same phrase is used to describe the endowment of Betzalel, the master craftsperson in charge of the Tabernacle project (Ex. 31:3; 35:31).

In addition, there are deep structural features attesting to the influence of seven-fold repetitions, heptadic patterns that are the characteristic rhythm of the creation of the world in Genesis and, subsequently, the construction of the Tabernacle in Exodus. These include the most obvious, such as the basic six-day-plus-one-day structure of the creation account, as well as the seven-fold occurrence of *tov*, "good," six times, capped by "very good."[21] The biblical narrator embedded heptadic rhythm deeply and skillfully in Genesis 1:1–2:3, so that its sonic beat resonates with the six-plus-one leitmotif, in manifold ways.[22]

---

20. *Midrash Tanḥuma, Pekudei* 2; cf. Numbers Rabba on Numbers 7:1.

21. The word *tov* does not appear on the second day of creation (Gen. 1:6–8), but it occurs twice on the third day (1:9–13) and the sixth day (1:24–31), assuring a total of seven when the six days of creation have been tallied.

22. Other examples were discovered by the astute eye of twentieth-century scholar Umberto Cassuto, who found many key words in patterns of seven or multiples of seven. Perhaps the most compelling is in the paragraph devoted to the seventh day (Gen. 2:1–3), which "consists of thirty-five words (7x5), twenty-one of which (7x3) form three sentences of seven words, each of which includes the expression "the seventh day." I am drawing upon Levenson's summary of Cassuto's observations, *Creation*, 67.

Heptadic rhythm is the time signature of the cosmos.

Turning our attention to the Exodus foot of the arch spanning the first two books of the Torah, we find heptadic patterns there as well. Again, some are obvious, such as the seven-branched Menora (Ex. 25:32, 37). Others, while hardly hidden or arcane, take a bit more focused attention to notice. For example, in the final chapter of the book of Exodus, we are given the description of Moses assembling the parts of the Tabernacle (40:17ff). The description is divided into subsections, each ending with the refrain "just as the LORD had commanded Moses." Upon counting the repetitions of this refrain, one discovers seven instances.[23] After the seventh repetition, we are told that "*vayekhal Moshe et hamelakha*, Moses brought the *melakha* to conclusion" (Ex. 40:33), employing the verb *vayekhal* – precisely the word used in Genesis 2:2 for the bringing to closure of God's creative actions ("*vayekhal Elohim bayom hashevi'i melakhto ashar asa*").[24] The sonorously repetitive account of the Tabernacle's assembly at the end of Exodus mirrors the structure of the creation narrative at the beginning of Genesis.[25]

The connection between creation and Tabernacle is not only lexical and structural, it is conceptual. As Levenson says, the Tabernacle rite "builds and maintains order, transforms chaos into creation, ennobles

---

23. Exodus 40:19 (basic structure – boards, sockets, tent materials); 40:21 (Decalogue Tablets, Ark of the Covenant, *Kapporet*, partition veil), 40:23 (Table and Bread of the Presence); 40:25 (Menora), 40:27 (golden incense altar); 40:29 (outer altar and Tabernacle curtain); 40:32 (Laver).

24. For all this, see Peter J. Kearney, "Creation and Liturgy," *Zeitschrift fur die attestamentliche Wissenschaft* 89 (1977). Amazingly, it is not only the account of Moses's assembly and erection of the Tabernacle that embeds a heptadic pattern. Exodus 39, the section on the making of the priestly vestments, and Leviticus 8, the consecration and investiture of the priests, reveal the same seven-fold pattern, using the identical device of the repeated "just as the LORD had commanded Moses." Equally remarkably, each of these sections is followed by a capstone statement that summarizes and provides closure for the previous material (see Ex. 39:42–43 and Lev. 8:36).

25. Notably, after the seventh "just as the LORD had commanded Moses," the Torah describes further action by Moses – he erected the courtyard and the curtain at the courtyard's gate. But this is not followed by an eighth repetition of the phrase! For a deeply insightful hasidic interpretation of this, see Rabbi Mordecai Yosef Leiner of Izbica, *Mei HaShilo'ah* (Bnei Brak: Elhanan Goldhaber and Yehudah Spigelman, 5755/1995), vol. 1, 99, *Parashat Pekudei, s.v. vayakem et hehatzer saviv laMishkan.*

humanity" and enacts the worship of God in a manifest, visible manner.[26] The activities performed in the sacred precincts of the Tabernacle maintain cosmic order, link heaven and earth, and keep chaos – whose threat never disappears – at bay.

This multi-layered, tight linkage between Genesis's creation narrative and Exodus's Tabernacle verses helps clarify the elusive term *melakha*.

The Tabernacle passages in Exodus have much to teach us about how to read Genesis 1:31–2:3, and in particular how to understand the word *melakha* in those verses. A key feature of the Tabernacle furnishings and the vestments of the priests who serve there is beauty or splendor.

Exodus 28:2 calls for the making of sacred priestly vestments *lekhavod uletifaret*, "for splendor and for beauty" (following JPS 1917).[27] Indeed, the preciousness of the gold, silver, rare jewels, and fabrics that went into making the Tabernacle, its furnishings, and the priestly garments bespeak an emphasis on elegance and beauty. Time and again the text calls for craft skill and wisdom in the service of fashioning the parts and the whole for visual appeal, as an aspect of the dignity and reverence appropriate for sacred service by anointed persons in sacred space.

Skill and artistic design are central qualities necessary for the Tabernacle's construction. Here is Exodus 31, where God informs Moses of the designation of the master craftsperson Betzalel:

> v. 3: I have filled him with the spirit of God, in wisdom, and in understanding, and in knowledge, and in all manner of *melakha*.

> v. 4: To devise skillful designs [literally, "to think thoughts"] for work in gold, and in silver, and in copper.

---

26. Levenson, 127.

27. The phrase occurs again with reference to the garments of Aaron's children; see Exodus 28:40. It is deployed in the blessing after the chanting of the *haftara* on Shabbos, in which we thank God "for the Torah, for divine worship, for the prophets, and for this Shabbos day which You, LORD our God, have given us for holiness and for repose, *lekhavod uletifaret* – for splendor and for beauty." This is another indication of the close connection between the sacred space of the Tabernacle and its service and the sacred time of Shabbos and its ambience.

v. 5: And in cutting of stones for setting, and in carving of wood, to engage in all manner of *melakha.*

Betzalel is not described as a contractor supervising laborious work, but as an artist, a master craftsperson endowed with *ruah Elohim,* "the spirit of God." It is evident from these verses that *melakha* has little if anything to do with toilsome labor and everything to do with skillful creative activity. This indeed is exactly how the artist Ben Schachter translates the term in his insightful work on contemporary Jewish art.[28] The New Jewish Publication Society translation, recognizing the significance of artistry in the call to Betzalel, renders *melakha* in 31:3 and 31:5 as "craft." Yet in the very next section, Exodus 31:12–17, where Shabbos is presented as a visual sign (*ot*) of the covenantal relationship between God and Israel – a visible enactment of intimacy in the temporal domain, just as the Tabernacle is a visible realization of intimacy in space – *melakha* is translated as "work." This elides what should have been learned from the immediately preceding passage on the imaginative creativity and skill needed to fashion the Tabernacle and its materials, accomplishments that are called *melakha.*[29]

By *melakha* is meant skillful artistic endeavor and the result of such endeavor. *Melakha* points to both skilled activity (workmanship) and the product of such activity (*opus*), as shown by its occurrences throughout the chapters devoted to the Tabernacle.[30] Ibn Ezra on Genesis 2:2 says this explicitly: "God desisted from all God's *melakha*"

---

28. Ben Schachter, *Image, Action, and Idea in Contemporary Jewish Art* (University Park, PA: Pennsylvania State University Press, 2017), 40. See in particular his chapter entitled "Melakhot, Creative Activities, and Artistic Practice." I am grateful to my daughter Adina Polen for introducing me to this book.
29. Notably, in what is perhaps the most central of all Shabbos passages – that contained in the Decalogue – New JPS also translates *melakha* as "work" (Ex. 20:10).
30. We might also mention passages elsewhere in the Bible, such as Psalms 73:28. The psalmist, having shared with remarkable frankness his confusion at the apparent success of the wicked and the suffering of the pious, finds insight and refuge in "God's sanctuaries" (v. 17), the plural perhaps referring to the dual sanctuaries of Temple and Shabbos, linking as always place and time. In the psalm's final verse, the psalmist exclaims exultantly, "As for me, nearness to God is good...that I may recount all Your *malakhot*" – which might indeed be translated as "works," understood as

means, "from all the created works/creatures (*mikol habri'ot*) that God
had made," spotlighting God's accomplishments, the creative products
of the six days.

To summarize: *Melakha* is productive activity worthy of acclaim
and admiration, a maker-activity in which the agent takes pride and to
which he or she maintains relationship.[31] If you are the maker, you have
put yourself into the work; it represents you, reflects you, in some sense
it embodies you.

Melakha is a term of art. Perhaps it should be left untranslated,
but if we are to render it in English, I suggest the word "project" as a
replacement for "work," in line with the dictionary sense of a large and
significant undertaking, usually involving planning, care, and thoughtful implementation.[32] In this biblical setting, the word also conveys
aesthetic excellence and beauty, recalling that God saw the whole and,
with evident delight, proclaimed it "very good!"

BRINGING CREATION TO CLOSURE
AND TAKING PRIDE IN THE PROJECT

Let us now return to Genesis and bring together the insights developed
thus far. We recall that *vayekhulu* is meant to convey closure based on
intentionality, craft, pride, and responsibility. It is a volitional act of
reflection and assessment. *Vayekhulu* follows from the prior verse, "And
God saw all that God had made and behold (*vehineh*), it was very good"

---

accomplishments in which the maker may justifiably take pride, much as in the
Tabernacle passages. The psalmist exclaims: My closeness to God induces me to
sing the praises of all God's *malakhot* – creative activities, skillful accomplishments.

31. For this framing of "maker-activity," I am indebted to my daughter Adina Polen for
many fruitful discussions on this topic. Adina is a leader in the movement to advance
artistic excellence in Jewish culture. Her applied arts yeshiva is called *Atiq: Jewish
Makers Institute.*

32. There are other recent suggestions for finding a more apt word than "work" to translate *melakha*. Robert Alter renders it "task," but this is not much of an improvement,
as it intimates laborious activity, a chore to be finished. I prefer the suggestion of
Baruch Levine in the *JPS Bible Commentary: Leviticus* (Jewish Publication Society,
5749/1989), 238 (excursus 8), who translates *melakha* as "assigned tasks." Assignment
adds a dimension of purposiveness and social significance, a broader context of
meaning; this comes close to my choice of "project."

(Gen. 1:31). God apprised the whole and judged it apt and aesthetically pleasing. The parts fitted together into a harmonious whole. It is because God saw that what God had made was "very good" that *vayekhulu* could be stated.[33] We recall Cassuto's analogy to an "artist finishing a work, stepping back to consider the piece in its entirety, taking delight in the result, noting with satisfaction the elegant coherence of parts and whole." Taken in ensemble, our insights into *vayekhulu* and *melakha* (together with the now widely accepted translation of SH-B-T as "cease" or "desist," rather than "rest") confirm and reinforce each other. Scripture's narrative voice is not asserting a dry, inert fact, claiming that the work was over and that now God could take a rest. God is not depicted as exhausted in this passage, or as having nothing left to do. The *melakha* ceased not because the task was over, but because the opus was deemed worthy. This was not the end of a line, but the sense of an ending in the artistic spirit.[34]

What does all this have to do with Shabbos? Shabbos is first and foremost an act of *imitatio Dei*; just as God ceased from *melakha* on the seventh day, so should we (Ex. 20:11; 31:17). The aspirational ideal is to

---

33. Although there is a chapter break between Genesis 1:31 and 2:1, synagogue recitations of Torah never stop reading after verse 1:31; the reader (*baal koreh*) always continues with 2:1–3. Ziony Zevit, *What Really Happened in the Garden of Eden?* (New Haven and London: Yale University Press, 2013), 77, notes that "the reference to 'heavens and earth' in Genesis 2:1 echoes the introductory sentence of the creation story in Genesis 1:1–3: 'In the beginning of God's creating the heavens and the earth.'" That is, Genesis 2:1 echoes the language of 1:1 and brings it to closure. It follows that it is the sixth day that completes creation.

34. For the phrase, see Frank Kermode, *The Sense of an Ending: Studies in the Theory of Fiction* (Oxford, 1967; second edition, Oxford University Press, 2000). The idea that God took immense pride and joy in His handicraft and accomplishments is explicit in *Midrash Tanḥuma, Shemini* 2:

> When the blessed Holy One created His world, He was filled with great joy, as it is stated (Ps. 104:31), "The LORD shall be happy in His works." It also says (Gen. 1:31), "Then God saw everything which He had made and behold, it was very good." These verses teach you that the blessed Holy One took pride in His work and found it worthy of commendation (*mitga'eh umishtabe'aḥ bemaasav*).

An earlier midrashic source is Genesis Rabba 12:1 on Genesis 2:4: "God takes pride in God's world and says: 'Look at the creature I have created, at the figure I have shaped!'" Our text of Genesis Rabba softens the anthropopathism with the word *kevayakhol*, "as it were," but the point remains.

cease for the reason God ceased – not out of weariness, fatigue, and drained energies, but out of confidence that the facets of *melakha* – the maker-activities that fill the weekdays – have been well done and have achieved what we hoped they would accomplish, and that we can take satisfaction in the result.

In this reading, the Decalogue command of Shabbos – "Six days you should engage in work, and accomplish all your *melakha*/projects" – is as much an instruction for how to view weekday endeavors as it is about sanctifying the seventh day; indeed, the two are totally interdependent. When we aim for our weekday work to be "good," to be pleasing and beautiful along every dimension that matters – aesthetic, cultural, moral, as well as practical – then we will be able to bring it to closure, to finish it with pride, satisfaction, and confidence, and to enter Shabbos with joy and gratitude.

This spirit was captured by Franz Joseph Haydn in his oratorio *The Creation,* a choral work that celebrates God's creation of the world, drawing on the book of Genesis and related texts. Haydn's masterpiece begins with an orchestral introduction called "The Representation of Chaos" (*tohu vavohu*). Haydn depicts the state of formlessness and disorder by means of music that is "ambiguous and harmonically unmoored," inventively deploying "downright weird instrumental effects," in the words of music critic Anthony Tommasini. The eerie, uncanny notes conjure a mood of "riveting nothingness." I do not know if Haydn had any knowledge of Kabbala, but I cannot think of a better definition of *ayin,* the primordial state from which substantive creation emerged, than "riveting nothingness."[35] As creation proceeds and the chorus sings, "And there was light," the sound turns joyously triumphal, with luminosity announced by an expansive, powerful, and confidently melodious chord.

At the conclusion of God's creative activity, the chorus sings, "Achieved is the Glorious Work." The librettist of *The Creation* eloquently captures the sense of aesthetic satisfaction expressed by these verses. As Peter J. Gomes once observed, the words "Achieved is the Glorious Work"

---

35. I quote from Anthony Tommasini's review in the *New York Times* of a performance by the London Symphony Orchestra at Avery Fisher Hall: "At 80, Colin Davis Indulges in a Program of His Favorites," *New York Times,* October 23, 2007.

in the oratorio mark "a sense of accomplishment, of purpose fulfilled, of destiny reached, of something fully and finally done."[36] Haydn and his librettist have got this precisely right: *Vayekhulu* is not termination but achievement, an ending not because the string has run out but because the work of creation – the cosmos we inhabit – is glorious.

To achieve Shabbos is to enter a domain of contentment and confidence, not so much to rest but to *rest assured*.

This, of course, has a profound impact on the weekdays. The knowledge that I'm going to bring the project of the week to closure shapes my thinking every day; it assists me in being able to actually bring it to closure. It invites me to concentrate on what is really important and to defer or eliminate the trivial, the superficial, the distractive of my main purposes.[37]

The realization that Shabbos is the time to behold, consider, and appreciate encourages us to make the week into an opus, with each segment of every day fashioned with intention and awareness. The activities of the week are elevated to craftsmanship and artistry. Like God in Genesis 1:31, we want to be able to see all we have done and say, "Behold, it is very good!" Or, to move from elevated biblical language to a colloquial vernacular, we want to look and say, "Wow – that's amazing!"

As Ben Schachter puts it, "Those who honor the Sabbath recognize God's creation, but they also recognize the (creative) work they completed during the week, hoping that it can be found to be 'good,' just as God did at the end of the story of creation."[38]

To be sure, pursuit of livelihood and toilsome activity are ruled out on Shabbos as well, but not by the word *melakha*.[39]

There is a reciprocal relationship between Shabbos and weekday in this understanding. By setting a limit to the week and providing a time to behold and regard the world we have created, Shabbos gives

---

36. Peter J. Gomes, from a year-end Morning Prayer delivered at Harvard University Memorial Church.
37. I owe this formulation and insight to my son-in-law Elisha Mallard.
38. Schachter, *Image, Action, and Idea*, 43.
39. See Nahmanides's Torah commentary on Leviticus 23:24, s.v. *shabbaton*. The verse addresses those who use Shabbos to catch up on household chores or engage in commercial activities. For fuller discussion, see below, note 53.

definition and dignity to the weekdays. And the weekdays reciprocate by serving as the time that our actions may be elevated, transmuted, and directed to sacred projects, when tasks may become work-in-progress, may aspire to be *melakha,* by having a clear focus and aim – that aim being the hallowed and blessed moment when the week will come to closure, and the time to stop, to behold, to regard with admiration and appreciation, will have arrived. Shabbos is not an escape from the week, but rather a deeper appreciation of it. Shabbos is not an analgesic or a sedative. Shabbos is an invitation to alertness, attunement, and vitality.

Such are the gifts of biblical Shabbos.

VAYEVAREKH AND *VAYEKADESH*: BLESSING AND HALLOWING

Two key words describe the God-given attributes of the seventh day: blessing (*barekh*) and hallowing (*kadesh*).

Genesis 2:1–2 speaks of God finishing the project of creation and desisting (sh-b-t) from further activity on the project. These verses address God's activity or cessation from activity. The foci are God and the created cosmos, "the heavens and the earth and all their host." Only in the third verse of this section, Genesis 2:3, are we told that "God blessed the seventh day and hallowed it."

The verbs in this sentence (bless, hallow) are transitive, describing God's bestowal of qualities upon the *day*, indicating that the seventh day has identity, the capacity to accept and embrace the gifts bestowed. This idea is far from obvious; indeed, it is a revolutionary transformation in consciousness. Note that in Genesis chapter 1, God surveys the objects created on each day and sees that that they are "good," but God does not call the days themselves "good"; the days are not recipients of attributes. It is an enormous – and largely overlooked – conceptual leap to consider a day as having identity, as having the ability to absorb and retain qualities that remain stable over time. To call the day "blessed" is to give it ontological reality; it is to give the day a *face.* As legal theorists might put it, the seventh day has "standing." Even if we were to learn nothing more of biblical theology, this would be an extraordinary insight.

The individuated reality that the seventh day achieves in Genesis 2:3 entails periodicity, the cyclic return of the day with identity intact.

This periodicity invites the thoughtful reader to envision a temporal grid, a matrix comprised of rows and columns – much as the gridlike array of a calendar page displaying an entire month. The rows of the matrix contain the six days, assigned ordinal numbers (as in Genesis 1), with each row ending with the seventh day, the only day tagged with the qualities "blessed" and "hallowed." The heptadic rows are arrayed vertically, positioned one over the other, creating columns, so that each "seventh day" joins its predecessors in the vertical array and anticipates its successors. Thus, the rhythmic recurrence of this specially marked day gives not only a horizontal progression to each week, culminating in the day to be called (later in the Bible) "Shabbos," but also *a vertical direction to time*, allowing one to think of instantiations of days and weeks past, days and weeks yet to arrive, as well as one's situatedness in the current day and week.

In Exodus, with the emergence of the children of Israel as a people, the seventh day receives the proper name Shabbos, and the association with holiness is reaffirmed (see Ex. 16:23). In Exodus 20:8–11, the pivotal passage of the Decalogue, the centrality of Shabbos is underscored. Reference is made to the creation narrative of Genesis, and we are again told that God "blessed" and "hallowed" the day of Shabbos.

What do these terms mean? What are these qualities that Shabbos receives? The core meaning of blessing is greeting, acknowledgment, salutation. To bless is *to affirm personhood of the one blessed.* When God "blesses" the seventh day, God is *bestowing personhood on Shabbos,* affirming that this day has a personality that deserves to be recognized, honored, and cherished. Shabbos's personality emerges over time, growing and developing in each historical period, but the idea that Shabbos has an identity is entirely biblical.

Similar observations can be made regarding God's hallowing of Shabbos. *Kedusha* (holiness) entails marking off a particular domain – spatial, temporal, or social – as distinct, focusing attention upon it in order to positively affect the domains not so marked. *Kedusha* is not "separation" in the sense of segregation or isolation. It is not meant to be exclusionary. *Kedusha* has a buoyant, uplifting, attractive quality. Think of *kedusha* as "sublime force," with the term "force" used as it is in physics: a push or a pull upon an object resulting from the object's interaction with another object. "Sublime" has the dictionary sense of "of very great excellence or beauty"; "of such excellence, grandeur, or beauty as to inspire great admiration or awe."[40] And, we should add, that *kedusha* inspires goodness, compassion, and greater moral and aesthetic sensitivity. *Kedusha* is a non-coercive invitational force that radiates from God's Presence. This purposive, transformative intensity exerts a positive influence toward excellence, virtue, loftiness, and nobility.[41]

Kedusha is closely linked with *berakha*, blessing. *Berakha* and *kedusha* may be viewed as complementary sides of the same process: *Kedusha*'s transformative energy is centripetal, directed inward, while *berakha* faces outward. One could not exist without the other. *Kedusha* is not estrangement from the world, but engagement with it; the distinctiveness it calls for is to benefit those one serves and blesses. The centripetal impulse is purposive – to clear and activate inner space to bestow positive influence. The journey inward is in order to emerge empowered to bestow blessing. As the Lithuanian *rosh yeshiva* and halakhic theorist Rabbi Shimon Shkop (1860–1939) wrote, "Holiness means dedication to noble purpose – all one's deeds motivated not by self-interest but directed to the greater good, for the benefit of the world."[42]

Blessing and holiness are also alike in being ampliative and emergent; they are properties that grow over time, whose full meaning is always yet to be fathomed and discovered, whose radius of influence expands and encompasses ever more, inscribing expansive virtuous circles of positive influence. As the literary critic and bible scholar Harold Fisch writes, "Paradoxically, the day of rest is announced by a group of signifiers that suggest ceaseless activity, a willed intention to shape a future…a beginning rather than an ending…openness rather than closure. We are speaking of a day invested with purposes still to be fulfilled."[43]

---

40. *Oxford Dictionary Online.*

41. I have expanded upon these ideas in my essay, "Touches of Intimacy: Leviticus, Sacred Space, Torah's Center," in *A New Hasidism, Volume II: Branches*, ed. Arthur Green and Ariel Evan Mayse (Jewish Publication Society/University of Nebraska Press, 2019).

42. Rabbi Shimon Shkop, *Shaarei Yosher* (1925), author's introduction.

43. Harold Fisch, *Poetry with a Purpose* (Bloomington and Indianapolis: Indiana University Press, 1988), 22.

To conclude: At the end of the creation narrative, the seventh day is greeted by God ("blessed"), granted personhood, and given the gift of holiness. This capstone of creation reflects God's confidence in the cosmos as beautiful opus, as work of art worthy of acclaim. The covenantal intimacy between God, Shabbos as named day, and Israel, is yet to come; this is left for the book of Exodus, when Israel becomes a people.

SECTION TWO: MANNA, LOCATION, SHABBOS

While the introduction of the seventh day as special – as "blessed" and "hallowed" – occurs as the capstone of the creation story, at that point the seventh day has not yet received a proper name. We read that "God ceased/desisted [the activity of creation] on the seventh day" (Gen. 2:2, 3). The Hebrew root SH-B-T appears, but as a verb, not a noun. The seventh day has been blessed and hallowed, but it has not yet been assigned the name Shabbos; for this we must wait until Exodus chapter 16, the manna narrative.

At this point in the narrative, the children of Israel have left Egypt, have experienced the miracle of the splitting of the Sea (Ex. 14–15), and have spent some time at Elim, a lovely oasis with twelve springs of water and seventy palm trees. They leave Elim and arrive in the Wilderness of Sin[44] (Ex. 16:1), where the people complain that they have no food.

This episode is usually read as an early instance of the people's ingratitude, murmuring, and complaining, a constant pattern throughout the forty years of the desert trek. My sympathies, however, are with the people. It is now a month since the exodus from Egypt (Ex. 16:1), and they should have already reached the Promised Land. The journey should not take more than a few weeks, even traveling by foot (see Ex. 13:17; Deut. 1:2). The people have not been told about a divine Revelation at Mount Sinai, about Torah, about the Decalogue. All they know is the promise of returning to the land of their ancestors (Ex. 3:8, 17; 6:8; 12:25; 13:4, 11, 17). Looking out at this strange, vast, and forbidding expanse, they must surely be asking: Why are we here? As slaves in Egypt, the people had been living in a highly developed society of great antiquity, with buildings and

---

44. This name has nothing to do with the English word meaning transgression; it is likely associated with the soon-to-be-introduced Sinai.

monuments everywhere. Now they are looking out at a wasteland with no markers; they are emerging into the reality of wilderness, of no-place. The desert is not a destination, but rather a non-location. Seeing nothing but empty desert, they lack any sense of direction or hint of what to expect for the future. The fact that they have just left a lovely oasis with springs and palm trees would only have increased their frustration and confusion.

The children are crying!

Their complaints are totally understandable, justified.

Their grievances are not just about lack of water and food, reasonable as those are. The people are shocked by the total lack of orientation in the wilderness. This theme appears already in Exodus 14:3, where God tells Moses that Pharaoh will reverse his decision to let the people go. God informs Moses that Pharaoh will say, "They are confused/astray (*nevukhim*) in the land; the wilderness has closed in on them." As often throughout the narrative, the lines given to Pharaoh are astute and perceptive. The vastness of the wilderness actually "closes in" on the person lost within it; the radius of vision seems infinitely large and therefore shrinks to nothing. The eyes sweep the horizon, and finding nothing to hold on to, sight collapses in a swirling vertigo of disorientation.

The eminent thirteenth-century talmudist, kabbalist, and biblical commentator Nahmanides (Moses ben Nahman, 1194–1270) captures this sense precisely. Commenting on Exodus 16:2, "And the whole congregation of the children of Israel murmured against Moses and Aaron in the wilderness," he writes:

> In my opinion, the reason for their complaint is to be found in the scriptural expression, "and they came…unto the wilderness of Sin" (Ex. 16:1)…. It may be that at first they had thought that after a few days they would come to the cities round about them. Now that a month had gone by and they found no cities of habitation (Ps. 107:4), they said, "We will all die in the great wilderness into which we have come."

Nahmanides is telling us that the people's complaint was not just about the lack of food or water; it was provoked and intensified by wilderness disorientation.

He directs us to Psalms 107:4: "They wandered in the wilderness, in the desolation of the path; they found no inhabited city." This verse echoes the Song of Moses in Deuteronomy: "He [God] discovered him [Israel] in a wilderness land, in formless chaos (*tohu*), a howling desolation" (Deut. 32:10). This poetic retelling of the exodus story focuses on the chaotic conditions of the wilderness, evoking the *tohu* (formless chaos) that preceded creation in Genesis 1. The Deuteronomic version of the exodus story will eventually mention that God provided the people with delicious food (Deut. 32:13–14). But first, and evidently more importantly, we are told of God's loving response to the wilderness conditions: "He [God] surrounded him [Israel]; [God] gave [Israel] discernment; [God] guarded [Israel] as the apple of His eye" (Deut. 32:10). God's protective encirclement and imparting discernment were the antidotes to the *tohu*; God's first caring response was to provide a positional focus, a circumference of divine embrace.

The discomforts of the desert were real, but they were made more acute by the initial disorientation, and their complaints took the form of remembering Egypt fondly: "When we sat by the fleshpots, when we did eat bread to the full; for you have brought us forth into this wilderness, to kill this whole assembly with hunger" (Ex. 16:3). In their nostalgic imagination, the people recall savory meat meals, but their idealization does not merely concern food. The phrase "when we sat by the fleshpots" – more literally, "when we sat *on* the fleshpots" – is contrasted to the contemptuous "this wilderness." The Hebrew word for "when we sat" – *beshivteinu*, with the Hebrew root Y-SH-V – suggests locatedness, exactly what was missing in their current circumstance. The Israelites were experiencing nostalgia for Egypt, but this was not ingratitude; it was a natural response to finding themselves without bearing, without position, bereft of situatedness.[45]

---

45. Avivah Zornberg elegantly captures the challenge of the wilderness trek narrated in the book of Numbers in her deployment of the word "bewilderment." See Avivah Gottlieb Zornberg, *Bewilderments: Reflections on the Book of Numbers* (New York: Schocken Books, 2015). For Zornberg, the wilderness is landscape that "does not yield to human demands," frustrating "the basic demand for direction, for markings to indicate a human mapping of blank space" (xii). It is notable that while Exodus links manna with Shabbos, Numbers makes no mention of Shabbos in its manna

As we shall see, the word for sitting – Y-SH-V – figures prominently in connection with the manna.

SHABBOS AS DISCOVERY AND GIFT OF PLACE

In this light, Exodus chapter 16 is about more than sustenance in the wilderness. The manna not only provided food; it also enabled the Israelites to discover Shabbos and simultaneously imparted a secure location, a being-in-place that fosters confidence and trust.

At first glance, Exodus chapter 16 appears to plot an unsteady and confusing trajectory. In the initial response to the people's complaints about food, God says to Moses:

> I will rain down bread for you from the sky, and the people shall go out and gather each day that day's portion – that I may thus test them, to see whether they will follow My instructions or not. But on the sixth day, when they apportion what they have brought in, it shall prove to be double the amount they gather each day. (Ex. 16:4–5)

We are already puzzled: What is the "test"? And what is meant by the "sixth day"? Is the reference to the sixth day of the week? The sixth day of the manna's arrival? Both? And what is the significance of the "double portion" that, without the people's intending it, manifests on that sixth day – apparently miraculously?

These verses foreshadow the introduction of Shabbos as a well-defined practice, something that will indeed happen later in the narrative (see vv. 23, 25, 29). But what is the point of the vague allusion to Shabbos at the very start of the chapter, in verse 4?

Moses seems to be as puzzled as we are, for he does not mention the sixth day's double portion until the sixth day, and even then

---

narrative. Exodus 16 wishes to present Shabbos as embodied practice that positions the Israelites in a specific locale, with the manna's evident visibility providing a tangible anchor in both place and time. The Torah in this Exodus passage wishes us to keep in mind that for one day every week, there was no traveling, but rather a settling-in and staying-in-place that fostered stability, equipoise, and the creation of community, thus counteracting the desert's "bewilderment."

only when prompted by the questioning of the tribal chieftains, who report with surprise the preternatural increase of the manna collected on that day (v. 22).

Rabbi Hayim ben Attar (1696–1743; eminent talmudist, Torah expositor, and kabbalist; Morocco, Italy, and Jerusalem) addresses these questions in his commentary *Or HaHayim*:

> God wanted to implant the apt, essential rightness of Shabbos as coming directly from God Above, not through a command delivered by a messenger [even such a one as Moses]. This happened when the people went out to gather the manna on the sixth day as they had done every weekday, an amount sufficient for that day, and after measuring they found an amount double that of previous days. This was compelling visual evidence that God wanted them not to make effort on Shabbos, instead providing the seventh day's portion on the sixth day.... So Moses did not initially command the Israelites regarding Shabbos.

In other words, Moses did not convey to them God's anticipatory announcement in Exodus 16:5 that the yield of Friday's gathering would be double that of previous days, without their intending to collect more; he waited until they noticed this on their own, as reported in 16:22. Had Moses told them about Shabbos ahead of time, they would have intentionally collected a double portion on Friday. As it was, they stumbled upon the truth of Shabbos unawares, and this intensified its power and effect. Shabbos was revealed to them not as command, but as a gift, a discovery.

Or HaHayim picks up this theme in his comment on 16:29, God's words to Moses: "Look – God has given you the Shabbos":

> The institution of Shabbos does not require an explicit directive. You Israelites see its reality with your own eyes; it comes directly from God without any mediation, even the mediation of Moses. This is a feature that Shabbos has [above all other mitzvot and Torah institutions]: The Israelites would see the palpability of Shabbos as manifestly visible. The words *al yetze ish mimekomo*

bayom hashevi'i (Ex. 16:29) are not to be taken as a command: "No one should leave their place on the seventh day," but rather as a blessing: "No one will have need to depart from their home in search of food" [since a double portion will arrive on Friday].

We may add that "everyone should settle into their location" and "let no one go out of their place" are essential aspects of the blessing of Shabbos; they should be read as promises and invitations. On Shabbos, you will not need to run to and fro, neither to find food, nor to dissipate nervous energy by distracting yourself. You may put yourself at ease; you can rest easy! All this is in contrast to the confusion, anxiety, and disorientation of the Israelites' first experience of the desert.

Exodus 16, with its lurches, jolts, and retrograde movements, is, in the eyes of *Or HaHayim*, a literary enactment of the narrative, wherein the Israelites initially stumble into Shabbos, tumble into their gift, only later to fully realize its impact and significance, so that in the future they might learn to appreciate it, to prepare and accept it mindfully.

Or HaHayim's approach to reading this narrative is echoed in the writings of Benno Jacob (1862–1945), a rabbi trained at the Breslau seminary, who, with the rise of the Nazis, fled to England in 1939. Jacob's commentary is noted for its ability to join the apparent fault lines of biblical narrative into a seamless and meaningful whole. His expository skill is particularly evident in the manna story, and his interpretation of Exodus chapter 16 emphasizes the centrality of Shabbos to the narrative. He writes:

> The special nature of the Sabbath has also been emphasized by the divine request that everyone remain in his place and not move on the seventh day.... Here we do not have the style of a lawgiver or judge, but the warning words of a teacher and friend.... Since I yesterday provided a double portion of manna, you need not move from your place today. This [the rootedness in place] was God's gift and represented His watchful care, just like the double portion of manna.[46]

---

46. *The Second Book of the Bible: Exodus*, interpreted by Benno Jacob, translated with an introduction by Walter Jacob, in association with Yaakov Elman (Hoboken, NJ: Ktav Publishing House, 1992), 461, on Exodus 16:29.

The embeddedness-in-place is more a gift than a prohibition, more an opportunity than a limitation. This insight is reinforced in Jacob's comment on Exodus 16:29:

> See – the LORD has given you (*natan*) Shabbos; therefore He gives for you (*noten*) on the sixth day enough food for two days; everyone should settle into their location; let no one go out of their place on the seventh day.

Jacob points out that *natan* and *noten* are words of gift-giving. The institution of Shabbos is a gift – *matana* – just as the double portion of manna on Friday is a gift – *matana*.[47]

This understanding of Shabbos as the gift of place finds support from other biblical occurrences akin to the phrase *shevu ish tahtav*, "everyone should settle into their place," or a close variant. In II Samuel 7:10, we read:

---

47. The tight nexus between manna and Shabbos, and their mutual classification as gift graciously disclosed rather than commanded edict, is already found in the biblical book of Nehemiah: "You made known [not "commanded" – NP] Your sacred Shabbos to them…and You gave them/gifted them bread from heaven" (Neh. 9:14–15). It is also significant that in this chapter, manna is linked with the gift of preternatural wisdom: "You gave them/gifted them Your good spirit (*ruḥakha hatova*) to nurture their understanding (*lehaskilam*), and You did not withhold Your manna from their mouths" (9:20). *Ruḥakha hatova*, which I translate here as "good spirit," intends a heaven-sent faculty of intellection beyond normal human cognition, what in a later period is referred to as *ruaḥ hakodesh*. See Ibn Ezra on 9:14: "Among all the statements of the Decalogue, Shabbos is singled out, because Shabbos has the special virtue of repose and enhanced intellection (*tosefet sekhel*)." Ibn Ezra on 9:20: "The 'good spirit' alludes to the prophetic spirit bestowed upon the seventy elders in Numbers 11:25." *Baal HaTurim* on 9:20: "By ingesting the manna, the Israelites received supernal awareness [*de'ah*, based on Deut. 8:3]. This is the meaning of the rabbinic statement that 'the Torah was only given to manna-eaters' (*Mekhilta* on Ex. 16:4)." Normally taken to mean that Torah study can only flourish among those who have the time to pursue it, free of the demands of making a living, the *Baal HaTurim* points out the deeper significance of this early midrashic trope: The Torah can be comprehended only by those gifted with supernal intellection, as ingested and metabolized by the manna.
The phrase in Nehemiah 9:14, "*VeShabbat kodshekha hodata lahem*," is the source for the concluding words of the *Ata Yatzarta* liturgy recited as in Musaf when Shabbos and Rosh Hodesh coincide; see, e.g., *Koren Siddur*, 599. I am grateful to Rabbi Yisrael Torchin of the Kamenitz Yeshiva in Jerusalem for bringing these sources to my attention.

> I will establish a home [*makom,* literally, "a place"] for My people
> Israel, and will plant them firm so that they shall dwell in their
> place [*veshakhan taḥtav*] and shall tremble no more.

This verse is the prophet Nathan's promise to David, assuring him
his role as leader of Israel. Note the language of planting, suggesting rootedness, of finding a place, *makom,* with resonances on many
levels, and then, "they shall dwell in their place [*taḥtav*]." We might
even translate *veshakhan taḥtav* as "they shall dwell emplaced" – that
is, with the feeling of situatedness, security, balance, firmly centered
and buoyantly facing the future. The prophet Nathan, speaking in
the name of God, promises David that his "house" – his dynastic
successors – will continue after him, will lead the people Israel in
security, and will build a house for the Lord, a Sanctuary that will
be the focal point of the people's worship, devotion, and communal
life. The security, the rootedness, and the freedom from anxiety all
come together.

The phraseology of Exodus 16:29, "Everyone should settle into
their location [*taḥtav*]; let no one go out of their place on the seventh
day," closely parallels that of II Samuel 7:10 and makes much the same
point: The essential gift of Shabbos is to provide location, and the core
practice of Shabbos is to commit to a location.

This point is beautifully and succinctly captured in the midrashic
text *Sifrei Zuta* on Numbers (the earliest extant tannaitic Midrash, from
the school of R. Akiva). In the context of Numbers 15:32, "And the
children of Israel were in the wilderness," the midrash quotes Exodus
16:29, "Let no one go out of their place on the seventh day" (*al yetze
ish mimekomo*) and adds: *yehei lo makom,* "s/he will have a place." That
is, even in the wilderness, the desert expanse bereft of coordinates, the
Shabbos-keeper is given a place, a locale that provides security, orientation, and rootedness.

PREPARATION

Exodus 16 indicates that the situatedness that is the gift of Shabbos
involves preparation. This theme is introduced at the very beginning of
the narrative with God's words, "And it shall come to pass, on the sixth

day when they prepare what they bring in, that it shall be twice as much as they gather daily" (Ex. 16:5), and is elaborated upon later in the text:

> (22) And it came to pass that on the sixth day they gathered twice as much food, two omers for each one; and all the princes of the assembly came and told Moses. (23) And he said to them: "This is what the LORD has spoken: Tomorrow is a solemn cessation, a holy Shabbos to the LORD. Bake what you wish to bake, and cook what you wish to cook; and whatever is left over, put aside for yourselves as a safekeeping until the morning." (24) And they put it aside until the morning, as Moses had commanded; and it did not rot, and did not get wormy. (25) And Moses said: "Eat it today; for today is a Shabbos for the LORD; today you will not find it in the field. (26) Six days you will gather it; but the seventh day is Shabbos; on it there will be none."

The manna narrative connects Shabbos with the cosmic rhythm that was established at the beginning of Genesis at the creation of the world. This idea is underscored in the wording of God's statement "And it shall be that *on the sixth day* when they prepare what they bring, it will be double what they gather every day" (Ex. 16:4–5). The Hebrew for "on the sixth day" – *bayom hashishi* – occurs three times in the course of the manna narrative: in 16:5, 22, and 29. With the emphatic definite article, *the* sixth day, readers are meant to hear echoes of Genesis 1:31: *Vayehi erev vayehi voker, yom hashishi*, "And it was evening and it was morning, *the sixth day*." The double portion of manna on the sixth day and the absence of manna on the seventh day enacts divine rhythmic cessation, established at creation, before the eyes of the Israelites. The people are interested in food; Moses and Aaron are interested in managing their unruly crowd. God is more interested in introducing Shabbos as manifest reality.

The palpability of Shabbos's presence is reinforced for the people in three ways:

- The fact that "it happened on the sixth day that they gathered a double portion of food, two omers for each; and all the leaders of the assembly came and told Moses" (Ex. 16:22).

- The fact that on the sixth day leading up to the seventh, "they put [the extra portion] aside until the morning, as Moses had commanded; and it did not rot, and did not get wormy" (Ex. 16:24).
- The fact that "[It happened that some of the people went out to gather, and] they did not find" (Ex. 16:27). Note that it is because of the transgressors that we learn that the manna actually did not fall on the Sabbath day!

The people are told to *prepare* for Shabbos. This appears already in verse 5 and more fully in verse 23: "And he said to them: 'This is what the LORD has spoken: Tomorrow is a solemn cessation, a holy Shabbos to the LORD. Bake what you wish to bake, and cook what you wish to cook; and whatever is left over, put aside for yourselves as a safekeeping until the morning.'" And verse 25: "And Moses said: 'Eat it today; for today is a Shabbos for the LORD; today you will not find it in the field.'" The main emphasis appears to be the *preparation* for Shabbos.

In this context, the phrase "Let no one go out of their place on the seventh day" (16:29) means: You won't need to leave your place. You won't need to rearrange, because everyone and everything you need is already at hand, in range. Preparation is crucial. For a full day you are holding a place – your place.

EXISTENTIAL RESTLESSNESS

After Moses told the people that no manna would fall on the seventh day, some of the people decided to see for themselves: "And it came to pass on the seventh day, that some of the people went out to gather, and they found none" (Ex. 16:27).

It is at this point in the narrative that God more fully discloses the meaning of the manna's not falling on Shabbos with the words we have already cited: "See – the LORD has given you Shabbos; therefore He gives for you on the sixth day enough food for two days; everyone should settle into their location; let no one go out of their place on the seventh day" (16:29).

But as attentive readers, we should ask: What were they thinking? After all, the people had already seen the miraculous nature of the manna. No matter how vigorous or how lax they were in the gathering process, everyone got exactly one measure per day (16:18); anything left overnight was spoiled by the morning (v. 20); and on the sixth day, each person noticed that they had received a double portion (v. 22). The extra portion that had fallen on the sixth day was set aside for the seventh day, and this time, "it did not spoil, and there were no maggots in it" (v. 24). In light of all this evidence of the manna's miraculous nature and of the veracity and accuracy of God's directives as transmitted by Moses, why did some of the people go out to collect? Did they not realize that they would find nothing?

Perhaps they did not really expect to find anything. Perhaps they simply could not stay in place. Their gathering expedition was certainly not motivated by need; recall that they already had food for Shabbos (vv. 22–26). It may have been an expression of restlessness, of the need to fidget, to avoid focusing on what was already with them, available to them, securely in their tent. They could not still the impulse to *accumulate*. They had not allowed themselves to settle in, to find place; they had not given themselves the gift of presence.

Note throughout this chapter the interplay of the Hebrew roots SH-B-T (to pause, to stop, to cease) and Y-SH-B (to sit, to dwell, to settle in). This assonance is part of the force of verse 29: "See – the LORD has given you Shabbos [SH-B-T]; therefore He gives for you on the sixth day enough food for two days; everyone should settle [*shevu*, from the Hebrew root Y-SH-B] into their location; let no one go out of their place on the seventh day."

This should be taken together with verse 30, which we may translate as: "The people settled in [*vayishbetu*, from the Hebrew root SH-B-T] on the seventh day [*hashevi'i*, from the root SH-B-A]."

The three roots are different, but the sound-play is clear: *Shabbos/shevu/shevi'i*.

Etymologically, *Shabbos* is cessation, bringing to a stop; *shevi'i* is the seventh, an ordinal number, and *shevu* means to sit. But the Torah's narrative voice makes a deft sonic association highlighting the deep connection between Shabbos, the seventh day, and settling in place.

This connection is in contrast to the earlier *beshivteinu al sir habasar*, "when we sat on the fleshpots" (Ex. 16:3). In the people's idealized nostalgia for Egypt, they imagined sitting on fleshpots, providing not only food but anchorage in place. Now, with Shabbos, their anchor was real, not illusory. Having stilled the impulse to accumulate, they could genuinely inhabit their camp, their community, their tent, their bodies, their selves.

MANNA, SHABBOS, AND COMMUNITY

The social and communal dimension of Shabbos already appears in Exodus 16. Once again, Benno Jacob:

> The social component of this communal establishing a place of residence for Shabbat makes the collection of individuals rise to the level of the people called for the first time "the House of Israel" (v. 31).[48]

Jacob notices that the significant phrase *Beit Yisrael,* "the House of Israel," appears for the first time in Scripture here, just after the people have finally, collectively, understood and accepted and observed Shabbos as a communal practice: *Vayishbetu haam bayom hashevi'i* (v. 30).

The translations of this sentence are instructive. The Jewish Publication Society *Tanakh* (1917) has: "So the people rested on the seventh day." But, as we've seen, the root SH-V-T does not mean "to rest" in the standard sense. New JPS and *The Jewish Study Bible,* evidently responding to this concern, have: "So the people remained inactive on the seventh day." But this also misses the mark. The people were not told to be inactive, just to stay in place and not to leave the camp and attempt to gather food. The Hebrew should be understood to mean that the people set aside their regular weekday activities – in particular, venturing outside the camp, as well as cooking and baking.

Since the first Shabbos was not kept by the entire people, verse 30 can only be referring to the second Shabbos under the manna regime, an early indication that Shabbos-keeping requires practice and that communal coordination and consensus emerge gradually. When that consensus arose, the camp in the wilderness became a household, a unified residence.

---

48. Jacob, *Second Book of the Bible,* 390–91.

Now there was *there* (with apologies to Gertrude Stein). The disoriented escapees have now found their place.

Initially, Moses did not explain to the people the deep connection of manna to Shabbos. At first, as far as the Israelites are concerned, manna is just food. As the story unfolds, they are depicted as stumbling, lurching clumsily into a trusting relationship with God. Eventually, they will come to see that with manna, God was providing more than food. They were given a weekly gift of Shabbos and the opportunity to mindfully prepare for it.

The people had been gathering manna daily, beginning on the first day of the week (what is now called Sunday). On the sixth day (Friday), they gathered manna and were surprised to find, after they came home, a double portion in their containers. The leaders came to Moses and reported their puzzlement about the double portion. Only at this point did Moses explain that "tomorrow is a cessation, a Sabbath of Holiness unto the LORD; bake what you wish to bake and cook what you wish to cook, and whatever is left over, put aside for yourselves as a safekeeping until the morning" (16:23).

Although God had intimated to Moses the specialness of the seventh day at the very beginning of this episode (16:5), Moses did not convey the information to the people initially. The first time the concept of Shabbos emerges is when the people see the double portion in their gathering buckets. The evidence of Shabbos emerges in front of their eyes!

The narrative voice tells us that on that Friday, the people followed Moses's instructions and saved manna to eat for the following day – Shabbos. Unlike a previous incident, when some individuals had hoarded manna overnight and it rotted, this time it did not spoil (16:24). The people had taken nearly an entire week to learn the lesson of trust – that they should not attempt to stockpile manna, and if they did, their effort would be futile. Now they were learning a complementary lesson – that their effort to get ready for Shabbos ahead of time was not greedy hoarding, but rather sacred preparation, a practice that would be met with success and blessing. Moses encourages them as follows: "Moses said, 'Eat it today, today is Shabbos unto the LORD; today you will not find it in the field'" (16:25).

I understand this as Moses saying to the people: Even though you will be enjoying manna, your eating will be devotional, sacred – not merely gustatory or utilitarian, but a holy act of surrender even as you take delight.

Shabbos is cessation, stopping that is *directed*; it is a vector of intentionality focused on God, aimed and lovingly handed up to God as offering, as gift.

The gifts of manna and Shabbos have transformed the wilderness. No longer facing a terrifying, featureless colossus in isolation, the people are now neighbors in a joint enterprise. Arranging their lives with Shabbos in mind, they are situated communally, partners in a collective household.

SECTION THREE: THE DECALOGUE

The next mention of Shabbos is in the Decalogue (the "Ten Commandments").[49] Exodus 19 and 20 introduce the covenant between God and Israel. In Exodus 19:4–6, God makes a specific proposal to Israel: If they accept and observe what God calls "My covenant," they will become a "kingdom of priests and a holy nation." The people have little idea at this time what that means. The Decalogue begins the process of providing specifics, but the Decalogue is essentially an outline, a

---

49. The Talmud (Shabbat 86–87; Yoma 4a–b) discusses the biblical account of the arrival at Sinai and the preparations for the revelation of the Decalogue (Ex. 19). While there is considerable debate about how to read the narrative timetable given there and how to reconcile chapter 19 with the related passage in Exodus 24, all rabbinic opinions concur with the assertion that "the Torah was given on Shabbos." As Rashi explains, the Decalogue's "Remember the Shabbos day to hallow it" is read self-referentially: We are to remember the day in light of the fact that the commandment was given *on that very day*. As Rashi puts it: "We were told to remember Shabbos on the very day of Shabbos itself (*be'aztmo shel yom hazekhira*). See Rashi, Shabbat 86b, s.v. *mah lehalan*.

This reminds us that Shabbos already existed before the Sinai event. The Decalogue presupposes Shabbos, relies on it as a given. The fourth commandment underscores Shabbos's centrality and amplifies it, but does not treat it as a new revelation. Shabbos is the essential basis for the entirety of the Jewish religion, the foundational frame upon which every other aspect of Judaism stands.

kind of executive summary of the full set of commandments. The only overt ritual in the Decalogue is the observance of Shabbos.

On Exodus 20:8 ("Remember the Shabbos day to hallow it"), Nahmanides comments as follows:

> "Remembering" Shabbos entails viewing the day as sacred, in line with the verse "If you call the Shabbos 'pleasure,' the LORD's holy day 'honored'" (Is. 58:13). This means that we should view our desisting as motivated by the day's sanctity, clearing our minds of business entanglements and time-killing diversions. We give delight to our spirits by following a Godly itinerary, seeking wisdom from sages and prophets.

Nahmanides is telling us that letting go of weekday concerns is the very essence of the Decalogue's call to Shabbos. Letting go is not just a pious embellishment or supererogatory afterthought, and it is certainly not a functional strategy to enable one to return to work refreshed, in service to a market economy and a culture of consumption. Nahmanides's deployment of Isaiah 58 means that the prophetic call to desist from weekday pursuits, to steer clear of conversational topics involving business, and to avoid the frenzied rush to acquire material goods results in an expansive appreciation of the world and all its inhabitants, especially the needy (Is. 58:6ff.), and this is the central aim of Shabbos's regulations. Nahmanides makes clear that Isaiah's word *oneg* ("pleasure" or "delight") does not primarily intend indulging in earthly delights, but the pleasure of breathing clear Edenic air in a body that is open and free, after having dropped the heavy encumbrances and rigid constraints of the weekday.[50]

Here is Sforno's comment on the same verse:

> This is what you should do in order to be able to hallow Shabbos: Be sure to arrange your affairs during the [six] weekdays in such a way that you will be able to detach your mind from those affairs on the Shabbos day.

---

50. See also Radak on Isaiah 58:14: *Vehataanug al Hashem hu taanug hanefesh*, "The 'pleasure' is spiritual pleasure."

For Sforno, this verse is a call to organize the week to make room for Shabbos, to make Shabbos *feasible*. It takes careful planning and thoughtful organization to ensure that what needs to be accomplished is done in six days rather than seven, that by Friday afternoon one can reasonably and responsibly call the workweek finished. The game of worldly pursuits is called – not on account of bad weather, nor on account of weariness or missed opportunities – but in order to honor the day of sanctity that is about to arrive.

Sforno adds an essential element to Rashi's observation that when Shabbos comes, "it should be in your eyes as if all your work is done; you should not be thinking about work."[51] As usual, Rashi's comment (based on the early Midrash *Mekhilta*) summarizes the entire rabbinic perspective on Shabbos in a single well-chosen phrase. What is left unstated in this oft-cited comment, however, is how such an enviable state of inner freedom is to be achieved. One cannot simply prevent the mind from thinking weekday thoughts by an act of will. If a week hasn't been planned to culminate in a hard stop by late Friday afternoon, it will be difficult – and possibly irresponsible – to call a halt to all weekday activity at sunset. One cannot lurch into Shabbos by slamming on the brakes and expect to enter into a state of blissful repose using mental effort alone. Sforno makes clear that Shabbos-consciousness must pervade the entire week, beginning on Sunday. It is not only (once again quoting Rashi, from talmudic sources) that when on a weekday you come across a hard-to-find food item, you should set it aside for Shabbos.[52] Shabbos awareness shapes the architecture of every aspect of your embodied existence – temporal, spatial, phenomenological. Your mind's executive function always operates with awareness of the next Shabbos – at times focally, at other times peripherally. Starting on Sunday, you are already in Shabbos's field of force; having set your sights on Shabbos, your week's trajectory is calibrated to reach the sacred target, to dock at the destination.

---

51. Rashi on Exodus 20:9.
52. Beitza 16a.

SHABBOS IN THE PROPHETS

Each of the major literary prophets makes a strong prophetic call to observe Shabbos. This is true for Isaiah, Jeremiah, and Ezekiel.

Isaiah chapter 58, the great prophetic call for justice for the poor as the essence of true repentance, is read in the synagogue on Yom Kippur day. The coda to that chapter highlights a series of core elements of Shabbos, including fixing one's position, abstaining from commerce and all weekday occupations, and elevated speech on Shabbos:

> If you restrain, because of Shabbos, your feet; refrain from pursuing your affairs on My holy day; if you proclaim Shabbos as delight, the LORD's holy day as honored, and you honor it by not engaging in your own ways, not attending to your own affairs, nor speaking of material matters, then you shall delight yourself in the LORD; and I will mount you upon the heights of the earth, and nourish you with the heritage of Jacob your father, for the mouth of the LORD has spoken. (Is. 58:13–14)

The linkage of these final verses to the preceding verses of the chapter, with their ringing call for inclusion and vigilant attentiveness to society's vulnerable and marginalized, is a reminder that Shabbos is for service to our fellow human beings as much as to God, and that, as always in Scripture and later Judaism, the two foci are not just linked in the tightest way, but are two expressions of the same posture of humility and self-transcendence.

Jeremiah 17:19–27 is an astonishing passage, in that the prophet makes the fate of Jerusalem, the Temple, and the Davidic dynasty dependent on one mitzva – Shabbos:

> Thus said the LORD: Guard yourselves for your own sake against carrying burdens on the Shabbos day, and bringing them through the gates of Jerusalem. Nor shall you carry out burdens from your houses on the Shabbos day, or do any *melakha*, but you shall hallow the Shabbos day, as I commanded your fathers. (Jer. 17:21–22)

The prophet continues with the exultant promise that if the people keep Shabbos, Jerusalem, its leaders, and citizens will flourish eternally! As Jeremiah continues, "And this city shall be inhabited for all time."

Jeremiah's language echoes the terminology of the Deuteronomy Decalogue (Deut. 5:12–15). Ezekiel, for his part, is equally insistent on the centrality of Shabbos, but draws upon Exodus 31:12–17, where Shabbos is singled out as the central sign of the covenant between God and Israel:

> I gave them [the Israelites] My rules and taught them My statutes, so that people will follow them and live. Moreover, I gave them My Shabbos days to serve as a sign between Me and them, that they might know that it is I the LORD who sanctifies them. (Ezek. 20:11–12)

See also Amos 8:5, where the prophet mocks people for their impatience for Shabbos to end so that they can get back to business – which includes dishonest trading and cheating the poor! For Amos, Shabbos is incompatible with even *thinking about commerce,* and fidelity to Shabbos demands ethical behavior.

In the third major division of Scripture, the *Ketuvim* (Sacred Writings), we find the post-exilic book of Nehemiah, a memoir of the Jewish leader, who, under Persian authorization, directed the restoration of Jerusalem and the reconstruction of the Temple. Prominent among the legislative enactments of Nehemiah is the strict prohibition of conducting business on Shabbos (Neh. 13:15–22).[53] A revealing incident is found

---

53. This passage in Nehemiah 13 is cited by Rabbi Moshe Schreiber (the Ḥatam Sofer) as a source for halakha. See *Responsa Ḥatam Sofer, Hashmatot,* no. 195, on the question of keeping a store open on Shabbos, which Rabbi Schreiber rules is a violation of biblical, not just rabbinic, law. In addition to the passage in Nehemiah, Ḥatam Sofer cites Nahmanides's Torah commentary on Leviticus 23:24, s.v. *shabbaton.* According to Nahmanides, the verse addresses those who, while avoiding technical violations of *melakha* as defined in Mishna Shabbat, ch. 7, use Shabbos to catch up on household chores or engage in commercial activities. Nahmanides asserts that the word *shabbaton* ("complete cessation") requires completely desisting from weekday activities of all kinds, any activity incompatible with Shabbos's total repose. The idea of desisting from *melakha* on Shabbos was never seen as merely avoiding technical violations, but rather a call for complete immersion in Shabbos ambience. While

in verses 13:20–21. Nehemiah has ordered that the gates to Jerusalem be closed on Shabbos, to ensure that no commercial traffic enter. But "the vendors of all sorts of wares spent the night outside Jerusalem ... alongside the wall," positioning themselves to have immediate access to the city as soon as the holy day would conclude. When he saw that the merchants were starting to make a habit of this stratagem, Nehemiah ordered them to desist. He objected to the merchants' beckoning presence, the distraction of camping just outside the wall, pre-positioning their wares on Shabbos. What Nehemiah objected to was the same impatience condemned by Amos, betraying an eagerness to get Shabbos over with so that the merchants could move on to what they obviously considered more important matters. Nehemiah, like the prophets before him, asserts Shabbos as a supreme value to be honored not only in action but in word and thought.

Shabbos calls a halt to business as usual.

These passages remind us how prophets and civil leaders considered Shabbos central to the people's very survival during all periods recorded in the Bible. The roots of what our age might term spirituality are clearly evident in these passages – for example, in Isaiah, who not only urges desisting from weekday occupations on Shabbos, but admonishes us to give honor to Shabbos by refraining from even talking about business. We are asked to disentangle from commerce; in our day, this entails refraining from the activity called shopping. Isaiah asks that we proclaim Shabbos "*oneg,*" delight – delight in the beauty of Shabbos, in Shabbos's otherworldly sweetness, cultivating a different way of thinking and speaking – with greater care and sensitivity, avoiding the slightest trace of bitterness, sarcasm, harshness, deceit. Delight is supple, not brittle.

The taste of Shabbos's delight has propelled the Jewish people in every generation to seek even deeper encounter with it, to be unsatisfied with minimal fulfillment of Shabbos regulations. Ḥibbat hakodesh – the preciousness of the sacred – spurs a yearning for growth that goes beyond merely duplicating the Shabbos achievements of the past, however worthy.

---

this totally immersive spirit is a core teaching of Hasidism, the hasidic masters are continuing and enriching a spiritual perspective about Shabbos that goes back to our earliest sources.

Indeed, Jewish encounter with Shabbos has continued to unfold throughout the Bible, into Second Temple and Rabbinic Judaism, the medieval and modern periods, up to our day and beyond. No one thinks that ancient Israelites sang *Lekha Dodi*. This is the contribution of a Safed kabbalist in the sixteenth century. The hasidic master Rabbi Aaron of Karlin composed the hauntingly evocative *Yah Ekhsof No'am Shabbos* in the eighteenth century. The process continues into the twentieth and twenty-first centuries, up to our own day. The love story remains fresh, a constant source of renewed vitality and passion. But it all began with the verses in Genesis, when God saw the artistry of the world, declared it "very good," and set in motion the six/one, six/one time signature of the cosmos.

Chapter 3

Rediscovering Hasidism – Masters, Practices, Dispositions

As we have noted, the essential posture of Shabbos is trust in God and the gifts of presence and intimacy cultivated by shared space within community. These gifts are precisely the core values of the early hasidic masters, the Baal Shem Tov and his disciples. These masters foregrounded prayer, storytelling, open-hearted Torah, and sacred melody (*niggun*) as vehicles to create deep personal presence and shared communal space. Hasidic practices are particularly powerful on Shabbos and effective for the cultivation of the spirit and embodied reality of Shabbos.

The teachings of the foundational figures of Hasidism inform hasidic practices, which in turn reflect hasidic core dispositions, including joy, love, generosity, equanimity, respect, and non-judgmentalism. These qualities are precisely the treasures of Shabbos. Hasidic practices are a suite of attainments that mutually reinforce each other and that flower most verdantly on Shabbos, deepening meaningful Shabbos engagement.

HASIDIC MASTERS

Hasidic masters have shown us how to inhabit our own selves, how to genuinely be in one place, how to build community, how to fuse body and spirit, how to trust God and our own inner selves.

Baal Shem Tov

Hasidism traces its origins to Rabbi Israel ben Eliezer (d. 1760), known as the Baal Shem Tov, a uniquely gifted teacher and healer who was sought out by the masses for paranormal powers of blessing and by the scholarly elite for an electrifying, transformative mystical reading of Judaism's canonical texts. The Baal Shem Tov breathed new life into the ancient words and traditions of Judaism, foregrounding love of God, Torah, and Israel, emphasizing ecstatic fervor in prayer and study, and promoting a theology of divine immanence, the teaching that all the universe is permeated with God's Glory – the indwelling Presence of the Divine – so that no place is void of God.

Core teachings, practices, and dispositions of the Baal Shem Tov include:

- God is everywhere, and evil is ultimately an illusion. This fosters an attitude of fearlessness and trust; the only one to fear is God.
- We are encouraged to embrace this world joyfully as God's arena. This physical world is enthusiastically accepted as the vehicle for one's approach to God, and nothing and no one is excluded.
- Every religious act must bestow pleasure, an ecstatic flow of intense communion, joining with the Divine.
- We are encouraged to appreciate humor, puns, bon mots, and wordplays as expressions of suppleness and surprise. This attitude is in marked contrast to the somber, even dour, tone of much religious culture. In Hasidism, jokes and good humor are serious business; they provide buoyancy and joyous momentum and can provide the spark that kindles illumination.
- The uniqueness of each individual person is treasured; every human being is embraced as sacred. Everyone has something to teach; this includes (especially) people who are not typically considered scholarly or overtly spiritual. Furthermore, each person has a unique

voice and perspective, a characteristic signature that is essential for the world. Humanity comprises a densely connected network of mutually enriching and reciprocal associations of endless learning and teaching.

- The religious path is *simple*, but not *easy*. Before Hasidism, the great spiritual movement in mystical Judaism was Lurianic kabbala, a profound system of complex, interconnected symbols, and meditative practices that grew enormously in intricacy, to the point that only the most adept and accomplished practitioners could navigate the system. The Baal Shem Tov advocated a "simple" approach to God – but the grasping of this straightforward, uncluttered approach is very challenging!

- Hasidism anticipates and embraces cyclic variation in the religious life. The Baal Shem Tov is quoted as teaching that "constant pleasure is no pleasure." The life of the spiritual seeker shifts between moments of illumination and dry times, and each pole of the cycle has something to teach the other. The real gift is the rhythm itself, the movement, the awareness of the in-between and the bond between the poles.

Central to the Baal Shem Tov's approach is the integration of all aspects of the self, including traits perceived to be undesirable, in a spirituality that is the capstone of, but not a replacement for, the physical.

One example of a Baal Shem Tov approach to Scripture is his reading of Ecclesiastes 9:10, conventionally translated as, "Whatsoever your hand attains to do by your strength, do so," or (another version), "Whatever it is in your power to do, do it with all your might." The Baal Shem Tov's reading is: "Whatsoever your hand finds to do, do it with all your mindful awareness."[1] He grounds this reading in the kabbalistic tradition that understands the Hebrew word *koʾaḥ* ("strength" or "power")

---

1. As quoted by his disciple, Rabbi Jacob Joseph of Polonoyye, *Toledot Yaakov Yosef* (first edition, 1780), *Parashat Vayera* 17:4, 81; cited by Rabbi Aaron ben Zvi Hirsch of Apta, ed., *Keter Shem Tov. Keter Shem Tov* is an early anthology of the Baal Shem Tov's teachings, first published in Zolkiew, 1794–1795. My quotes are from the revised Kehot edition (New York, 2016), no. 91, 251–52.

as mental faculty/thought/mindful awareness. Thus, this verse, conventionally understood as akin to the maxim "Seize the day," is reframed as a call to unite bodily action with conscious awareness and intentional presence. The praxis suggested here is not particularly "mystical"; there is no focusing on names of God or angelic beings, no *gematria*, and no invocation of the 613 canonical commandments. It is simply – *simply indeed!* – that by uniting hand and mind, action and intention, by synchronization of external movement with total inner focus, that one unifies the self – and the cosmos.

This approach goes beyond the oft-repeated directive that one must have *kavana* (intention) in the performance of a mitzva and in prayer. First of all, the Baal Shem Tov's application of the Ecclesiastes verse is not limited to an overt ritual action, but applies to the entirety of human activity. Furthermore, action and intention are not merely placed on parallel tracks, but are bonded together in a fusion that releases sacred energy and blessing, redounding to oneself, others, and the cosmos.

This call to total presence and focus is at the heart of many classic hasidic stories. For example, take this tale of Rabbi Hayim Krasner, a disciple of the Baal Shem Tov:

> One time, a tightrope walker came to town. He set up his rope, stretching it over the local river. The rabbi stood there watching how the man performed wondrous deeds – dancing on the rope. The Rabbi gazed in deep concentration. He appeared to become so absorbed in his thoughts that his students noticed him reaching the stage of divesting himself of corporeality.
>
> Finally, the students asked him, "What about this is so deeply engaging to the Master?"
>
> He answered, "I was pondering this person risking his life – but why? For this performance, he will earn, let's say, one hundred gold coins. But if he thinks of this, he will fall into the river for sure. He can only walk the tightrope by disentangling his thoughts from everything other than what he is doing. He must focus only on balance, on not leaning too much to any one side. Any other thought would bring disaster. But if he's not thinking of his earnings, then is he not foolish to risk his life for no reason?"

There are different versions of this story.[2] I have presented the version that appears in *Tiferet HaYehudi* because here the story leaves off with the questions unanswered: Why walk the tightrope, and why was the rabbi so captivated by the performance?

The story may be saying that only by disregarding goals, benefits, designs, and plans can the walker keep his balance. Perhaps there was a hat on one side of the river, into which the townspeople were throwing coins. If the tightrope walker were to glance at the money in the hat, he would certainly lose his balance and fall into the river. He could not allow himself to be distracted by thoughts of mouths to feed, rent to pay, wood for the stove, and the coming winter. Success demands total presence, total focus. This is a metaphor for life. Most of our actions focus on some long-term goal that deflects us from living in the moment, so that we become decoupled from our own lives.

Even watching the total focus of another gives us a sense of deep presence. With the intensity of his gaze on the tightrope dancer, the rabbi entered the fusion of mind and body that enabled the successful traversal of the rope. The story opens an aperture of successive observational frames: the rabbi entering the delicate balance of the performer; the students learning from the rabbi; the narrator relating the story to us; and finally, we the auditors/readers entering the world of the tale and, through the magic of narrative, coming to our own balance and presence.

What assures the successful passage from one side of the river to the other is total connection to oneself, exactly where one is. It is only by inhabiting one's own self at a moment that distances can be spanned, gaps compressed.

This is the call of Shabbos, especially at its onset, at sunset on Friday. Shabbos is the greatest meditative immersion we have. Total presence is the deep meaning of **Stop**.

It is common in religious discourse to distinguish physicality from spirituality, body from soul, lower appetites from cerebral cognition, and to promote the latter at the expense of the former. However,

---

2. *Tiferet HaYehudi* ([Warsaw, 1912] Jerusalem, 1987), no. 3. Compare the version in Buber's *Tales of the Hasidim: The Early Masters* (New York: Schocken Books, 1991), 174: "From the Circle of the Baal Shem Tov: The Rope Dancer."

the mysticism of the Baal Shem Tov does not privilege soul over body. The Baal Shem Tov's approach is non-dualistic, cultivating a unitive state achieved when the person simultaneously holds together deed and thought, action and cognition, body and spirit, linking the different states but not collapsing one into the other. Inhabiting the linkage engenders a kind of apotheosis that channels blessing and unlocks power.

Closely related to this is the Baal Shem Tov's understanding of Proverbs 3:6, "In all your ways acknowledge Him [God]," which is heard as a call to recognize God not simply in all aspects of life, but in all levels of one's being. Total recognition of the Divine fosters a holistic integration of one's corporeal and spiritual sides so that their respective yearnings are satisfied – not just serially or even in tandem, but in mindful embrace of their fusion, enabling one to inhabit a unified self.

Meant as a directive for every aspect of life, this teaching finds particularly rich expression and fulfillment on Shabbos. It is precisely this unified self that Shabbos encourages us to aim for and bring to realization.

The Baal Shem Tov's mystical monism had a strong interpersonal dimension. Precisely because God is everywhere, it follows that higher realizations of unity lead to the softening of boundaries and the overcoming of distinctions, eventually culminating in the unity of opposites.[3] The implications of these realizations for human relationships are profound. The Baal Shem Tov taught that those we perceive as our adversaries carry hidden parts of our own selves; instead of striving to suppress our "enemies," we should pray for them, for in redeeming them we redeem the lost parts of ourselves.[4] If you detect a flaw in someone else, know that the same flaw is within you; otherwise, you would not have noticed it. Rather than attempting to change the other person, search yourself, and you will find an area to rectify. By improving yourself, you will elevate the other person as well, and, as a bonus, you will have made peace between you.[5]

---

3. *Keter Shem Tov,* no. 51a, 148–49. This and further citations of *Keter Shem Tov* are from the revised Kehot edition (New York, 2016).

4. Rabbi Jacob Joseph of Polonoyye, *Ben Porat Yosef, Parashat Noaḥ,* no. 6; cited in *Keter Shem Tov,* no. 18, 69–70.

5. *Keter Shem Tov,* no. 89, 247–48.

An aphorism:

If you are moved to praise someone, then praise God [or, "This is praise of God"], and if you are moved to disparage someone, then disparage yourself [or, "This is tantamount to self-disparagement"]. For when you praise, you are acknowledging the unity of being, and this itself is worthy, honorable. But if you insult and demean, then simply by abusing another person, you separate yourself from the unity of being.[6]

These aphorisms and others like them establish that the way of the Baal Shem Tov requires an open-hearted benevolence to all people without exception, a non-judgmentalism that shines a gentle light on the world as a whole, on other people in one's circle, and, most importantly, into one's own heart. The cultivation of a non-censorious spirit and a benevolent gaze are core hasidic dispositions at all times, but especially on Shabbos.

The library of hasidic classics is bountiful and deep, overflowing with essential insight into the spiritual path in general and Shabbos in particular. Each of the great masters brings fresh perspective, astoundingly creative and provocative exegesis, and inspiring example to help guide us toward a meaningful Jewish life as a whole, and Shabbos observance in particular. I cannot attempt to survey them all here. Necessarily, my selection must be partial, idiosyncratic, reflective of my personal interests and experiences. Without in any way slighting the vast treasury of hasidic teachers and texts, I focus here on a few masters subsequent to the Baal Shem Tov who have had particular formative influence on me and my understanding of Shabbos, and I endeavor to summarize some of their teachings.

Meor Einayim

Rabbi Menahem Nahum of Chernobyl (1730–1797) was a disciple of the Baal Shem Tov and Rabbi Dov Ber, the Great Maggid of Mezritsh.[7] He

---

6. *Keter Shem Tov*, no. 54, 156–57; from *Ben Porat Yosef, Parashat Vayigash*, no. 2.
7. Rabbi Dov Ber (d. 1772) is credited as taking the mystical ideas and ecstatic practices of the Baal Shem Tov and fashioning the movement that would in a few decades transform traditional Judaism throughout Eastern Europe. Rabbi Dov Ber combined

was the founder of the widespread and influential Chernobyl dynasty, whose family surname is Twersky. To this day, many scions of the Twersky dynasty are prominent figures in Jewish religious leadership. (My own family was privileged to pray at the small *shtibel* of the late Rabbi Yitzhak [Isadore] Twersky in Brighton/Brookline, Massachusetts, where we were inspired by his intensely focused, awe-inspiring prayer and hasidic-inflected teachings. Rabbi Twersky was also a famed Maimonides scholar, and he achieved great distinction as a revered Harvard professor for decades, teaching generations of students.)

In his work *Meor Einayim*, Rabbi Menahem Nahum of Chernobyl taught on Exodus 31:13 ("You [Moses] speak to the children of Israel, saying: Above all you shall observe my Sabbaths, for it is a sign between Me and you throughout your generations, that you may know [*ladaat*] that I am the LORD who sanctifies you") that the very point of Shabbos is performing all actions from a state of interiority, *daat*, with awareness that the energy to act in the world comes from God and is to be returned to God. Shabbos-consciousness entails speaking mindfully, choosing words carefully and thoughtfully, inhabiting each one with compassion and full presence. Rabbi Menahem Nahum states that this mode of intentional inhabitation of embodied action is the central call of Torah, and this is the deep meaning of the rabbinic dictum that "the Torah was given on Shabbos."[8] We all begin our religious lives in a state of immaturity (*katnut*, "small mind"), but Shabbos affords us the opportunity to move to greater maturity – to closeness between action and intention, between spoken word and

---

dazzling spiritual intensity with depth of traditional talmudic learning. Known as the Great Maggid ("preacher" or "homilist"), he is remembered as awe-inspiring and intense, deeply intellectual and gifted, with manifest paranormal powers, such as clairvoyance. Unlike the Baal Shem Tov, who did much traveling, the Maggid generally stayed in one place, establishing a center where gifted disciples came to learn Torah and receive guidance. His teachings were intensely demanding, focusing on surrendering the self and returning to the *Ayin*, the divine Nothing. Yet his parables were warmly appealing; he often spoke of God as a doting parent, lovingly and patiently teaching us, much as parents train their child to walk. See Ariel Evan Mayse, *Speaking Infinities: God and Language in the Teachings of Rabbi Dov Ber of Mezritsh* (University of Pennsylvania Press, 2020).

8. Shabbat 86b.

sacred sonic reverberation – in an endless path of achieving alignment and fusion of all levels of our being.

Hasidic Revival in the Modern Era

Hasidism began as a radical movement of religious renewal, but over the course of the generations, and in part as a reaction to the trauma of the Holocaust, many Hasidim have become deeply conservative in outlook, favoring allegiance to the external signs of their family's tradition over the quest for direct experience of divinity. Loyalty to lineage may overshadow interiority and the search for God. Still, there are pockets of Hasidism in which the intensity of religious quest continues unabated.

Seekers (like myself) who do not formally belong to a hasidic community can learn from all the great masters, beginning with the Baal Shem Tov and his early disciples, as well as from the enormous store of teachings, wisdom tales, sacred melodies, and practices that have been transmitted throughout the generations. Each master has a characteristic voice, each adding a new emphasis and style to the rich legacy of Hasidism.

There has been a rediscovery of hasidic teachings and practices in circles that are not insular, but rather influenced by modern modes of thought and a broadly cosmopolitan spirit. Two relatively recent masters from the late-nineteenth and early-twentieth centuries have had tremendous influence on many contemporary seekers, including me. Perhaps surprisingly, on the basis of their social setting and dynastic commitments, these Hasidic masters appear to be deeply entrenched in traditionalism, yet they nevertheless succeeded in recovering the fresh, dynamic, appealingly provocative voice of early Hasidism, transposed to a new register. I refer in particular to Rabbi Yehudah Aryeh Leib Alter and Rabbi Kalonymos Kalmish Shapiro.

Sefat Emet: The Inner Point

The Gerer Rebbe, Rabbi Yehudah Aryeh Leib Alter (1847–1905), was a notable exemplar of the Przysucha school of Polish Hasidism, which emphasized intellectual attainment in talmudic study, cultivated independence of thinking, demoted the emphasis of belief in paranormal powers, and stressed (as Abraham Joshua Heschel put it) a "passion for truth." The collection of the Gerer Rebbe's Torah discourses, *Sefat Emet*, published shortly after his death, is widely considered one of the greatest hasidic Torah commentaries, distinguished by mastery of classic sources, profundity and freshness of insight, literary flair, economy of expression, and mystical intensity. Eschewing technical kabbalistic terminology, *Sefat Emet* is elusive without being arcane or esoteric, a breathtaking combination of concise exposition and sublime spiritual vision. *Sefat Emet's* popularity has grown to the point that the master is frequently referred to by the name of his work.[9]

An example of the *Sefat Emet's* fresh reading of a traditional source is his interpretation of the talmudic dictum, "Those who give delight to Shabbos are rewarded with the desires of their heart."[10] In conventional understanding, the statement is an encouragement to take delight in Shabbos, with the assurance that Heaven will grant reward by fulfilling one's desires (*ratzon*). The *Sefat Emet's* shift in reading is subtle but transformative: Observe the Shabbos with delight, and Heaven will reward you with *deeper, nobler, more sublime desires of the heart*. Rather than a promise of bounty bestowed on the Shabbos-keeper, the heavenly gift is to have one's heart opened, so that *one knows what to ask for*; one is granted *the wisdom to yearn for what really matters*. In the hands of the Gerer Rebbe, the talmudic dictum is a promise of deepening one's spiritual sensibilities and perceptions. Shabbos observance is a path of ever-higher awareness, a virtuous circle wherein each level of comprehension sets the stage for yet another even more sublime horizon, in a never-ending trajectory of heart-expansion and inner growth.[11]

---

9. English-language readers can access *Sefat Emet* through Arthur Green's translation and annotation of selected teachings, *The Language of Truth: The Torah Commentary of the Sefat Emet, Rabbi Yehudah Leib Alter of Ger* (Philadelphia: Jewish Publication Society, 5759/1998). See also *idem*, "Three Warsaw Mystics," in *Rivkah Shatz-Uffenheimer Memorial Volume*, ed. Rachel Elior and Joseph Dan (Jerusalem, 1996), vol. 2, 6–21.

10. Shabbat 118b. See Isaiah 58:14; Psalms 37:4.

11. *Sefat Emet, Parashat Beshallaḥ* 5662–5663 [1902–1903], s.v. *uvamidrash pote'aḥ et yadekha umasbia lekhol ḥai ratzon*. What is presented here is an excerpt from a more far-ranging piece, which begins by quoting Psalms 145:16, "You open Your hand and satisfy the desire of every living thing." There is a subtle wordplay here on *ratzon* as either "favor" or "desire." The favor or grace that God bestows is a more elevated

A key term in *Sefat Emet*, with special relevance to Shabbos, is *nekuda penimit,* the "inner point." The *nekuda penimit* is a beckoning to interiority, a reminder to avoid superficiality of all kinds. As Arthur Green has noted, the term has a range of meanings and can be variously translated "core of being," "inward reality," or, when combined with another key term, *ḥiyut,* "inner life-point."[12] The *nekuda* is a fundamental element of consciousness that, when recognized and nurtured, opens the individual to more profound awareness of self, the world, and divinity. Rabbi Aryeh Leib invites his readers (originally his audience) to develop sublime perception and to inhabit a gracious, inclusive mode of seeing ever more robustly, opening eyes to the truth of the ultimate unity of all things.

An important aspect of that truth is that the innermost point always existed within the individual who discovers it, waiting to be awakened, and the process of discovery and awakening never ends. We already possess *nekuda penimit,* but at the same time, we need to work to make it manifest. As Michael Fishbane has noted, Shabbos is at the core of this spiritual quest. He writes that "to penetrate the mystery of Shabbos is to bring to mindfulness the transcendental unity and totality of divine Reality that lies at the core of all things – despite the apparent multiplicity of the phenomenal world and the scattered perceptions of an unfocused mind."[13] This monistic (non-dualistic) approach to Shabbos is one reason that *Sefat Emet* appeals to so many contemporary readers.

Sefat Emet understands place as the essential Shabbos modality. In a teaching based on Ezekiel 46:1, he develops a typology of "two gates" that open into the domain of the sacred, one related to time

---

desire. In the midrash that launches this *Sefat Emet,* the *ratzon* is connected to the manna's changeable flavor, responding to the desire of the individual eating it. See Exodus Rabba on Exodus 16:4.

12. See Arthur Green, *The Language of Truth,* introduction, xv–lviii. The discussion of the term *nekuda* can be found on pp. xxxi–xxxix. My thanks to Rabbi Jonathan Slater for a fruitful discussion on *nekuda penimit.*

13. Michael Fishbane, "Transcendental Consciousness and Stillness in the Mystical Theology of R. Yehudah Arieh Leib of Gur," in *Sabbath: Idea, History, Reality,* ed. Gerald J. Blidstein (Beer Sheva: Ben-Gurion University of the Negev Press, 2004), 119–29; quotation on 120–21.

(New Moon) and one centered on place (Shabbos). In support of the idea that the essence of Shabbos is embeddedness in place, he cites Exodus 16:29, "Let no one go out of their place on the seventh day," a verse we have discussed above, as well as Leviticus 23:3, "It is Shabbos for the LORD in all your dwelling places." He also points to Exodus 31:17, "The children of Israel shall observe the Shabbos, to make the Shabbos *ledorotam.*" The Hebrew *dorotam* is typically translated "their generations," conveying a succession of temporal periods, but *Sefat Emet* understands it as related to *dira* – "residence" or "dwelling place." He therefore reads the verse to mean: "The children of Israel shall observe the Shabbos, to make the Shabbos in all their places of residence."[14] For *Sefat Emet*, we make Shabbos happen by affording Shabbos entry into our neighborhoods, our homes, our hearts.

Piaseczner Rebbe: Connoisseurship of the Sacred

Rabbi Kalonymos Kalmish Shapiro (1889–1943), known as the Piaseczner Rebbe, was a twentieth-century hasidic master who lived and taught in Warsaw and the nearby town of Piaseczna. Many know of his profound writings from the dark years of the Warsaw Ghetto during the Holocaust, but he was equally prominent before the war as a hasidic educational theorist and practitioner. His guides to hasidic practice introduced beginning students to hasidic spirituality and Kabbala, while advanced students were given meditative techniques, such as visualization, guided imagery, and quieting the mind (*hashkata*). Rabbi Shapiro encouraged the formation of small fellowships for Hasidim seriously interested in developing a gentle type of inner spirituality within communities of fellow seekers. His approach might be called "Sensitization to Holiness," stressing the imperative to cultivate one's personal spiritual signature.

Rabbi Shapiro is located entirely within traditional Hasidism, yet he writes with a surprisingly modern voice. His prescient pedagogical

---

14. *Sefat Emet Parashat Mattot-Masei* 5659/1899, *Rosh Ḥodesh Av.* The association of *dorotam* with *dira* is etymologically sound and biblically attested. See, for example, Isaiah 38:12, "My habitation is plucked up and carried away from me as a shepherd's tent" (JPS 1917), where the Hebrew *dori* is rendered by JPS and many other translations as "habitation."

methodology, his deep awareness of contemporary sensibilities (Warsaw in the 1930s was a cosmopolitan, acculturated metropolis), his psychological astuteness, personal warmth, and caring heart, as well as his spiritual heroism and astounding theological writings from the Holocaust period, have combined to make him a figure of great scholarly interest and an inspiring personal model.

Rabbi Shapiro encouraged his Hasidim to develop an acuity of sacred perception, the ability to discern subtle distinctions in the texture of holiness. As he put it, "Saintly people are aware of the difference in taste between one mitzva and the next."[15] He understands the response to the "wise child" in the Passover Haggada as an invitation to grow in discernment of the subtle taste distinctions between types of mitzvot, to aspire to ever more sensitive appreciation for the overtones and timbres of each mitzva. This growth is a process that takes place deep within the individual and is ultimately inexpressible in words.[16] A teacher can point to the path but can never fully specify his or her uniquely personal experience.

Rabbi Shapiro's teachings are especially applicable for Shabbos. He invited his Hasidim, and now invites his readers, to savor Shabbos's inner texture, not just conceptually but experientially, evoking the ambience of each stage of the day with rich sensory specificity. As he writes:

> The stages of Shabbos are distinct; the evening has its own taste, appearance, and holiness; the day has its own taste, appearance, and holiness; and the third Shabbos meal (*Shalosh Seudos*) has its own taste, appearance, and holiness. This is like the soul in Paradise [which experiences not a frozen, eternally static bliss, but] an endless itinerary of epiphanies and realizations.[17]

---

15. Rabbi Kalonymos Shapiro, *Derekh HaMelekh, Parashat Tzav (Shabbos HaGadol)* (Jerusalem: Vaad Hasidei Piaseczna, 1991), 124.

16. Ibid.

17. "Essay Three: Some Thoughts about the Holy Shabbos," in *Ḥovat HaTalmidim* (Warsaw, 5692/1932), part 3, near the end. Rabbi Shapiro evokes the ambience of the third Shabbos meal frequently in his writings. (Technically, this meal is called *Seuda Shelishit*, but he refers to it as *Shalosh Seudos*, "Three Meals," as was common in the Yiddish of Eastern Europe.) See *Hakhsharat HaAvreikhim* (Jerusalem: Vaad

A mature Hasid's religious phenomenology includes the ability to savor Shabbos's variegated sensory textures, aspects, and ambiences.

Rabbi Shapiro stressed that Shabbos should not be seized upon as an instrumental tool for self-centered aims, as a day of leisure and amusement in order to return to weekday pursuits refreshed and energized.[18] His view of Shabbos as divine gift, sacred offering, and – in its higher registers – as transcendent self-surrender is what makes Shabbos a genuine spiritual practice.

Generosity of Spirit and an Open Heart

In interpersonal relationships, hasidic masters urge cultivation of generosity and openheartedness, at all times and especially on Shabbos. As we noted above, the Baal Shem Tov taught that we have no right to judge others; the failings we see in others are projections of our own flaws.[19] Rabbi Kalonymos Kalman Epstein of Krakow (c. 1751–1823) taught that

---

Hasidei Piaseczna, 5726/1966], ch. 4, 16b–18b (note the suggestion that the room should be dark [*"uvaḥoshekh atem yoshevim"*] on 17b); ch. 11, 61b–62a ("the third Shabbos meal is the Yom Kippur of the week"); *Tzav VaZiruz* (Jerusalem: Vaad Hasidei Piaseczna, 1966), nos. 47, 52–53. For more on *Seuda Shelishit*, see below, chapter 6, section "The Piaseczner Rebbe on *Shalosh Seudos*."

18. *Derasha LeShabbat Shuva*, delivered in Piaseczna, 1936. Published in *Shalosh Derashot Asher Darash … R. Kalonymos Kalmish Shapiro* (Tel Aviv: Merkaz Hasidei Koznitz VaAnafeha Grodzisk Piaseczna, n.d.), 32–42; also in *Derekh haMelekh* (Jerusalem: Vaad Hasidei Piaseczna, 1991), 374–82.

19. See the impressive range of teachings on this theme collected in *Sefer Baal Shem Tov*, ed. Shimon Menaḥem Mendel Wodnik of Gevartshav, *Parashat Kedoshim*, s.v. *betzedek tishpot amitekha* (on Lev. 19:15). This comprehensive anthology was first published in Lodz, Poland in 1938 and has been reprinted many times since. I am consulting the edition of Jerusalem, 1992, vol. 2, 425–28, entries 2–6.

For a powerful statement of non-judgment of others, especially those one is tempted to classify as "wicked," see Rabbi Menaḥem Mendel of Vitebsk, *Peri HaAretz, Parashat Shofetim*. For contemporary discussion, see Avraham Yitzhak (Arthur) Green, "Judaism as a Path of Love," in *BeRon Yaḥad: Studies in Jewish Thought and Theology in Honor of Nehemia Polen*, ed. Ariel Evan Mayse and Arthur Green (Boston: Academic Studies Press, 2019), 1–26. Cf. Rabbi Gedalya of Linitz, *Teshuot Ḥen* and *Imrei Pinḥas HaShalem* on the Messiah's vindication of the "wicked." For a suggestive early source, see Mishna Nega'im 1:4 on the avoidance of judging *nega tzaraat* on Shabbos.

this was the sin in the Garden of Eden.[20] By eating the fruit of the Tree of Knowledge, Adam became arrogant, considering himself wise enough to have figured out other people, assuming he could discern their inner motivations. The lesson of the story, says Rabbi Epstein in his *Maor VaShemesh,* is that we must refrain from judging others; we must humbly acknowledge that we have no access to other people's hearts and that judging people is the sole prerogative of God.[21] If we wish to touch the spirit of prelapsarian Eden on Shabbos, we must be vigilant in cultivating the gaze of benevolence, the eyes of grace, compassion, and acceptance.

The *zemer Menuḥa VeSimḥa* (sung at the first Shabbos meal in the evening) provides a poetic sampling of the rites, benedictions, and prayers associated with Shabbos observance. At the end of the list, and as a capstone, the poet speaks of *ruaḥ nediva* – "the spirit of generosity."[22] The disposition of generosity – not just sharing material resources, but also the humble, non-critical acceptance of the variety of ways of being human – is what the entirety of Shabbos practice leads to. This is the cherished prize at the pinnacle of the interior Shabbos journey.

Hasidism is a path of sensitization to holiness; in Hebrew this is called *ḥibbat hakodesh,* "cherishing the holy." While perceptive acuity to the holy is a hasidic desideratum at all times, it reaches a peak on Shabbos. As the *zemer Barukh El Elyon* by Rabbi Barukh ben Samuel of Mayence (d. 1221) puts it, whoever keeps Shabbos fully "is endowed with a predisposition of loving sensitivity to the sacred" (*Kol shomer Shabbos kadat mehallelo/hen hekhsher ḥibbat kodesh goralo*).[23] These faculties and dispositions are not easily achieved. They are not self-evident, even to those who have grown up in a traditional Shabbos community. The cultivation of these inner qualities requires an ambience of study,

---

20. Rabbi Kalonymos Kalman HaLevi Epstein of Krakow was one of the early masters of Hasidism in Poland. A disciple of Rabbi Elimelekh of Lyzhansk and the Seer of Lublin, his *Maor VaShemesh* is a fundamental work that encapsulates the core ideas of Hasidism's classical period. He was the great-great-great-grandfather of Rabbi Kalonymos Kalmish Shapiro, the Piaseczner Rebbe.

21. *Sefer Maor VaShemesh HaShalem VehaMefo'ar* (Jerusalem: Even Yisrael, 5752/1992), vol. 1, 12, s.v. *vayetzav Hashem* (on Gen. 2:16–17).

22. See *Koren Siddur,* 432–33.

23. Ibid., 632–33.

story, and *niggun,* and a willingness to take time, linger, and savor the spirit – in all, a pedagogy of interiority[24] that nourishes the public liturgy.

Franz Rosenzweig wrote: "The highest things cannot be planned; for them, readiness is everything. Readiness is the one thing we can offer to the Jewish individual within us, the individual we aim at."[25] If there is one thing that unites all the hasidic personalities in this section, it is their state of readiness. And readiness for Shabbos is the deep meaning of *shomer Shabbos.*

HASIDIC PRACTICES AND SHABBOS

Hasidism did not invent any of the practices commonly associated with the movement. Joy, fervent prayer, reverence for teachers, sacred song and dance, ecstatic communion with God, fellowship and solidarity, and storytelling are all to be found elsewhere in Judaism, usually well before the advent of the hasidic movement. That said, Hasidism brought new vitality and enhanced focus to all these dispositions and practices. Here we explore several practices that are particularly relevant to Shabbos.

Throughout the centuries, preachers who wanted to intensify the spiritual dimension of Jewish practice would speak of *kavana,* "intention." The hasidic movement and its teachers went farther, emphasizing *presence.*

Presence is more than *kavana. Kavana* is how carefully I aim the arrow of my intention. Presence is how firmly I hold the bow.

Linking the core of all hasidic practices is the ideal that might be called "common ground" – the sense of being securely and palpably held, grounded in place, not just in ethereal ideals.

This grounded spirituality is located in community. From the beginning, Hasidism emphasized three essential bonds: *dibbuk ḥaverim* ("connecting with friends," camaraderie), *devekut* (attachment to God), and *hitkashrut* (bonding with the central figure of the community). Indeed, the three bonds – with friends, with God, and with inspirational

---

24. This lovely phrase is from Irish poet John O'Donohue.
25. Franz Rosenzweig, "On Being a Jewish Person," in Nahum N. Glatzer, ed., *Franz Rosenzweig: His Life and Thought* (New York: Schocken Books, 1972), 222.

teacher – act as a cohesive, internally consistent, and mutually reinforcing structure that defines its own sacred space. The community of fellow-seekers supplies a network of support and encouragement, a safety net in times of crisis and a slipstream of propulsive energy and buoyancy in times of joy.

Each of the three practices I now introduce are part of the Hasid's weekday as well, but on Shabbos these practices benefit from and contribute to the formation of Shabbos community, sacred ambience, and collective energy. They all cultivate the common ground that Shabbos-keepers inhabit.

Niggun

Niggun (sacred melody; plural *niggunim*) is an essential component of Shabbos observance. There is sheer pleasure in this noble and gracious practice that enables one to be both the producer and the receiver of great beauty and depth. With *niggun* in our hearts, we carry within us the sublime notes of soul-expression that one may choose to share with others or embrace within. *Niggun* allows us to feel the body's resonant cavities richly; it opens the spirit and points both high and deep with the promise of ever-greater alertness and aliveness.

The *Sefat Emet* points to the relationship between *niggun* and recognition, awareness of the divine vitality in all things. We know that Hasidism speaks of sparks of light everywhere, but the *Sefat Emet* suggests that there are notes of sacred song everywhere. Our task is to listen intently, to discover, to recover. When we link the notes of our attentive listening in melody, our voice becomes resonant with the song of all creation. Each day, each moment, has its own song. The song is as old as the cosmos and as new as this moment's breath.

The practice begins in listening and continues with sound production. The reason, according to the *Sefat Emet*, that the first words of the Decalogue (Ex. 20:2) mention *hotzetikha*, "taking out," rather than "creation," is that while divinity is everywhere, our focus is *hotzetikha* – to bring about emergence, release from bondage. This means *expression* – the production and emission of sound, especially in sacred song, stringing a sonic holy thread, setting notes into line and ourselves into alignment.

When we produce tones, we are our own instrument. Our vocal cavity resonates with the vibration of our vocal cords, carried by the rushing column of air emitted by our lungs and pushed out by our diaphragm. The making of sound – any sound, and certainly musical tone – is quite miraculous. There is an exquisite blend of active and passive effects; our muscles do not directly make the vocal cords vibrate at a rate of hundreds of cycles a second (hertz), but the pulling and stretching they engage in allow the flow of air to activate and vibrate the cords. There is further shaping as the column of air proceeds through and past palate, tongue, and lips. We may not have cognitive knowledge of the physics, but as embodied humans we all have some intuitive awareness of this awe-inspiring process, which leads us both deeper into ourselves and beyond ourselves.

I believe this is what the Baal Shem Tov was referring to when he said that every phoneme – every spoken letter – is comprised of "Worlds," "Souls," and "Divinity." And when the sounds are linked together in the patterns we perceive as musical, the result is utter magic! In singing a *niggun*, we are privileged to participate in all this with a vehicle that, in addition to aesthetic aspects, foregrounds the sacred dimension and is expressly designed to enable us to touch our own souls and the souls of others.

Not just singing, but also *learning* a *niggun* is sacred practice. When learning a *niggun*, we must be attentive to the *niggun*'s flow, contours, and dynamic unfolding. Most *niggunim* are quite singable and do not require that much technical expertise. But the simplicity can mislead; there is almost always a surprise, a cadence, tempo shift, or tonal transition that is unexpected. It is precisely the quality of attentiveness that *niggun* wishes to cultivate, so remain alive and present. Don't be misled by deceptive simplicity!

As we learn the *niggun*, the *niggun* is shaping our soul. Our spirits learn new modes of suppleness, new inner pathways, new delightful postures to inhabit and embody.

While being attentive to the precise unfolding of the *niggun*, we must allow each realization of the *niggun* to be unique. The subtle differences reflect the fact that we and the world are constantly changing; we are in motion, and our awareness of the Divine and what it means to reach for the sacred is also constantly in motion. Our *niggun* practice is a shuttling between discipline and freedom, between meticulous devotion and creative openness, between bestowal and receptivity.

Carrying a *niggun* in the heart throughout an entire week is a particularly powerful practice. The *niggun* becomes our anchor, our anthem, our lifeline during this period. Whatever else happens, we know we can find splendor and joy in the *niggun*. When appropriate – and with permission of family and friends – we may sing in full-throated exultation; other times may find us humming quietly, to ourselves, luxuriating in resonances that are totally internal. *Niggun* enables us to be involved in inner work and still be present to the world, to the sights, sounds and fragrance of nature, to the smiles of passersby. We may simultaneously maintain both an inner and outer presence.

The practice is focused yet expansive. Each note is carefully chosen and intoned; the sequence must be precise, rhythmic, just so. There is *gevura* (self-control and restraint) here! At the same time, there must be openness of body and heart, a spirit of *ḥesed* (compassionate expansiveness). Stretch your mind and your rib cage and find space that you didn't know you had; remember to breathe!

As *niggun* awakens and deepens our total being – body/emotions/spirit/divine soul – it simultaneously assists in cultivating greater compassion, for ourselves and for others, as it gently peels away layers of calcification and stiffness. It promotes *simḥa,* joy – the joyous satisfaction of learning and internalizing this simple-yet-challenging form, and the *simḥa* of the dynamic energy of the *niggun* itself. If the *niggun* is slowly restful, it can promote richer, more balanced contemplation. And just about every *niggun* embodies and expresses nobility, yearning, spiritual grace. All this means that *niggun* is a vehicle for *middot*, the character traits and dispositions that we are likely attempting to realize and embrace throughout our lives. The inner change catalyzed by *niggun* assists in working toward equanimity, empathy, energy, focused determination, and commitment.

And there is *teshuva*, return. Most *niggunim* invite repetition; the final notes and the last cadence set the stage for a return to the beginning. As *Sefer Yetzira* says, "The end is wedged in the beginning." This return is always at a different level. As we revisit and start anew, we recall where we've been and build on it; we have learned something from the experience and grow into it, from it, *up* from it but not *away* from it. We contemplate where we've been and where we would like to go next, and this is the essence of *teshuva*.

Beyond the sheer beauty of *niggunim*, there is a visionary element – there is a mission, sometimes expressed, sometimes implied, of sharing these core values with the world. The Piaseczner Rebbe taught that it is the Jewish mission to teach the world how to sing.

Niggunim should be sung with deep emotional engagement, not simply for aesthetic delight. We should endeavor to channel joy, yearning, aspiration, wonder, fulfillment, longing, and reaching for insight beyond our grasp. *Niggunim* convey both confidence and brokenness, quest as much as certainty. With voice and words, we coax ourselves out of indifference and into deeper encounter with our own souls, without easy answers. The depth cannot be simplified or reduced to any one feeling – such as "love" or "joy" – no matter how important. The expressiveness should involve our eyes, our posture, our entire body language. We must be aware of the range of religious emotions and the keen intensity that our voices can convey, aspiring to touch the deepest places of the soul.

The best *niggunim* have a compelling combination of elegant simplicity, propulsive inevitability, and deep emotional expressiveness.

The Piaseczner Rebbe taught that the *niggun* assists in the process of sensitization to holiness, in "softening the soul" from calcification, cultivating joy and *eidelkeit* – nobility of soul and spirit. It is an essential way of becoming aware of the presence of the Divine in the world. The *niggun* is a spiritual tone poem, a meditative induction, beckoning the chanter – the intoner – to enter an ethereal, dreamlike world of holiness and tenderness.

Note that the gentle, quiet, delicate quality of the *niggunim* is quite purposeful; they are simple chants, to open up the heart, to *enter* a phrase of Bible or other sacred text. Perhaps the secret of the power of the hasidic *niggun* lies not in musical sophistication or complexity, but in the opposite – in simplicity, in the ability to reach deep into the human soul and reveal its primal power and delicacy.

They are to be savored, entered into with all one's senses, with all the levels of one's being. Hasidism means to take the time to experience deeply, to immerse oneself so fully that the waters of holiness seep through the very pores of the skin. *Niggunim* are therefore often sung for long periods of time – twenty minutes, an hour. Then there are the pauses, the thoughtful silences, providing opportunities for reflection and integration.

The Hebrew word used by Rabbi Nahman of Bratslav (1772–1810) for the notes of the *niggun* is *nekudot* – literally, points or dots. This enables him to say that to connect the notes of a melody is to connect the dots of one's own life – to bring oneself to integration, wholeness, and understanding, and to find and to celebrate the good points of one's soul.

The notes of a *niggun* are indeed alive; they each have their personality, their story to tell. The singer, the intoner, must participate in the process of bringing the notes to life. When this happens, each note of the *niggun* looks back at the note that preceded it, turns to it, and says:

"Thank you for being my rebbe, my teacher."

And then, each note turns to the note to follow and says:

"I give you permission to be even more beautiful than I am!"

There is a *niggun* posture that impacts everything – all of life.

The *niggun* sensibility involves openheartedness, suppleness, and nobility of spirit.

Niggun and joy

It is worth exploring more deeply how *niggun* helps cultivate and sustain *simha*, joy.

Simha is founded on optimism, buoyancy, and a positive outlook with regard to the world. Its qualities include openness, the sunniness of an inner smile, and sensing the propulsion of wind at our backs.

Almost every *niggun* can contain these qualities, including melodies that are slow, contemplative, or introspective. We experience a positive momentum, a forward-leaning stance that says "yes" to God and the world.

As we continue in our *niggun* practice, we may cross over from quietly optimistic directionality into overt happiness. Our joy becomes visible; it takes physical expression through a smile, through movement, or in a warm hug. *Niggunim* that lend themselves to this stage tend to be faster paced, overtly upbeat – in the Yiddish language of Klezmer music, *freilich*.

But there is more. The unexpected or unanticipated melodic interval, syncopation, or dynamic shift found in many *niggunim* can lead us toward a still more intense state. Now there is a moment of emergence, a breaking of the bonds of expectancy. Something eruptive occurs that transcends conventional boundaries and reconfigures the world. Now *simḥa* goes beyond positive affect, beyond happiness, into an inner beaming, perhaps expressed outwardly in a radiance visible on one's face. The *niggun* has accomplished a physical and spiritual transformation, a phase transition that has transformed ballast to buoyancy, heaviness into open heart.

When a *niggun* fully expresses this kind of *simḥa*, it is a rare experience indeed – manna from heaven, beyond categorization.

Afterglow in silence

Rabbi Zev Wolf of Zhitomir (d. 1800; disciple of the Maggid of Mezritsh) comments on the phrase from the blessing of *Yishtabaḥ*, "*haboḥer beshirei zimra*," which he creatively rereads as, "*haboḥer beshiyarei zimra*" – God chooses what is left over from song. Rabbi Zev Wolf explains that the "remains of song" are the resonances that linger after the singing stops, the rich, eloquent silence after the song ceases to be intoned. The walls of the room continue to reverberate, as does one's vocal cavity and the recesses of one's heart. This is most precious; this is the most holy of all. This is what God chooses, and that is what we should cherish, hold on to, and internalize.

Nothing is more important in *niggun*-practice than savoring the silence after the melody stops.

Niggun, sacred space, and Shabbos

Niggun is an embodied practice that allows people who might not be able to talk to each other amicably to join together in sound. The embodied practice of singing *niggunim* together builds community and rises from community. *Niggun*'s reverberative power emerges best in a chorus of voices and in an enclosed space. To be sure, you can hum a melody walking alone in a field, but the richness and complexity of ambient sound reflected from manifold surfaces and emerging from multiple singers yields unparalleled depth and fullness in tone. Singing together creates sacred space; it carries forward the great biblical mandate mentioned above to settle in place and form the "House of Israel."

Tefilla

The Baal Shem Tov, the Great Maggid of Mezritsh, and their disciples devoted much attention to *tefilla*, prayer. Hasidic prayer shares much in common with *niggun* as explored above, but adds the elements of fixed liturgy and ritual structure. When we pray in community – especially on Shabbos – we join other contemporary Shabbos communities throughout the world, as well as all similar communities past and future. We bear collective witness to our fidelity to Shabbos. In addition, the rich semantic content of the words of prayer adds a deep ideational element that bonds the praying congregation together.

The following are some main points of emphasis.

Tefilla is a practice anchored in the physical; it is a set of physical activities, leading beyond the physical. It begins when the pray-er offers physical energy in producing utterances; it flowers when those utterances are linked with intentionality (a mental/spiritual state); and it climaxes when it bestows a manifestation of the sacred (a state of divinity). This practice aims to take ego (*ani*) and transform it into sacred emptiness (*Ayin*).

As a physical practice, prayer begins in units of sound produced and emitted by the vocal cavity, vibrating the column of breath/vapor ("the white smoke column of the altar's fire") emitted by the lungs and diaphragm (*neshima/neshama*). This breath is a gift of God, and this production is meant to return it as a gift to God, thus closing a circle. It is constituted of elemental units of sound (spoken letters), which only later aggregate into larger units of meaning (spoken words).

The emphasis on *tefilla* as a physical practice encompasses much more than speech. There is the silent sitting before and after prayer ("*Ashrei yoshevei veitekha*"); there is the bowing/prostration when one enters and leaves the prayer location to acknowledge the sacredness of the space (compare the *reverence* of classical ballet); the standing (*Amida* – "here I stand") as well as the bowing (slowly, with attentiveness and awareness, feeling the opening up of the vertebrae);[26] the *shoklen* – either the broad rhythmic swaying in loving motion, or the tremorous shaking in awe of the Ultimate; the wrapping oneself in the tallit; lifting of the Torah, opening it wide and ceremonially displaying it to the congregation; dancing; the angelic fluttering on tiptoes during *Kedusha*, and so on.

In the Jewish mystical tradition, the twenty-two letters of the Hebrew language are the basic elements of the universe. The letters are alive. They are not, in the first instance, graphic marks on a page, but elemental sounds. To pronounce, to shape a sound in one's vocal cavity with intentionality in a sacred context, is thus to bring a dead letter to life.

As living entities, the letters have three aspects: physical form, spirit, and a divine origin. Inspirited articulation links these levels together, giving the letters their full stature and dignity. As living entities, the letters also join with each other. This joining or coupling has an erotic element; it is intensely pleasurable for them and for us.

As with all spiritual activities, the goal and aim of *tefilla* must be immediate, not deferred. The "payoff" comes here and now. Every prayer is answered – at the moment it is uttered (Baal Shem Tov). This is because when prayer is uttered *behitlahavut* – with fervor – it is no longer prayer to the Divine, it is divinity itself (Rabbi Nahman).

When we pray in a communal setting, the sounds are the vehicle that enables the individual pray-ers to join with each other (*"beshem kol Yisrael"*). Rabbi Pinhas of Koretz teaches that the entire congregation bonds together by means of melodious prayer. The strong human bond enables us to link with the Divine as well, to bring God among us, within us. We create sacred space through collective sound and silence.

Since we must all join together to create sacred space, we are all responsible for one another, to one another. When we enter the prayer space, we must feel joined, mingled (*arevim*) with everyone in the room, with all of Israel, with all the world. In hasidic discourse, *arvut*, "mutual responsibility," is also *arevut*, "sweetness." We must all be sweet for one other.

---

26. See Berakhot 28b.

The Maggid of Kozienice, Rabbi Yisrael ben Shabbetai Hapstein (c. 1737–1814),[27] has a profound insight on the regulation that in order to constitute a *minyan* (prayer quorum), the ten pray-ers must be "in one place."[28] The straightforward meaning of this law is that it is not sufficient to have ten people in one synagogue building – for example, seven people in the sanctuary, one in the social hall, another in the office, yet another in the kitchen. They must all be in the same place in order to constitute the *minyan*.

The Kozienicer Maggid gives this law a hasidic turn. He observes that when people gather to pray, it is often the case that they come with different foci of attention; one person is worried about health, another about business, a third about a child at risk. They may be together physically but far apart emotionally and spiritually. It is the task of the prayer leader to bring the aggregation of individuals together, to form community on all levels. As the *Shulḥan Arukh* states (now heard in a new register), "All ten people must be in the same place – and the prayer leader is with them."[29] While this is a desideratum on weekdays as well, it is a greater imperative on Shabbos, when we are called upon to leave our weekday baggage behind and to enter a shared space of blessing and holy aspiration.

Storytelling

Hasidic stories open our hearts. They can transform space.

---

27. The Maggid (preacher) of Kozienice was a founder of Hasidism in Poland, an erudite talmudic scholar and kabbalist who was famed for his ability to lead others in ecstatic prayer. Among the personalities who were profoundly influenced at an early stage in their careers by the Maggid of Kozienice was Rabbi Isaac Meir (Rothenberg) Alter, the founder of the famed Ger dynasty and grandfather of the author of *Sefat Emet*. The Maggid of Kozienice combined in one person all the ideals of the early hasidic master: selfless devotion in service of God and other human beings; mastery of Talmud and codes; cultivation of a rich inner life of mystical practice; reputed paranormal powers, especially the ability to grant efficacious blessings; the mentoring of disciples and followers; and finally, saintly prestige and influence in the gentile as well as the Jewish world, deployed for the benefit and protection of his community.

28. *Shulḥan Arukh* (Code of Jewish Law), *Oraḥ Ḥayim* 55:13.

29. Rabbi Yisrael ben Shabbetai Hapstein, *Avodat Yisrael* (Jerusalem: 5756/1996), *Likkutim*, 220–21.

Hasidic stories convey wisdom and sacred insight that resonate beyond the original context, hinting at universal values and meaning. The story is a guide, gently challenging us and pointing us to insight. Stories are not mere entertainment or edifying tales; they are meant to assist us in cultivating an inner voice. When we reach a situation similar to that of the story in some respect, we may hear the voice of our teacher in the voice of the story. That voice provides perspective, poise, grounding, and a new purchase on the circumstance, and it assists us in proceeding with wisdom and integrity.[30]

Hasidic wisdom tales typically have an aphoristic quality, hinging on a play on words, a pun or *aperçu*. These tales may pivot around a new understanding of a scriptural verse, a talmudic passage, or a life experience. The point is to surprise, to startle, to create an opening for new perception, for a change of perspective. The change within the story is meant to provoke a change within one's own spirit.

Hasidic stories open our eyes to the obvious, lead to a reversal of expectations, and uncover inner levels of meaning, allowing the tellers and the listeners to effect inner transformation. Stories are often enigmatic, open-ended, allusive, and elusive. They may use the secular as a metaphor for the sacred, and they often have a self-referential quality, a paradoxical and provocative self-mirroring that invites analysis and reflection. Stories emphasize the interconnectedness of everyone and everything; they teach that we are all pieces of someone else's puzzle.

Hasidic stories embody values such as faith in God and in spiritual mentors (*tzaddikim*); the power of prayer, inwardness, devotion, and simplicity; and the importance of seeing things from another vantage point. That almost invariably means seeing things from the side of the powerless, the disenfranchised, those who otherwise would not have a voice.

Telling a story is a sacred act accompanied by a spirit of reverence, but reverence does not preclude joy and humor. To the contrary,

---

30. This analysis of the power of hasidic tales is influenced by an essay on mentoring. See Michael Zeldin, "Touching the Future: The Promise of Mentoring," in *Touching the Future: Mentoring and the Jewish Professional*, ed. Michael Zeldin and Sara S. Lee (Los Angeles: Rhea Hirsch School of Education, HUC-JIR, 1995), 12–27.

the stories themselves are often filled with humor and work precisely by getting us to laugh at our own foibles and misconceptions. In the hasidic tradition, joy is among the most sacred and cherished of emotions. Laughter is the lubricant that helps us to move ourselves in the direction of growth.

When listening to a hasidic story, one should listen respectfully, non-judgmentally. Try to hear the story from the perspective of the teller, who is putting trust in the story, and in you. Try carrying the story with you – in your heart, in your belly – all day, so that the story may open up to you, and you to it, on a deeper transformative level.

The storyteller should leave space for ambiguity and uncertainty. Listeners should leave space in their hearts for change while maintaining the firm integrity of their most inner convictions. In sum, both the teller and the listener should attempt to open up new possibilities, with respect for one's interlocutor, as well as for the self that one may yet become.

To illustrate, I present a hasidic story about Rabbi Elimelekh of Lizhensk (1717–1787), master of the third generation, disciple of the Great Maggid of Mezritsh, venerated for sanctity, selfless devotion to God and community, and charismatic gifts. Hasidic tradition attributes to Rabbi Elimelekh powers akin to those of the biblical prophets. His grave site is to this day a pilgrimage destination for both Jews and non-Jews who seek his intercession on matters spiritual or mundane, or simply the merit of communing with the spirit of a great saint.

The story is told that many years after his death, an elderly woman who had once served as a cook in Rabbi Elimelekh's household was asked to share memories of the great master. She replied that she knew nothing about Rabbi Elimelekh's mystical practices or esoteric teachings, but she recalled one thing. The kitchen, tasked with preparing large meals for family and guests, was constantly busy, and like all such kitchens, was a frequent arena of tension between the staff. This would have been especially true on Friday, with the added pressure of the onset of Shabbos. Yet, she recalled, as the sun began to set and Friday turned into Shabbos, the atmosphere changed. The mood was like the entry into Yom Kippur; the entire staff was overcome with warmth and kindness. People who had previously shouted at each other now sought forgiveness and reconciliation. Shabbos spirit swept over the entire kitchen, transforming the ambience to love and grace. This happened, she concluded, every Erev Shabbos (Friday).

This story allows us to feel the erstwhile cook's astonishment at the change in mood that swept over her and her coworkers just before the arrival of Shabbos: This was indeed a miracle!

But there is more to learn from the story, a version of which is presented by Y. A. Kamelhar and cited by Abraham Joshua Heschel. For Rabbi Elimelekh, the onset of Shabbos was indeed akin to the onset of Yom Kippur, both times engendering awe and reverence, a homecoming to the most nobly gracious and forgiving places in one's own psyche. In his framing of the story, Kamelhar emphasizes the theme of *eimat Shabbat* – "reverence for Shabbos." The Hebrew *eima* actually denotes something beyond reverence; perhaps the word "trepidation" captures the intensity of emotion. Most versions of the story, which apparently circulated widely in pre-Holocaust Eastern Europe, underscore *eima* as a key factor inducing the mood of love and compassion.[31]

The parallel to Yom Kippur is indeed instructive. It is precisely Yom Kippur's palpable sanctity, its passageway back to origins, to First Things and Final Things – in a word, to the Holy of Holies – that spurs individuals to seek each other out in contrition and humility. There is a

---

31. Yekutiel Aryeh Kamelhar, *Dor De'ah* ([Bilgoraj, 1933] New York, 1952), 126; see n. 5. Kamelhar is cited by Abraham Joshua Heschel, *The Sabbath* (New York: Meridian Books, 1963), 31. Another version appears in Avraham Hayim Simhah Bunem Michaelson, *Ohel Elimelekh*, no. 246, 95–96. Yet another presentation is found in *Niflaot HaTiferet Shlomo* (Pietrokow, 1923), no. 253, 101. The variations are not surprising, as they capture cultural memories of persons and events from over a hundred years earlier; Rabbi Elimelekh died in 1787, and the published versions date from the early-twentieth century. What is remarkable is the consistency of the core: the spirit of peace and reconciliation that permeated the entirety of Rabbi Elimelekh's environs with the onset of Shabbos. Most transmitters of the tale also emphasize the overwhelming awe that seized the kitchen staff. *Niflaot HaTiferet Shlomo* is particularly emphatic on this point. The way it tells the tale, two workers who used to quarrel bitterly over division of chores were turned around to mutual love and generosity, vowing to assist and support each other. Due to the reverence for Shabbos that seized them, "their hands would tremble in awe as they jointly carried the pot of *cholent* (bean stew)" (p. 102).

Martin Buber anthologized the story in *Tales of the Hasidim: The Early Masters* (New York: Schocken Books, 1947), 254, under the title "The Servants."

sense of momentousness, of encounter with long-obscured truths that are both reassuring and frightening, of being called to seriousness and self-scrutiny, all of which evoke intense sobriety, transparent clarity, as well as joy.[32]

One might think of a wedding day as a helpful analogy. The couple and their parents are filled with joy, but for anyone not blithely indifferent to the weightiness of an all-embracing life-commitment, there is also trepidation.

The same is true for Shabbos. As the *Sefat Emet* teaches, every Shabbos is a *Lekh-Lekha* moment – a moment of embarkation on a great journey, like that of Abraham, surrendering the reassurances of weekday routine unconditionally for the sake of an itinerary inward and upward, whose full implications are not entirely clear at the outset.[33] As God said to Abraham, the destination is "to the land that I will show you" (Gen. 12:1). Along with loving trust and joy, such a venture necessarily evokes a measure of trepidation.

As we retell the story, we endeavor to conjure that same surprise, that same transformative *eima*. The story invites us to melt frozen patterns into supple movements and open portals, to embrace a beckoning horizon, to be transported to a new relational space.

The "harmony and peace," the "sympathy for all things"[34] of which Heschel speaks are so desirable, but the transformation does not happen of its own accord. The state of grace in Rabbi Elimelekh's household that the story invites us to emulate is a result of setting tone and articulating expectations, likely by subtle gesture more than by words.

---

32. The close connection between Shabbos and Yom Kippur is already clear in the Bible, which calls Yom Kippur *Shabbat shabbaton*, "A Shabbos of complete cessation" (Lev. 16:31; 23:32). In the medieval period, Rabbi Baḥya ben Asher points to the similarity between Shabbos and Yom Kippur in that each has unique liturgy for each phase of the day. See *Kad HaKemaḥ*, in *Kitvei Rabbenu Baḥya*, ed. Hayim Dov Chavel (Jerusalem: Mossad HaRav Kook, 1970), 224. Rabbi Kalonymos Shapiro speaks of the third Shabbos meal as "the Yom Kippur of the week"; see *Tzav VeZiruz*, no. 47, 52–53.

33. *Sefat Emet, Parashat Lekh Lekha*, 5637/1876, s.v. *bamidrash shimi bat*.

34. Heschel, *The Sabbath*, 31.

Most of all, it is a posture of reverential anticipation, a palpable awe for the great Guest who is arriving.

Of all the dispositions that Shabbos entails, perhaps reverence is among the hardest for us to achieve. In his book *Reverence: Renewing a Forgotten Virtue*, Paul Woodruff notes that we live in a culture that celebrates irreverence. Woodruff asserts that reverence is needed not only in religion but in all worthwhile cultural activities. Some features of this virtue according to Woodruff are: harmonious group-engagement with a project in a structured, ceremonious way, without ego and in willing submission to a higher goal, leading to "a shared feeling of inarticulate awe."[35] The story of Rabbi Elimelekh prods us to consider how we might better foster this reverential awe in our own homes, so as to enter Shabbos as we enter Yom Kippur: free of hatreds, grudges, and pettiness of all kinds, and open to immensity, to mystery, to our own limits, to infinite compassion, acceptance, and embrace.

Summary: Shabbos, Embodied Practice, Common Ground

The practices that we have discussed – *niggun*, intense prayer, and storytelling – are embodied practices that foster mindful awareness, enhance presence and centeredness, and grow out of and nurture community. They cultivate common ground.

As our analysis of the manna passage (Ex. 16) has indicated, common ground is precisely the gift that Shabbos gives us. It turns a fractious, disoriented multitude adrift in the wilderness into the "House of Israel," enabling them to settle in, connect to themselves and each other, find personal place and shared space, and develop into a worthy receptacle for the indwelling of the Divine Presence, the *Shekhina*. Shabbos-keepers overcome the "buffered self of modernity";[36] they count their days with awareness, acquire a heart of wisdom (Psalm 90), and find their place in society and the cosmos.

---

35. Paul Woodruff, *Reverence: Renewing a Forgotten Virtue* (Oxford and New York: Oxford University Press, 2002), 48–49.
36. The phrase is from Charles Taylor, *A Secular Age* (Cambridge, MA: Harvard University Press, 2007).

Chapter 4

Stop – Preparation, Anticipation, and Love

THE THREE STAGES OF SHABBOS: STOP, LOOK, LISTEN

In the previous chapter, we explored some of the core practices of the hasidic movement: *niggun*, prayer, and storytelling. Each practice is certainly found elsewhere in Judaism, but is given a special resonance within Hasidism. The common theme of these practices is embodied spirituality and finding presence. Central to the Baal Shem Tov's spirituality is the fusion of action and intention, body and spirit, form and matter.

Each practice creates a holy domain, a zone of sacred time fused with a region of sacred space. By uniting the participants in heart, mind, spirit, and bodily presence, a radius emerges, emanating from a central point of holiness. The circumference is the sacred envelope formed by singing, listening, and prayer. The central point is the energetic, attractive core of each practice. The space that is swept by the radius is then filled with *daat* – mindful awareness, presence.

Once we are mindfully aware in our prayer, study of Torah, story-sharing, and singing, we inhabit our own bodies more richly and resonantly, and we form, foster, cultivate and enhance communal bonds. Our families and friends become a *ḥevreh* – a society of trust, deep sharing, and intimacy. That is the goal of the hasidic practices and dispositions, and the goal dovetails elegantly and precisely with the mood and spirit of Shabbos, which is all about presence and coming into place – orientation and location in one's physical, emotional, and spiritual topography.

This orientation and settling-in has three distinct stages; one might see them as movements in the musical composition that is Shabbos.

The eminent modern Jewish philosopher Franz Rosenzweig (1886–1929), in his work *The Star of Redemption*, highlighted three motifs of Shabbos, as found in our liturgy: **Creation, Revelation,** and **Redemption.**[1] Rosenzweig's basic insight was already pointed out by Rabbi Jacob ben Asher, a late thirteenth- early fourteenth-century Bible commentator and author of the *Arbaa Turim*, the classic work that serves as the template for the Code of Jewish Law in four major sections.

The *Tur* writes:

> The Sages instituted three distinct prayers for the three Shabbos services:
>
> - For the evening service, *Ata Kidashta* ["You have sanctified the seventh day for Your sake." The prayer speaks of cessation on the seventh day, the goal of all creation, and God's blessing and hallowing this day above all others, quoting Gen. 2:1–3.]
> - For Shabbos morning, *Yismah Moshe* ["Moses rejoices," speaking of Moses on Sinai in intimate relationship with God, receiving a bestowal of divine luminous glow that emanated from his face (Ex. 34:29), as well as the Decalogue with specific reference to Shabbos, and quoting Ex. 31:16–17.]
> - *Ata Ehad* ["You are One," speaking of the unity of God, the name of God as One, and Israel's uniqueness. The prayer continues with a rapturous description of Shabbos's *menuha* (serenity), described as "serenity of love and generosity, serenity of truth and faith, serenity of peace, tranquility, stillness, and calm."][2]

1. Franz Rosenzweig, *The Star of Redemption*, trans. William W. Hallo (Notre Dame: University of Notre Dame Press, 1985), 310–14.
2. Rabbi Jacob ben Asher (c. 1269–1340), *Tur Orah Hayyim*, sec. 292.

This is in contrast to the prayers for the Festivals – Passover, Shavuot, and Sukkot – all of which have the same base text, *Ata Beḥartanu* ("You have chosen us") that remains uniform for the evening, morning, and afternoon of each Festival day. The reason for the assignment of three distinct prayers for the three services on Shabbos is their correspondence to three foundational themes of Shabbos:

- The evening service corresponds to the Shabbos of Creation (Gen. 2:1–3).
- The morning service corresponds to the Shabbos of the Revelation of Torah at Sinai (Ex. 19–20), in accordance with the talmudic teaching that "the Torah was given on Shabbos."[3]
- The afternoon service corresponds to the eschatological Shabbos – the Shabbos of Redemption.

Rabbi Jacob ben Asher in the thirteenth century and Franz Rosenzweig in the twentieth were quite correct in pointing out the three stages of the unfolding of Shabbos's arc. This is an important and underappreciated aspect of the spirit and significance of the day. Shabbos unfolds gradually, incrementally, sequentially. Each stage assumes and builds upon the prior stage. We are meant to absorb and sustain the lessons of Friday evening when we experience Shabbos morning, and likewise we are to build upon the first two stages as we move to the culminating moments toward the end of the day. The day has a propulsive trajectory, a progressive deployment.

The schema of **Creation, Revelation, Redemption** is reflected in our liturgy, it has wise expositors, and it makes sense from a theological perspective. That said, I would like to suggest a parallel but somewhat different way of approaching the three stages of Shabbos's unfolding. I call the stages **Stop, Look, Listen**. These words point to a sequential arc of awareness and perception. They are three experiential postures that choreograph mood and ambience of Shabbos, synchronized with the path of the setting sun late Friday afternoon, the rising of the sun in

---

3. Shabbat 86b.

the morning, and the gradual fading of sunlight on Shabbos afternoon at a time when, paradoxically, Shabbos achieves fullness as it is about to disappear.

There is a sensory progression of the Shabbos experience – three postures that embrace us as we inhabit them, surrender to them. The impress they leave on our bodies and spirits is the gift of Shabbos, the great bestowal.

The reason for augmenting the triad of **Creation, Revelation, Redemption** with my schema of **Stop, Look, Listen** is that the latter three more directly focus on embodied practice, on actual physical actions, postures, and sensory awareness. **Creation, Revelation,** and **Redemption** are theological affirmations that invite us to enter the ideational states of Shabbos. **Stop, Look,** and **Listen** allow us to embrace these states in a phased, sequential manner with our bodies and our senses, with total experiential immersion.

STOP

Erev Shabbos

We are about to turn our attention to **Stop,** the focus of Friday evening, but first we must revisit the notion of "Friday." Let us return for a moment to Genesis chapter 1. At the conclusion of the account of each day, the Torah speaks of "one day, a second day, a third day, a fourth day, a fifth day." But the next day breaks the pattern. After humans were created and blessed, God assessed all that He had made, "and behold it was very good." This is followed by the refrain, "There was evening and there was morning," but instead of the expected "a sixth day," the biblical text has "**the** sixth day," *yom hashishi* (Gen. 1:31). The definite article indicates that the activity of world-making has now reached its conclusion; all the prior days were leading up to this one.[4] As Rabbi Samson Raphael Hirsch put it:

> We are clearly meant to regard this day as one for which the others were preparatory, one to which they led up to, in which the list of creations found a goal and came to an end.... The seventh

---

4. See Rashbam, *Ḥizkuni,* and Rabbi David Zvi Hoffman.

day, accordingly, is simply the result of the sixth; it presupposes its existence.[5]

Shabbos-observers know Friday as Erev Shabbos. These two alternate designations for the sixth day of the week are not equivalent. Erev Shabbos is the time that anticipates Shabbos, sets the stage for Shabbos, alerts us to what we need to do in order to be ready for Shabbos, and, in its waning moments, humbly salutes and welcomes Shabbos.[6] As the sun starts to hug the horizon, Erev Shabbos bows reverently, exits the stage walking backward, and makes gracious room for Shabbos to arrive.

Erev Shabbos attunes us to solar movement. This is of particular relevance for city dwellers, especially in our age, when artificial illumination has nearly erased awareness of the natural diurnal cycle and when the worlds of employment and commerce display hardly any concern for seasonal changes in sunset/sunrise. The sun sets later in summer and earlier in the winter, and Shabbos observers learn to adjust their Friday schedule accordingly.

The Big Ask

We have now come to what might be the most challenging aspect of Shabbos observance in our society. Readiness for Shabbos entails arranging your Friday so that you arrive home before sunset. Not many employers attempt to control what their workers do on Saturday. Most supervisors will be indifferent to whether you spend your weekend shopping, at an entertainment venue, or at synagogue. But Friday is different; Friday is the last day of the workweek, and leaving early may be a big ask.

---

5. Samson Raphael Hirsch, *Genesis*, trans. Isaac Levy, 2nd ed. (Gateshead: Judaica Press, 1989), 39–40. This conclusion is supported by the three-fold occurrence of the phrase *bayom hashishi*, "on the sixth day," in the manna chapter, each time focusing on the preparatory activity to be accomplished before the arrival of Shabbos; see Exodus 16:5; 16:22; 16:29. With regard to mindful awareness, the preparatory day may carry even more weight than the day of Shabbos!

6. See the impassioned words of Rabbi Joseph Soloveitchik, as cited in Pinchas Peli, ed. *On Repentance* (Jerusalem: Maggid Books, 2017), 32, n. 1: "It is not for the Sabbath that my heart aches; it is for the forgotten 'eve of the Sabbath.' There are Sabbath-observing Jews in America, but there are not 'eve-of-the-Sabbath' Jews who go out to greet the Sabbath with beating hearts and pulsating souls."

Only commitment to Shabbos, to Shabbos's holiness, blessing, venerable antiquity, and gravitas, will grant you the stature and confidence, the firmness and courtesy, to request to leave work early on winter Fridays.

If Shabbos is to happen at all, it happens on Friday, on Erev Shabbos. Converting what might have been a seventh weekday into Shabbos is the essence of what the sixth day is meant to accomplish. This is the deeper meaning of the Big Ask: Shabbos asks us to move to a state of readiness before Shabbos arrives, in loving and thoughtful anticipation.

The practice that we have been calling **Stop** demands planning to responsibly bring oneself to a controlled and balanced equilibrium as the brakes are being applied. This is certainly true on a practical level; preparations of all kinds must be made in order to enter Shabbos repose. As the Talmud puts it, "One who takes the trouble to prepare on Erev Shabbos will have food on Shabbos."[7] On an existential level, anticipating **Stop** on Friday conveys to oneself and others that the agendas of the week are provisional, contingent, and limited, and that they must subordinate themselves to ancestral practice, to the prior truth of Shabbos. Indeed, weekday goals only find meaning when in service to the transcendent, when they readily bow to the higher horizon of Shabbos – "last in action, first in thought."[8] The willingness to adjust schedules to accommodate Shabbos signals that regimes of commerce, transactional marketplaces, dreams of economic expansion, and grasping for competitive advantage do not lay final claim on our time and our attention; appetites for acquisition and consumption can be reined in and stilled. They are not ultimate goals; they cannot convey lasting meaning to human lives or nurture souls. By setting the stage for Shabbos on Friday, you are breaking free of the shackles of labor; you are, in the spirit of Sabbatical year and Jubilee, "proclaiming liberty throughout the land,"[9] and first and foremost, in your own soul.

---

7. Avoda Zara 3a.
8. A phrase from *Lekha Dodi*, the poem composed by the Safed Kabbalist Rabbi Shlomo Halevi Alkabetz, for the liturgy of welcoming the Shabbos. See Reuven Kimelman, *The Mystical Meaning of Lekha Dodi and Kabbalat Shabbat* (Jerusalem: Hebrew University Magnes Press, 2003) [Hebrew with English summary], p. 34, n. 10.
9. Leviticus 25:10.

The promotion of Friday into Erev Shabbos accords with the most general principle of spiritual practice: setting one's intention first, committing to the practice before entering it, thereby framing a space and establishing a safe harbor, a refuge from distractions, a sheltered cove in which to dock and store provision.

PREPARING BODY, MIND, AND SPIRIT

Meal preparation is the most salient aspect of Friday's to-do list, already mentioned in Scripture in the manna story: "And it shall come to pass on the sixth day that they shall prepare (*vehekhinu*) that which they bring in, and it shall be twice as much as they gather daily" (Ex. 16:5; cf. 16:23).

It is interesting to observe, however, that food preparation has already come into play earlier in the Bible, in Genesis's story of Joseph and his brothers. In chapter 43 of Genesis, the brothers return to Egypt for a second purchase of grain, this time bringing Benjamin, at the insistence of the harsh Grand Vizier, who they do not recognize to be Joseph. Father Jacob has sent along a gift, choice products of Canaan such as date honey, nuts, and spices. Puzzlingly, the brothers are invited to a formal dinner at noon with the Vizier. They prepare the gift (*vayakhinu et haminḥa*) (Gen. 43:25), freshening up the items after the long journey from Canaan and arranging them attractively. Joseph also instructs his staff to prepare a banquet (*vehakhen*) for the guests (43:16).

We see from this that "preparation" involves more than merely the action of making food ready. There is a strong emotional component and a vector of intentionality in the act of preparation. The brothers, carrying with them Jacob's fervent hopes, yearn to find favor in the eyes of the inscrutable Egyptian (see 43:14), while Joseph for his part is testing his brothers, challenging them to display the fraternal love that had failed them years earlier when they sold him into slavery. Food preparation is the enactment of hope in physical substance, in this case hope for family reconciliation and reunification in a way that neither the brothers nor Joseph could fully anticipate nor imagine.

Less dramatic yet equally meaningful, your Erev Shabbos food preparation expresses the hope that your Shabbos meals will be occasions of gathering, sharing, and lovingly accessing layers of soul, all in ways that cannot be fully envisioned or predicted. Much like the honey and nuts carried from Canaan, the prior day's Shabbos-meal preparation is the materialized embodiment of heart-yearning for intimacy and restoration of lost parts of the self, a message from one time and place to another. Conversely, when you sit down to your Shabbos meals, you will recall with gratitude the person or persons (likely including you) who injected so much love into the very foods you eat now. Food preparation is the ultimate arena of intentionality, linking with love two people – the person you were once and the person you are now – bridging the gap with filaments of heart and soul.

The *Sefat Emet* advances the remarkable principle that preparation for a mitzva is more transformative than actually performing the mitzva.[10] This is because the mitzva may be done in a moment, but preparation is ongoing, a constant process of making oneself ready for right action in alignment with the will of God; preparedness never ceases. In addition, the *Sefat Emet* continues, preparation is primarily an inner activity, a posture of joyous anticipation and spiritual desire, which, as he says, is "very precious."

All this applies to Erev Shabbos food preparation. Your peeling, slicing, cooking, and baking are intentional activities, outward expressions of interior states, depositing sacred energies to be released once the sun has set and Shabbos has arrived.

Give *tzedaka* (charity). Reach out to out-of-town relatives and friends and wish them, "Good Shabbos!" Place a call or make a visit to someone who cannot leave their house or hospital bed. Make sure they have food for Shabbos.

Hasidim are particularly keen on the practice of immersing in a *mikve* (ritual bath), allowing the primal waters to flow over the entire body and emerge reborn.[11] If you want to have skin in this game, make sure every bit of skin is in!

---

10. *Sefat Emet, Parashat Haazinu* 5634/1874, s.v. *baTur hevi hamidrash.*

11. For the idea that bathing in the *mikve* is a return to one's mother's womb and that the moment of emergence from the *mikve* is a moment of rebirth, see Rabbi Eliyahu de Vidas, *Reshit Ḥokhma, Shaar HaAhava* (The Gate of Love), ch. 11, par. 29. Vidas writes, "When you emerge from the *mikve*, your limbs and your soul are restored to their pristine state, so you are a new being! You should feel a new spirit within, a spark of the soul that has been returned to you (cleansed and refreshed)." Vidas

If Saturday is to be Shabbos, then Friday must be Erev Shabbos. Most important: Arrive at your destination ahead of time – before sunset.

There is an extended talmudic passage discussing the visual signs of Shabbos's approach. The time to light the Shabbos lamp is when the sun is at the top of the palm trees. But, the Talmud asks, how can one determine the approach of Shabbos on a cloudy day? The answer is, by looking at the roosters in one's yard or the ravens in the meadow. When they settle down, it is time to light. The Talmud also mentions a plant called *adanei* or *aronei*.[12] Rashi explains that *adanei* is highly sensitive to the path of the sun; in the morning, the leaves bend eastward, at noon they rise straight up, and at sunset the plant displays a sharp westward tilt.[13]

Living as we do with devices that measure time with the utmost precision and accuracy, and accustomed to relying on algorithmically calculated tables of sunset and sunrise, the talmudic indications seem quaint and archaic. But what we have gained in precision, we may have lost in connectedness to the basic rhythms that regulate life on our planet and to the phototropism that guides plants and animals. There is something profound in being alert to signals from the natural world, reminding us to stop the workweek and enter into Shabbos space and

---

also counsels repentance before immersion, "so that nothing leave a barrier in your soul." There are many editions of *Reshit Ḥokhma*; I consulted the three-volume edition (Jerusalem, 5740/1980) published by Hayim Yosef Waldman, vol. 1:614. For a hasidic articulation of this theme, see *Likkutim Yekarim* (Jerusalem: Toledot Aharon, 5734/1974), no. 42, no. 56 (pp. 134a–135b; 142b–143b). This text, an anthology of Baal Shem Tov and Maggidic traditions compiled by Rabbi Meshullam Feivush of Zbaraz (first published in Zolkiew in 1796), provides kabbalistic sacred name-permutations for *mikve* and adds that "the main intention is intimate attachment (*devekut*) to God; broken-hearted humility shatters all barriers between the human being and the Divine. This is the preparatory intention that is crucial for the efficacy of the *mikve*-immersion. After such an immersion, one emerges a newly born person, a pure-hearted creation." He adduces the verse in Psalms, "Create in me a pure heart, O God" (Ps. 51:12). In the Hebrew verse, the first letters of the words *lev tahor bera* can be arranged to form an acronym for *taval*, "immersed."

12. Shabbat 35b.
13. Rashi, ad loc., s.v. *adanei*.

time. As Rashi puts it, *"veḥal alav haShabbos"* – at this time of phase-transition, Shabbos takes hold of the person.

Take a cue from light-sensitive flora – bend to earth with the setting arc of the sun, and welcome Shabbos into your body and spirit.

PRACTICES FOR THE ENTRY OF SHABBOS

Lighting Candles

Lighting candles (in ancient times, oil lamps) before sunset is an essential aspect of welcoming Shabbos. The practice honors Exodus 35:3, "You shall not kindle fire throughout your residences on the Shabbos day," as interpreted by the Pharisaic-rabbinic tradition that the prohibition applies to igniting a new fire on Shabbos, while a flame already burning before sunset may continue to burn (so long as no more fuel is added on Shabbos). This distinction is important, because the Karaites (an anti-rabbinic sect emphasizing a literalist reading of Scripture) understood the verse as teaching that the Shabbos home may have no fire burning at all. This meant that their homes were dark and their food cold. The rabbinic tradition makes it possible to enjoy the Friday night meal illuminated by lamps or candles lit prior to Shabbos's entry, before sunset.

The original intent of the kindling, then, is largely practical – so that food can be enjoyed during the evening meal and the members of the family do not bump into each other in the dark. The Talmud calls this *shalom bayit*, "peace in the household." Another consequence of the Pharisaic-rabbinic interpretation is that the second Shabbos meal in the daytime can include hot foods that have been kept warm by a fire burning since late Friday afternoon.

Over the centuries, however, pre-Shabbos candle lighting has taken on a more ritualized, ceremonial character. It is the time to welcome Shabbos peace and holiness and to give thanks for all aspects of one's life, to focus on sending light and blessing into one's home and household. In Eastern Europe especially, a tradition developed of the parent (usually the mother) kindling the lamps and entering a state of grace, asking to be worthy to raise children and grandchildren who are "wise and discerning, in love with and in awe of God, embodying truth, holy seed, intimate with the Divine, enlightening the world with Torah, good deeds, and all aspects of God's work." The poignancy, tenderness, and expressiveness of the moment and the practice – performed with eyes closed, and with the most personal aspects of the prayer kept as a soft murmur or silently in the heart – are unforgettable. The house is bathed in light and in love, and now Shabbos can begin.

The candles will continue to burn into the night, illuminating the evening meal, the first of the three Shabbos meals. Rabbi Moses Isserles (eminent Polish rabbi and halakhic authority, author of a work that became a key component of the expanded Code of Jewish Law, *Shulḥan Arukh;* d. 1572) calls for the practice of gazing at the lit candles, especially during Kiddush (which will be discussed below). He writes:

> During Kiddush, one should fix one's eyes upon the candles and gaze into them. The Talmud tells us that rushing around [literally, "taking huge strides"] during the weekdays clouds one's vision [literally, "takes away one five-hundredth of the light of the eyes"]. The remedy is to gaze at the flame of the two Shabbos candles.[14]

It was already true in antiquity; the relentless pace of daily activity, generally directed to economic pursuits, blurs one's vision. How much more so in our own age! Transfixed all week by the flicker of glowing screens, our eyes are drained of clarity and focus; we lose sight of the actual world we inhabit, even the people around us who most deeply share our lives. The remedy, the Talmud tells us, is to gaze intently, caressingly at a different flicker – the natural, warm, and gentle glow of Shabbos candles. Kindled with love and grace and blessed with eyes closed, they are the perfect restorative of sight, a soothing eyebath, an elixir of vision, an immersive meditation practice.

Gaze and absorb; gaze to find lucidity.

Stop in the Name of Love: Chanting Song of Songs

The spirit of love pervades Shabbos. Many synagogues, as an introduction to the Friday evening liturgy, have the custom of chanting *Shir HaShirim* (Song of Songs), the biblical love-poem saturated with ecstatic

---

14. *Darkhei Moshe* on *Tur, Oraḥ Ḥayim* 276:8.

passion and longing. As Ellen Davis has written, "The Song returns us to Eden with the intent of imaginatively healing the ruptures that occurred there between man and woman, between humanity and God, between human and nonhuman creation."[15] It is in this spirit that *Shir HaShirim* is chanted as we enter Shabbos. The love we feel for family and friends; passionate love for one's life partner; love of God, Torah, and people; love of sacred practices; love of our beautiful, fragile, vulnerable world; love of life itself – all these are embraced in *Shir HaShirim's* haunting lines.

Shir HaShirim underscores that all love is embodied, including spiritual love. Love affects physiology, breathing, pulse, hormonal balance. Love propels mood and mental state in the deepest, most transformative way. To link *Shir HaShirim* with Shabbos is to affirm that equivalence, to express the hope that the Shabbos we are entering *now* – *at this moment* – will be felt compellingly on every level of our being, in our bodies, in all of our senses.

The allusions to the Garden of Eden in *Shir HaShirim* bring us back to Paradise as we enter Shabbos. Again quoting Ellen Davis:

> The garden was a place characterized by complementarity and companionship, by mutual responsiveness among the creatures human and nonhuman, and between all creatures and their Creator. ... Humans enjoyed companionship with God, who walked with them in "the breezy time of day."[16]

---

15. Ellen Davis, "Reading the Song Iconographically," in *Scrolls of Love: Ruth and the Song of Songs*, ed. Peter S. Hawkins and Lesleigh Cushing Stahlberg (New York: Fordham University Press, 2006), 172–84; quote on 173–74. In contrast to the prevailing academic view that Song of Songs is a collection of secular love poems that made its way into the Hebrew Bible by means of an allegorical rereading, Davis argues that "the Song was correctly understood by those who accorded it a place among Israel's Scriptures," that "it really is, in large part, about the love that obtains between God and Israel – or, more broadly, between God and humanity." Davis is "convinced that the rabbis correctly judged the genre of the Song and heard a message that did not deviate widely from the theological vision of the poet who gave us the Song in its present form." See also Ellen F. Davis, "The Ecstasy of Intimacy – Song of Songs," in *Opening Israel's Scriptures* (New York: Oxford University Press, 2019), 360–75.

16. Davis, *Opening Israel's Scriptures*, 371.

While chanting *Shir HaShirim*, the resonances of Eden, the allusions to the aromas of the Garden's vegetation, surround us with a paradisic ambience.

Toward the end of *Shir HaShirim*, we read, "Mighty waters cannot extinguish love; rivers cannot sweep it away. If a person were to give all their wealth for love, they would be laughed to scorn" (Song. 8:7). This verse captures love's intensity, knowing no boundaries or limits. Utilitarian, practical considerations are swept aside. We enter this enchanted space as we embrace Shabbos in love. As Michael Fishbane writes, "Love cannot be purchased; it is not a commodity for exchange.... It flares up from one's inmost depth."[17]

The resonance between love and Shabbos gives power to the thought expressed elegantly by Fishbane that "Love exceeds all bounds"; it is an "ineffable force." Quoting Ibn Sahula, Fishbane writes that "nothing in the 'flood' of experience can overwhelm it." It is precisely this irresistible palpability of love/Shabbos that we desire to inhabit.

Return to Eden: Paradise Not Lost

The evocation of Eden in the Shabbos liturgy has strong roots in classic rabbinic thought on the Garden of Eden narrative, a story that continues to fascinate not only religious devotees but secular thinkers as well. One recent treatment is that of Stephen Greenblatt, who has elegantly traced the influence of the Garden story on Western culture in his work *The Rise and Fall of Adam and Eve*, drawing on theology, literature, and art, with special emphasis on Augustine and Milton.[18] While he does not neglect Judaism entirely, his treatment of rabbinic literature is sparse and largely based on secondary sources. He might have noted that in rabbinic understanding, the expulsion from the Garden and the attendant degradation of the cosmos are delayed until after Shabbos. As the early Midrash Genesis Rabba teaches, the glorious luminosity that pervaded the Garden (and is now hidden) remained with Adam and Eve until the end of Shabbos,

---

17. *The JPS Bible Commentary: Song of Songs* (University of Nebraska Press and the Jewish Publication Society, 2015), 212–13.

18. Stephen Greenblatt, *The Rise and Fall of Adam and Eve* (New York: W. W. Norton, 2017).

at which time they were expelled and experienced darkness for the first time.[19] Building on this motif, the later Midrash on Psalms asserts that after Adam sinned on the first day of his life – the sixth day of the week – God decreed upon Adam expulsion from the Garden in the late afternoon of that first Friday, and the verdict was about to be carried out. But Shabbos, personified, appeared, taking the role of an advocate and interceding:

> Shabbos made the following argument: "During the six days of creation, no one suffered punishment. And you want to begin with me? Is this my blessing? Is this my repose?" [God relented] and because of Shabbos, Adam was saved from Gehenna. When Adam saw the power of Shabbos, he began singing, "A psalm, a song for the Shabbos day" (Ps. 92:1).[20]

Psalm 92 was composed by Adam, according to this midrash! Continuing this line, *Or HaḤayim* explains:

> "Remembering" the Shabbos day means being grateful to Shabbos for the very existence of humankind. This is not only a memory from the primordial past, but a living reality today. Shabbos continues to put us on our feet.
>
> When a person experiences miraculous deliverance from danger on a certain day, they commemorate that day by making it a holiday year after year.
>
> This impulse to celebratory gratitude is even more compelling in our case, since according to the midrash, it was Shabbos personified that interceded and won [for Adam and Eve a reprieve and an amelioration of the original verdict of expulsion and all that expulsion entailed].[21]

---

19. Genesis Rabba 11:2 on Genesis 2:3.
20. *Midrash Tehillim* on Psalms 92:1, no. 4, ed. Solomon Buber (Vilna: Romm, 5651 [1891]), 404; compare the English version in *The Midrash on Psalms*, trans. William G. Braude (New Haven and London: Yale University Press, 1987), vol. 2, 112.
21. *Or HaḤayim* on Exodus 20:8.

On Shabbos, we get a taste of what it means to return to primordial situatedness. With periodic regularity, we return to Edenic existence, prior to displacement, before alienation from the natural world, before estrangement from those we love the most, before the corrosive whispers of cynicism and mistrust (what the narrative calls the words of the serpent) open a gap between us and God. Expulsion from Eden meant rupture and decoherence. Shabbos brings healing and reunion. With Shabbos we know that Paradise is not lost.

Kabbalas Shabbos

The suite of prayers that serves as overture to Shabbos is called *Kabbalas Shabbos*, "Receiving Shabbos." This collection of psalms and poetry invites the worshipper to transition from weekday to sacred consciousness. The first six psalms recited (Psalms 95–99, Psalm 29) parallel the six days of the week.[22] We recall each day with gratitude, taking insights and illuminations with us into Shabbos.

Lekhu Neranena

The *Kabbalas Shabbos* service opens with Psalm 95, beginning with the words *Lekhu neranena*, "Come, let us sing joyously to the LORD, raise a shout for the Rock of our deliverance." Acclaiming God as Creator and sovereign of the universe, this psalm appropriately celebrates the week that has just come to an end. As the Piaseczner Rebbe (Rabbi Kalonymos Shapiro, mentioned in ch. 3) points out, biblical verses such as this one are in the imperative mood. The liturgy asks us to address the world and invite all creation to unite in joyous exultation of the God of all existence. As Rabbi Shapiro puts it, "It is not enough to be thinking of the meaning of each word. You must imagine yourself at this moment standing in front of the entire

---

22. For the text of the psalms with English translation, see *Koren Siddur*, 356–63. Regarding the parallel with the six days of the week, see *Siddur Tefilla Yeshara VeKeter Nehora HaShalem* (Berditchev), ed. Rabbi Aaron of Zelichov, new edition (Jerusalem, 2006), 133; *Siddur Ḥelkat Yehoshua LeShabbatot UMo'adim* (Biala), ed. Meir Yehezkel Weiner (Jerusalem, 5778/2018), 118.

world, face-to-face, proclaiming the words as a full-throated invitation" to lift up voices in song.[23]

But what about the last lines, where the tone changes and the psalmist pivots to channeling God's voice?[24] We now read of God uttering a complaint against God's people, recalling the time in the wilderness after the exodus from Egypt. God says (vv. 10–11), "For forty years I was wearied with that generation, and said: They are a people of errant heart, and they have not known My ways. Concerning them I swore in My anger [Hebrew, *api* – the first-person possessive of *af*] that they should not enter into My rest."

What is the purpose of the psalmist giving us this rare access to the divine perspective and, in particular, reminding us of a time of dismay and anger? In light of its placement at the start of the *Kabbalas Shabbos* service, we can understand this verse as giving us insight into how to enter into Shabbos. When Scripture pulls aside the curtain on God's thinking, as it were, we are certainly invited to learn a lesson on what to do and what to avoid.

The last word of the psalm, *menuḥati*, "My rest," has a double meaning here. Its overt denotation (*peshat*) refers to the Promised Land, called *menuḥa*, "the place of rest," in Deuteronomy 12:9.[25] In the context of welcoming Shabbos, however, the word carries another valence – a

---

23. Rabbi Kalonymos Kalmish Shapiro, *Shelosha Maamarim* [*Three Discourses*, published as an appendix to *Ḥovat HaTalmidim*], Discourse no. 2: "Torah, Prayer, and Song to God," section B. In the Tel Aviv, 1956 edition published by Rabbi Nahman Geshaid, this appears on p. 96. The specific example given there is *Hodu* (I Chr. 16:8–36), which begins the *Pesukei DeZimra* section of the morning service, but the intention is for the example to be broadly applied to similar passages of opening and invitation. See also *idem, Derekh HaMelekh* (Jerusalem, 1991), *Shavuot 5689* [1929], discourse for first day of the holiday, p. 351, where Rabbi Shapiro refers to *Lekhu Neranena* specifically and makes clear that our invitation to sing praise to God is addressed not only to fellow humans, but to all of nature – sun, moon, and stars; fire, hail, snow, and mist; mountains, trees, and animals (following Psalm 148). Rabbi Shapiro avers that all these beings have souls [*neshamot*].

24. As noted by Rabbi Barukh HaLevi Epstein in his siddur commentary, *Barukh SheAmar* (Tel Aviv: Am Olam, 1940), 226.

25. Rashi on Psalms 95:11 notes that the Land of Israel and Jerusalem are called *menuḥa* in Psalms 132:14: "This [Zion] is My resting place (*menuḥati*) for ever; Here will I dwell, for I have desired it."

sense pointing to the *menuḥa* (repose) of Shabbos! The deployment of this verse in a pivotal location of *Kabbalas Shabbos* with its play on words on *menuḥa* alerts us to the resonant overtones of *menuḥa* on linked spatial and temporal axes, calling us to rest in the most fulsome, most inclusive way that a human being can. The word *menuḥa* instructs us that if we wish to enter into Shabbos repose, we should avoid misdirecting our heart (v. 10). We should avoid *af* – that is, a state of feeling disgruntled and disaffected, disappointed and frustrated with life, such as the Israelites lapsed into during the wilderness trek, thereby provoking God's *af*, anthropomorphically speaking. God's *af* is a reflection of human *af*, and the way to enter God's *menuḥa*/repose is to bring ourselves to repose and equanimity.

To understand this more fully, consider a teaching of the Piaseczner Rebbe on this key word *af*. He discusses Shabbos as cessation, a letting go, entering the state of contentment that comes when we surrender control and express gratitude to God. He draws upon a midrashic teaching that the interior states of tranquility, calm, serenity, and stillness appeared in the world *after* the onset of the seventh day of creation. What is troublesome about life is any effort that centers on the interests of the individual rather than a higher horizon. This inevitably leads to frustration, work without satisfaction, mental and emotional anguish. Rabbi Shapiro develops the implications of two contrasting states – "toil and weariness" on the one hand, versus "tranquility, calm, serenity, and stillness" on the other. He writes:

> The world itself is not problematical, worrisome; what is worrisome is the fraught fragility of it, always poised between good and evil. Yet God, knowing all this, still created the world, for the sake of singular individuals who would live lives of sacred service and righteousness.
>
> Scripture states, "Humans are born to toil" (Job 5:7). But there are two kinds of toil that a person might experience: toil of sacred service (*avoda*) or toil of worry, anxiety (*de'aga*).
>
> It all depends what you want to receive from the world. For the self-absorbed individual immersed in their own material wants – for such a person, since the world involves toil of

anxiety (*amal*) and weariness (*yegia*), all their days are days of vexation and bitterness (*kaas vetamrurim*). They may not even be confronted with problems, yet they never know satisfaction (*seva ratzon*), never have contentment from the world. They are always looking to calm their tormented soul. This leads to an endless search for pleasure, entertainment as distraction from a profound, unstated anxiety.

But if you remember that God sent you here for a higher purpose – to acquire Torah wisdom and live a life of service – and that is what you seek from the world, then you are above anxiety and weariness. You are in the state of tranquility, calm, serenity, stillness (*shaanan, naḥat, shalva, vehashket*)....

We are situated in the world poised between the good of holiness and the distractions presented by the world. If holiness is our main focus, then that is our primary experience. We place first things first, and we feel the serenity and calm, the goodness, and the supernal pleasure.

God [anthropomorphically speaking] has existential anxiety about creation – the freedom that lies at the core of human personhood. Nevertheless, God did create the world – overcoming God's anxiety, as it were – for the sake of even one virtuous person.

The realization that so much is at stake in God's creation should increase our sense of responsibility.

Happiness (*simḥa*) is not carousing, merriment, revelry (*holelut*). Nor is it the case that the person serving God should be in a state of misery or sadness. The truth is that revelry comes from inner worry – frustration and weariness, inner disquiet and existential anxiety.

By contrast, the person serving God experiences the inner state of tranquility and quiet.

Even worries – one's own or others – are like chaff in wheat. When such a person wishes to sum up the state of the world from a personal perspective, they arrive at the formulation of Genesis: "God saw all that God had made – and behold, it is very good!"

The world consists of Torah, prayer, good deeds, Shabbos, Passover, and the other Holy Days – this is the world! It is all good, pleasure, satisfaction. There is also chaff and husk, and we can deal with them as well.[26]

Applying this teaching to *Kabbalas Shabbos*: Since Shabbos is *me'ein olam haba* (a foretaste and essence of the World to Come), we endeavor to reach this state of repose on Shabbos. We are called to move forward on the basis of the sacred work that we have done during the week. We see the path ahead clearly, without confusion, so there is no *amal veyegia*, "toil and weariness," just *shaanan, nahat, shalva vehashket*, "tranquility, calm, serenity, and stillness." These are positive states, states of alertness and vitality, not states of lethargy or inertia.

What is the meaning of the concluding verse of Psalm 95, "Concerning them I swore in My anger (*api*) that they should not enter into My rest," in light of Rabbi Shapiro's teaching? If we want to enter into God's *menuha* – divine tranquility and repose, the repose of Shabbos – we must adopt the posture of *shaanan, nahat, shalva vehashket* – tranquility, calm, serenity, and stillness – which can only be accomplished if we have avoided *af* – the habit of reacting to everything with frustration, disgruntlement, and disappointment.

The key to receiving Shabbos and being allowed entry into Shabbos's blessings and repose is the attitude of affirmation – of saying the "Yes!" of a joyous heart – not *af* – endless regrets, resentment, and discontent.

In astronomy, "perturbation" describes what happens when a celestial body deviates from a regular orbit due to the influence of some other celestial body. In psychology, perturbation describes mental agitation and unsteadiness, the source of which may be subtle and elusive, of which the affected individual may not be entirely aware. Unlike stars and planets governed by the laws of celestial mechanics, however, humans can examine and control the forces that contribute to their unease and lack of centeredness; we can choose to reframe and disregard annoyances and frustrations that warp perceptions and endanger relationships. In this quest for poise and balance, we are greatly aided by Shabbos. Shabbos's stability enables us to choose to overlook minor

---

26. Rabbi Kalonymos Kalmish Shapiro, *Derekh HaMelekh, Parashat Hayei Sara*, 5691/1930.

slights and grievances, to get beyond grudges and regrets, to find the centered equilibrium that only *blessing* and *sanctity,* only sublime relationship and loving affection can bring.

On Shabbos, we can choose not to be perturbed.

Lekha Dodi

The highpoint of the *Kabbalas Shabbos* service is the singing of *Lekha Dodi,* a hymn by the sixteenth-century kabbalist Rabbi Shlomo Alkabetz, who lived in the town of Safed in northern Israel, in the scenic Galilean hills. Written in biblical Hebrew, its individual words are immediately comprehensible to anyone with basic familiarity with the language, but, as Reuven Kimelman has shown in his exposition of the poem, its full meaning is grasped only by attending to its carefully crafted web of kabbalistic allusions. As Kimelman writes, the poem "operates on four levels simultaneously: the spatial, the temporal, the human, and the sefirotic."[27]

As mentioned above, celebration of Shabbos enables one to enter into an Edenic state of restoration and wholeness. From the perspective of spiritual practice, this means a reversal of the consequences of exile from Eden: estrangement from place; from one's fellow human beings, especially one's life partner; from meaningful accomplishment; from God; from one's own deepest self.

Of particular relevance is the fifth stanza of *Lekha Dodi,* which alludes to a kabbalistic myth based on an early rabbinic midrash, that in the Garden of Eden the first couple was blessed with garments of light (Hebrew *or,* spelled with an *alef*), and only after they sinned did they have to resort to garments of animal hide or leather (*or* spelled with an *ayin*).[28] The implications of this are manifold, woven into Alkabetz's

---

27. The *sefirot* are the ten manifestations of divinity, cosmic symbols found in the classical Kabbala. Readers interested in a full explication of the poem and its kabbalistic allusions are invited to consult Reuven Kimelman, *The Mystical Meaning of Lekha Dodi and Kabbalat Shabbat* (Jerusalem: Hebrew University Magnes Press, 2003) [Hebrew with English summary], vii–xiii.

28. Genesis Rabba 20:12, on Gen. 3:2, *Midrash Bereshit Rabba, Critical Edition with Notes and Commentary,* ed. J. Theodor and Ch. Albeck (Jerusalem: Wahrmann Books, 1965), 196–97; see discussion in Kimelman, *Mystical Meaning,* 137, n. 15.

poem with deft elegance and concision.[29] For our purposes, we may understand this motif as reflecting a pervasive aspect of the human condition – the tendency to wrap our true selves in "garments" that signal our roles in society. While garments can be totally appropriate manifestations of who we are, sometimes we are tempted to pose, to hide behind a cloak of pretense and deception. In our day, this tendency is reinforced by social media, which enable the posting of a flatteringly curated image. The self is masked in the selfie and the persona becomes an installation to be exhibited. This stanza invites us to recover the ideal of genuine transparency radiating from within, the garments of light.

Shabbos is the time for true luminosity of spirit, at home in sacred time and sacred space, centered and in focus, not cloaked in the false glitter of celebrity.

Who is the *dod*, the beloved, in the phrase *Lekha dodi likrat kalla*, "Go forth, my beloved, to greet the bride"? Arthur Green suggests that the beloved is the *neshama yetera*, the extra soul, the expanded capacity for spiritual sensitivity that enters the individual upon the arrival of Shabbos. "As Shabbat begins, we call it [the *neshama yetera*] forth, telling it that it is now safe to let itself be revealed. *Lekha Dodi* may be read…as a flirtation or seduction song to the *neshama yetera*, seeking to coax her out of hiding."[30] The idea here is that our everyday lives do not always allow us to tap our inner reservoir of spiritual yearning, our aspiration for the sublime and the sacred, and that *Lekha Dodi* is a love song, beckoning to our deep thirst for the sacred.

Green's insight is especially apt in our contemporary world, with the pace of life moving ever more quickly, with discourse crude and coarse, with little time or interest in things not commodified or subject to quantification. To express interest in spirit for its own sake is an act

---

29. See Kimelman *Mystical Meaning*, chapter 5 (pp. 134–84).
30. Arthur Green, "Kabbalat Shabbat: A Brief History," in *Kabbalat Shabbat: The Grand Unification*, illuminations and commentary by Debra Band, translations and literary commentary by Raymond P. Scheindlin (Honeybee in the Garden, 5776/2016), 3–5. See also Arthur Green, "Some Aspects of Qabbalat Shabbat," in *Sabbath: Idea, History, Reality*, ed. Gerald J. Blidstein (Beer Sheva: Ben-Gurion University of the Negev Press, 2004), 95–118.

of courage that goes against the grain of a culture besotted with materialism and the toys of technology.

In addition to addressing the *neshama yetera,* as Rabbi Green proposes, I suggest that the *dod* is the *kahal,* the community of like-minded pray-ers who have gathered in testimony to their aspiration for the sublime, the sacred, the treasured value of the created world. Surrounded by friends who share this deep conviction, singing in unison, each member of the *kahal* feels safe to disclose what really matters, giving witness to their steadfast conviction that whispers of transcendence are real and not delusional, taking a stand against pervasive cynicism and the insensitivity of those consumed by consumerism. *Lekha Dodi* gives permission to each pray-er to come out as a person animated by spirit, as native to the land of interiority.

We have discussed the first half of the refrain "*Lekha dodi likrat kalla.*" The second half of the refrain reads, "*Penei Shabbat nekabla,* Let us receive the Presence/Face of Shabbos." This phrase makes clear that we are addressing Shabbos as more than temporal duration; Shabbos is a personality that is invited into oneself for indwelling. We are asking Shabbos to move in, to take up residence in our neighborhood, our home, our body. We not only welcome Shabbos; we also aspire to become Shabbos-beings.

"Awaken, awaken – for your light has come, rise and shine!" (*Lekha Dodi*).

Psalm 92

Psalm 92 appears in the liturgy three times over the course of Shabbos: once in the early morning "Verses of Melody" (*Pesukei DeZimra*);[31] once as the Psalm of the Day;[32] and now for the first time, just after *Lekha Dodi,*[33] to proclaim that Shabbos has indeed arrived and we have entered a different, more elevated state, a temporal domain of sanctity. The psalm celebrates the profundity and intricacy of creation, called God's "handiwork" (v. 5), and is thus entirely appropriate for the

---

31. *Koren Siddur,* 470–71.
32. Ibid., 544–45.
33. Ibid., 370–71.

day that is the capstone of God's creative process (Gen. 1; 2:1–3). Contrasting the fleeting nature of human life with God's permanence, the psalm assures us that the apparent flourishing of wickedness is temporary, whereas the righteous partake of God's stability and permanence. In a double simile, the righteous are compared to a fruitful date palm and to a stately cedar of Lebanon, "planted in the house of the LORD" (vv. 13–14). In contrast to the infirmities of age-related decline depicted so unsparingly in Ecclesiastes chapter 12, the last lines of Psalm 92 are much more optimistic, promising that the righteous, nurtured by their rootedness in holy ground, can continue flourishing and producing fruit in old age, "full of sap and freshness" (v. 15).

In an incisive exposition of this psalm, Harold Fisch points to the keyword *lehaggid,* which both begins (v. 2) and concludes (v. 15) the psalm. The word means more than "to relate" or "to declare." Citing other biblical occurrences, Fisch offers "expounding," "solving a riddle," "interpreting a dream," and "making a connection."[34] The psalm invites us to address the riddle of existence and life's dreamlike evanescence by making connections, noticing patterns of meaning that may not be fully articulable but that nevertheless give rise to a sense of direction and sweet purposiveness. Our full **Stop** on Friday evening provides the emotional, cognitive, and social space for precisely this kind of connection-making and discovery of meaning to occur. This is the firm ground, the sacred courtyard (v. 13), upon which Shabbos enables us to stand.

The hasidic tradition affords yet further access to the riches of this psalm. One of the most famous teachings attributed to the Baal Shem Tov is known as the "Parable of the Walls of the Palace." As presented by his disciple Rabbi Jacob Joseph of Polonoye (c. 1710–1784), the teaching begins by citing Zoharic passages about the ascent of prayer to heaven by way of "palaces of prayer" assisted by angelic beings. The question arises: Why is there a need for angelic assistants and stages of ascents, when God's Glory is present everywhere? Why don't we have direct access to God? In response, the following parable is offered:

---

34. Harold Fisch, *Poetry with a Purpose* (Bloomington and Indianapolis: Indiana University Press, 1988), 128.

There was a great and wise king, who, by means of legerdemain [Heb. *aḥizat einayim*]³⁵ created an effect of walls, towers, and gates. He commanded that he should be approached by means of the gates and towers. He further commanded that treasures from the king's coffers should be placed at each gate. Some [seekers] went as far as the first gate, found money, took it, and turned back. Others [proceeded farther but eventually noticed a treasure that was too good to pass up, took it, and turned back]. Finally, his son, his beloved child, summoned his full determination to avoid being distracted by treasures and committed himself to proceed until he would reach his father, the king. Then he saw that that there was no barrier between him and his father, since all the partitions were effects of legerdemain.

The meaning of the parable: God hides in all types of garments and partitions. God's Glory fill the world (Is. 6:3); every move we make and every thought we have has its origin in God. Similarly, all angelic beings and all heavenly palaces are created out of God's own Self, like the snail whose shell is secreted from its very self.³⁶ It follows that there is no partition separating the person from the blessed Creator. With this awareness, "all the workers of iniquity shall be scattered" (Ps. 92:10).

The precise meaning of the parable has been widely discussed by interpreters of Hasidism. Some have seen in it the doctrine of pantheism, others panentheism (God is immanent everywhere in the universe but also transcends it). Some have compared it to the Eastern "veil of Maya." Rather than weighing in on this dispute directly, I wish to focus

---

35. I do not translate this term as "illusion," as some presentations of this teaching do. Illusion (Hebrew *dimyon*) generally suggests an image falsely considered to be real. However it is produced, it is not grounded in reality. By legerdemain or sleight of hand, I understand an effect produced by artful manipulation of real objects that tricks the eye into seeing something different than what is actually there. The distinction is key to understanding the Baal Shem Tov's intent, as we explain.

36. Genesis Rabba 21:5; more literally, "like the snail whose garment is part of its body." See Marcus Jastrow, *A Dictionary of the Targumim, the Talmud Babli and Yerushalmi, and the Midrashic Literature* (New York: Judaica Press, 1975 [1903]), s.v. *kamtza*, 1386.

on the biblical phrase that is deployed, essentially a direct quote from Psalms 92:10. According to the Baal Shem Tov as transmitted by Rabbi Jacob Joseph, the "workers of iniquity" are the distractions that seduce us into forgetting our goal of perceiving God everywhere and thereby achieving intimacy with our divine Parent. It is not so much that the world is illusion, but that the physical and mental entities that constitute our phenomenal world deflect our attention from the reality of God's Presence everywhere, *even in the distractions themselves*. Once the "walls and towers" are perceived to be of the divine essence, like the snail whose casing is self-secreted, the barriers cease to be barriers and the sought-for One stands revealed in full majesty. The angelic beings and heavenly palaces, just like more mundane treasures, are deceptive only insofar as they deflect our focus. When we cease to allow our attention to be divided, we concentrate on the One, and the walls dissipate. Partitions that were meant to be provisional and not hard-and-fast barricades have achieved their purpose and now allow clear passage.

Applying the wisdom embedded in this verse to its original context – the psalm for the Shabbos day – we may say that the delights of the world are only barriers to God if we allow them to distract us from the deeper truth that "the snail's garment is part of the snail," that the world emerges seamlessly from its divine source. If we keep our mind on God, then distractions need not be forcefully suppressed; they simply melt away. And it is Shabbos's repose, Shabbos's **Stop**, that affords us the inner freedom and spaciousness to arrive at and sustain this realization. By giving us the gift of time, Shabbos clears place for truer perception. The static of everyday life is removed, interior bandwidth is expanded, and the signal of sacred reverberation is received in its full range and richness.

"All the workers of iniquity shall be scattered" (Psalms 92:10).

TRANSITION TO HOME AS SACRED SPACE

At the end of evening services, warmly greet your fellow congregants. Together, you have embarked on the great Shabbos journey; you have joined your voices in a chorus of praise, thanksgiving, and arrival, requesting that the sacred canopy of peace cover all existence. Now is the time to make it personal, seeking out every member of the community, extending the hand of friendship, and bestowing upon each a brief but sincere Shabbos blessing. I am familiar with the Yiddish, "*Gut Shabbos!*" Many people say, "*Shabbat Shalom!*" English works very well – "Good Shabbos!" However you say it, enter into the words and meet the eyes and heart of your neighbor. Without attachment or agenda, in the fullness of your being, express your wish that the next twenty-four hours should be a taste of the World to Come, an immersive encounter foreshadowing the day of endless repose that the prophets envisioned.

As you walk home, you are already in the ambience of Shabbos. Your senses are more acute, yet more mellow; the world reveals itself with softness, compassion, and warmth.

You arrive home from synagogue services. Open the door and fill your heart with gratitude. Greet your family, greet the house itself, with the same blessing you gave your fellow neighbors-in-prayer.

Shalom Aleikhem

The history of the welcoming hymn *Shalom Aleikhem* – chanted upon returning home from the synagogue service on Friday evening – begins with the oft-quoted passage in the Talmud:

> Two ministering angels accompany the person on the eve of Shabbos from the synagogue to the home, one a good angel and one evil. When the person arrives home and finds the lamp lit, the table set, and the bed covered with a spread, the good angel exclaims, "May it be thus on another Shabbos too," and the evil angel has no choice but to answer, "Amen." But if the house has not been prepared for Shabbos, then the evil angel exclaims, "May it be thus on another Shabbos as well," and the good angel is forced to respond, "Amen."[37]

Shalom Aleikhem first appeared in 1641. Adopted with great enthusiasm by Jewish communities all over the world, it has also been the subject of controversy and even opposition. Rabbi Jacob Emden (1697–1776) was quite uncomfortable with the requests made of the angels, and he

---

37. Shabbat 119b.

was entirely puzzled by the last stanza, which reads, *Tzethem leshalom,* "May you leave in peace." Emden writes: "Why should we send the angels away? Let them stay and rejoice in the Sabbath meal. Their joy would increase, as would their blessing." Perhaps, Emden suggests, we want them to depart before something improper takes place, which might make them leave in anger.[38]

Rabbi Hayim Volozhiner (1749–1821), foremost disciple of the Gaon of Vilna[39] and founder of the famed Yeshiva of Volozhin, had even stronger reservations about *Shalom Aleikhem.* He writes: "It is forbidden to make any requests of angels, for they have no independent power whatsoever. When a person is worthy, the angels have no choice but to bless, and if a person is unworthy, they have no choice but to curse." He did not attempt to terminate the folk tradition entirely, but he himself never said the words *Barkhuni leshalom,* "Bless me for peace," the line that directly makes a request of the angels. In his view, this was too close to praying to beings other than God.[40]

The Hatam Sofer (Rabbi Moshe Schreiber, 1762–1839, one of the most prominent and influential juridical authorities of the last several centuries) did not sing *Shalom Aleikhem.* He is said to have explained, "We are no longer on the spiritual level to have angels accompany us!"

On the other hand, Polish hasidic masters were quite at ease with greeting the angels. Rabbi Shmuel of Sochotchov (1855–1926), known as the *Shem MiShmuel,* extolled the virtues of *Shalom Aleikhem.* He noted that all week long, the human being is not at peace, for the body pulls in one direction while the soul pulls in the other. But on Shabbos, the power of holiness is so strong that body and soul make peace with each other, so the angels bless us. This teaching suggests that the angels really represent aspects of our own natures, which on Shabbos finally reach the place of mutual understanding and harmony.

38. Emden is cited from Issachar Jacobson, *Netiv Bina* (Tel Aviv: Sinai Publishing, 1978), vol. 2, 115.

39. Rabbi Eliyahu ben Shlomo Zalman (1720–1797), towering talmudist and rabbinic figure, famed for his absolute devotion to Torah study, extreme piety, and opposition to the hasidic movement.

40. Jacobson, *Netiv Bina,* 114–15.

The Gerer Rebbe in *Sefat Emet* addresses the meaning of the goodbye to the angels in the last stanza. He writes that there are weekday angels and Shabbos angels. The weekday angels accompany us on our travels, as stated in Psalms 91:11 – "For He [God] will command His angels concerning you to guard you in all your paths" – while Shabbos angels form a circle of protection as we settle in for the day of repose: "The angel of the LORD encamps around those who revere Him, and He delivers them" (Ps. 34:8). At the start of Shabbos, there is a changing of the guard, and the send-off in the fourth stanza is to say goodbye to the weekday angels who are departing. Their mission has now been completed as the week rises to fruition with the arrival of Shabbos![41]

In light of these different views, how should we understand this most popular of Shabbos home melodies? Let's leave angels aside for a moment and talk about the significance of "home."

In her book, *The Sacred and the Feminine: Toward a Theology of Housework*, Kathryn Allen Rabuzzi has a chapter called "Home as Sacred Space." She writes: "Home holds things together by providing a familiar foundation within which you can orient yourself to the universe as a whole.... This ability to be at home with yourself relates directly to the fact that home, as opposed to a merely profane house, functions as ... above all a symbol of ultimate concern."[42] Building on her insights, I would add that home is the place where you reveal, enact, and convey your values, the place that reflects your hopes and aspirations, that cradles your nearest and dearest ones in love.

In Judaism, the home has an added element: It is sacred space. We mark our doorways with the mezuza, the parchment scroll on which a scribe has handwritten the *Shema* – the affirmation of the unity of God. The home provides sacred space not just for the individual, but even more crucially for the family.

The home-as-sacred-space contains books – not just manuals of technique that explain useful skills such as cooking, carpentry, photography, not just old college textbooks or entertaining fiction, but works

---

41. *Sefat Emet, Parashat Vayetzeh* 5661/1901, s.v. *bapasuk malakhei Elokim olim veyordim.*
42. *The Sacred and the Feminine: Toward a Theology of Housework* (New York: Seabury Press, 1982), 64–65.

of wisdom that challenge the mind and heart, are worthy of repeated readings, reward sustained scrutiny, and lend themselves to sharing with a study partner or partners (*ḥavruta*). In a word, I'm referring to *sefarim* – sacred books from the vast library of our people's engagement with Torah in all its forms. The *sefer* as a material object connects us not only to the sages whose thoughts are inscribed in the book, but also to all the book's owners and readers, to all those who held the book lovingly in their hands.

Our sacred texts have been a portable homeland. Throughout the ages, Jews have poured their hearts and souls into the study of the Bible and the Talmud and have found therein a vast treasury of law, ethics, philosophy, metaphysics, and esoteric teaching. Our books are sacred writ, the embodiment of a civilization so intoxicated with the notion of the holiness of the word that its aura was transmitted to the ink and parchment itself, and later to the paper of the bound book.

My father's library contained *sefarim* that he owned and used; some had belonged to his father and some to *his* ancestors from the old country. Holding those volumes gave me – and continues to give me – connection to my forebears and their learning, their experiences. The connection is tangible. I feel their hands as I turn the pages. (The oldest books are in surprisingly good shape, since the paper was made from rag, not acid pulp that self-destructs.) Occasionally I find a visible sign – a bookmark. The bookmark gains in meaning by its evident casualness, a sheet stuck in where a learning session came to a pause. One such place-marker is a receipt for a charity donation. I see my grandfather's name written on it – "Nehemia Polen" – in Hebrew characters. This is, of course, my name. (My grandfather died before I was born; I am named after him.) The charity is a yeshiva in Russia, located in a town that once flourished but is now gone, erased by the Holocaust. What is most striking is the amount of the donation – fifteen cents. This was evidently a significant enough contribution for the charity collector to write a receipt and evidently a meaningful donation for my grandfather, perhaps even a bit of a stretch. All this is captured in the slip of paper with faded ink, imprinted with a group photograph of the yeshiva students in the background. A slip of paper, probably chosen without much thought; it was simply on the table within reach, placed in a sacred book to mark a spot, but it now serves as an anchor connecting me to my grandfather, his world, his values.

My grandparents' modest tenement flat in the Lower East Side of Manhattan was open to guests and hosted gatherings of scholars, so my parents told me. My received family lore and associated tangible objects underscore that a home embodies the values that are lived within it. The hasidic belief is that walls and furniture reverberate with the spirit of all the sacred melodies that ever were sung there, all the words of Torah spoken there, all deeds of kindness and hospitality enacted there.[43] The walls and furnishings give testimony. Silently, they call for openness, generosity, benevolence, and acceptance.

The holiness of the house is shaped by the myriad small acts of kindness, consideration, and respect that the members of the household show for each other, for their guests and visitors.

One's home is sacred space, a local sanctuary, and the angels in the talmudic story and the *Shalom Aleikhem* hymn hold up a mirror to the kind of home we have constructed and consecrated. The angels testify to our ultimate concerns. When the home is filled with words and deeds of kindness, caring, generosity, welcome, sacred celebration, and joy – especially on Shabbos as we return from synagogue – then we rest assured that the angels are "angels of peace."

Similar thoughts on the meaning of the angels are expressed by the hasidic master Rabbi Shlomo of Radomsk (1801–1866). He writes:

> Our good deeds and good intentions throughout the week do not have wings to fly above until the arrival of Shabbos. Shabbos gives them a supernal vitality, a kind of *neshama yetera*, "supplemental spirit." The enhanced vitality is what is referred to as "angels." That is why we greet these "angels" with *Shalom Aleikhem* – on Shabbos, all our mitzvot – all our good deeds, all

---

43. See Rabbi Kalonymos Kalmish Shapiro, *Derekh HaMelekh, Parashat Pinḥas,* 157–59; Yehoshua Mondshine, *Migdal Oz* (Kfar Habad: Makhon Lubavitch, 1980), 160–61, on Rabbi Menahem Mendel of Vitebsk's preternatural ability when he passed by a house, to sense "every thought that had ever occurred in that house, and every thought that someone would think in the future till the end of time." This tradition is transmitted in the name of Rabbi Shneur Zalman of Liadi.

our good intentions – come to fruition; they ripen and achieve maturity and stability.[44]

Shalom Aleikhem expresses the hope that one's home is worthy of angels, that this is a home that brings out the better angels of our nature.[45]
That is the meaning of *Shalom Aleikhem*.

Parents Blessing Children on Friday Evening: A Moment of Great Intimacy

My father was from the "greatest generation." He came back from World War II toughened. He had been injured in combat; intimacy was hard for him. My memories of being a toddler do include a lot of sweet engagement, especially as he taught me the Hebrew alphabet by playing with blocks. But as I grew older, the relationship strained. Nevertheless, there was one time I could count on every week that I would experience genuine closeness with my father – Friday evening's parental blessing to children. I felt his breath, his hands on my head, the fragrance of his freshly shampooed hair. It was meaningful, warm, and powerful. The fact that it was scripted did not diminish the power; quite the opposite. The awkwardness and strain that accompanied other facets of our relationship did not appear here, because the ritual created a comfort zone of safety, of certainty, where we both knew what to expect and what to do. We knew that this was the time to **Stop,** and that cleared space in our hearts for a different mode of being with each other. All three siblings – my two brothers and I – received the same blessing.

---

44. Rabbi Shlomo of Radomsk, *Tiferet Shlomo, Parashat Yitro*, s.v. *leme'evad;* cited in Pinhas Spitser, *MiBo'o ve'ad Tzeito* (New Square, NY: Kaftor Publishing, 2004), 170.

45. I am, of course, borrowing a phrase from Abraham Lincoln, but the idea that the angels are produced by our own deeds and dispositions has ancient roots in Jewish tradition. See the excursus on *Shalom Aleikhem* in *Siddur Ḥelkat Yehoshua LeShabbatot UMo'adim*, 16–18. This siddur, which contains the traditions of the Biala hasidic lineage, draws upon *Tiferet Shlomo* on Festivals (25b), which suggests that Shabbos is the time when the Torah and mitzvot of the week ripen to their fullness and perfected state, thus creating angels. These are the angels we greet when we sing *Shalom Aleikhem*.

The core text of the parental blessing for children is the Priestly Blessing (Num. 6:24–26), striking in its simple, powerful diction, direct address to each individual, complete inclusiveness, and rhetorical elegance. While blessing in the Bible often refers to increase and fruitfulness, or (especially in Genesis) the bestowal of a privilege or position of leadership in the family, the core meaning of blessing is interpersonal salutation, greeting, and acknowledgment. For one human being to bless another is to convey honor; it is to respect the other's very personhood. When God blesses a human being, it indicates divine favor and recognition; to know that God is smiling at one is the greatest gift a human being can receive.[46]

When a parent blesses a child with the Priestly Blessing, the blessing engages these deep levels of acknowledgment and appreciation. What greater gift, what deeper intimacy, can there be? But there is more. Because the Priestly Blessing does not offer advice, suggestions, or direction – just (!) the affirmation that God will favor you, will smile upon you – there is genuine respect. The parent is not possessing the child, not placing burdens, and certainly not projecting needs or desires on the child. There is interiority, intimacy, but also letting go. The child is empowered, validated.

The parent places deep trust in the child, knowing that the child will go places, do things, see vistas, have realizations, and achieve accomplishments that the parent may not even dream of.[47]

Some specific suggestions for blessing children

Pause for a moment before giving the blessing. Tap into that superrational place of absolute trust, transparency, and sweetest love.

You may wish to close your eyes during the blessing. Closing the eyes helps to ensure that the blessing is not limited, not constrained by preconceptions of the person you think you see in front of you, the child

---

46. For more on this, see Nehemia Polen, "*Birkat Kohanim* in the S'fat Emet," in *Birkat Kohanim: The Priestly Blessing*, ed. David Birnbaum, Martin S. Cohen, and Saul J. Berman (New York: New Paradigm Matrix Publishing, 2016).

47. For more on this idea, see Rabbi Kalonymos Shapiro, *Derekh HaMelekh, Parashat Toledot* 5690/1929, 21–26.

you think you know. Your blessing is robust, ampliative, extending far into the future – a becoming, not a frozen stasis. Open to a horizon of sweet possibility. Your blessing provides a seedbed for growth, a window for opportunities that may emerge in the womb of time, perhaps only in some distant future. The very essence of your blessing is beckoning.

Be totally present; face your child directly. Speak with clarity, confidence, and without forcing the words, the moment, the feelings.

If you and your child are comfortable with this, place your hands on your child's head.

Go to the deepest, clearest, most transparent-to-the-light place inside yourself that you can reach at this moment. Know that this place may be beyond your conscious awareness, beyond anything that you might articulate or that you could manipulate or control.

Clear your mind of all other thoughts; totally focus on the recipients and their infinite light.

Bless with humility. Fill your heart with love.

Do not covet anything for yourself or your child. Cherish, but do not clutch. Be close, but do not crowd. Open space allows freedom for the blessing to grow and flourish. Letting go – even as you place your hands on your child's head – is an essential part of the process.

The person in your field of vision is much more than a freeze-frame captured at one place, one time, one stage of development. Aim for beyond-the-horizon vision.

Your blessing smiles at your child, with confidence in an indeterminate future. Your blessing is an ever-so-gentle gesture touching life's balance scale on the side of felicity.

Blessing children combines individualized attention to the person in front of you with the universal scope of the Priestly Blessing – each one complementing the other.

Conclude with humble silence, savoring the moment together.

Child's perspective

Invite yourself to feel addressed by the Ineffable. As you touch your own interiority, refrain from fastening your ego on any one specific image or concept of yourself, any one horizon of aspiration. Give yourself permission to reach a very deep place within – deeper every time you receive the words of the Priestly Blessing. The blessing helps you to realize that God has good things in store for you.

The meaning of naḥas

Parents often express the wish to "have *naḥas*" from their children. This is generally taken as the desire for the children to have success, so that the parents can bask in reflected glory. Sometimes it can even indicate the parents' desire to live vicariously through the child, projecting their own unfulfilled aspirations onto their offspring.

Berakha (blessing) offers a helpful corrective to this notion. The blessing for children is entirely open, non-coercive. It is an expression of love, admiration, acknowledgment, salutation, gratitude, recognition. On the deepest level, that is all that really matters.

The word *naḥas* comes from the Hebrew root N-V-Ḥ, to come to rest, the same root that gives us *menuḥa* – the word for Shabbos repose. In this context, it means that the parents can rest easy. They have confidence in their children, their wisdom and integrity. The parents do not wish to control outcomes or take credit for their children's achievements.

My *naḥas* is the knowledge that my children see beyond the horizon of my vision; it is my confidence in the wisdom and probity of the decisions that they make and the life they lead. It is the awareness that my children spread the light far beyond my reach, with a sweet illumination that I could not achieve.

It's Shabbos. Rest easy! Have *naḥas*![48]

Table as Sacred Space

Shabbos is the time for the entire family to come together, participate in the sacred rites of Kiddush, *ḥalla* (specially braided loaves, reminders of the manna, "bread from heaven"), and bond over a festive meal. To frame this in terms of American culture, think of Thanksgiving dinner – a family gathering that is fixed on the calendar, anticipated, and carefully planned and prepared, typically drawing a diverse and multigenerational group of participants and retaining a quasi-ritual character, a trace of civil religion in our secular society. Now think of Thanksgiving dinner

---

48. These thoughts are based on a teaching of Rabbi Kalonymos Shapiro, ibid.

every week. For many families, Shabbos may be the only time when all members can be counted on to be present, to be physically and mentally available to each other, to interact. That alone is an important part of the blessing of **Stop**. The arrival is coordinated, synchronized.

Shabbos is the time to invite guests, so in addition to the analogy of Thanksgiving, one must consider the analogy of the dinner party. When inviting guests to a dinner party, one can never predict which guests will hit it off, where the most scintillating conversation will arise. But there must be some shared understanding, an implied pact between host and guests. This surely includes the assumption that all participants will be open to camaraderie, discovery, and dialogue, in a spirit of respect.

The guests may not know each other, but they all know you or the members of your immediate family. You have invited them because you want to sustain or renew your relationship. Or you may want to strike up a new relationship that you hope may flower into a meaningful friendship.

Guests should not be invited with an eye to status, yours or theirs. Shabbos dinner is not a platform for networking, career advancement, or social climbing. The meal is celebratory and enjoyable, yes, but it is sacred – a tribute to Shabbos and an offering to God.

The Sages teach in the Talmud: "At the time when the Temple stood, the altar used to make atonement for a person; now a person's table makes atonement for him."[49] Rashi explains that this happens through hospitality extended to poor guests. It is important to invite those whom you may not view as your social peers or part of your preferred inner circle. It is precisely the outliers, the effectively invisible, the forgotten, who will most appreciate an invitation to your Shabbos table and who frequently will have the most to contribute. Consider inviting the just-moved-in couple; the new single grieving the loss of a partner or the breakup of a long-term relationship; the aging neighbor whose children are busy and whose grandchildren live far away; the socially awkward individual whose unconventionality make it easy to overlook the fact that he or she is an utterly delightful person. The presence of a diverse and inclusive group that may push the bounds of your comfort zone is what makes your table into an altar and your meal into a sacred offering.

---

49. Ḥagiga 27a.

Wine and Ḥalla: Biblical Symbols of Welcoming and Blessing
Bread and wine appear together as symbols of blessing early in the Bible.
In chapter 14 of Genesis, Melchizedek king of Salem (identified with
Jerusalem; see Ps. 76:3) greets Abram after the latter's victorious military campaign and rescue of his nephew Lot along with other residents
of Sodom. Melchizedek, who is described as a priest as well as a king,
blesses Abram (later Abraham) with these words: "Blessed be Abram
to the most-high God, possessor of heaven and earth. And blessed be
the most-high God, who has delivered your enemies into your hand"
(Gen. 14:19–20). This brings to mind the opening verses of Genesis 12,
God's charge to Abra(ha)m, which might be called the mission statement of Abrahamic religion: "And you shall be a blessing... and through
you shall be blessed all the families of the earth" (12:1).

It is worth pausing to contrast the way Melchizedek greets Abram
with the way the king of Sodom does, after Abram's successful rescue
of the captives.

Melchizedek brings out bread and wine and blesses Abram and
God supreme (14:18–20). Notably, bread and wine have appeared before
in biblical narrative. In the aftermath of disobedience in the Garden of
Eden, the ground is cursed and humans must toil for their sustenance:
"By the sweat of your brow shall you eat bread" (3:19). Bread serves to
remind humans of their initial failure and loss of Paradise. Wine has
also appeared before in biblical narrative. After emerging from the ark,
Noah planted a vineyard, drank wine to excess, and uncovered himself.
In a puzzling and unclear incident, Noah curses a grandchild (9:25–27).
Without entering into the huge body of commentary on the Garden
passage and the Noah story, it is clear that both bread and wine have
negative associations in the earliest biblical chapters. Yet Melchizedek
turns these items into expressions of welcoming and gratitude, conveyers of honor, esteem, recognition, *blessing*. The priest-king is inspired by
Abraham to transform reminders of human failure into radiant sources
of light and robust blessing.

Now let us turn to the king of Sodom, who has benefited from
Abram's courageous foray that resulted in the return of Sodom's residents,
including Lot, as well as much booty. The king of Sodom encounters
Abram, but instead of gratefully offering thanks and blessing, he makes

a crass offer to split the bounty of victory – the king taking the humans, and Abram taking the booty: "Give me the persons and take the goods to yourself" (14:21). The words are in the imperative – "Give me!" – and the statement as a whole is impertinent, not betraying a shred of gratitude. Abram summarily refuses the degrading offer and swears by God that he will not profit from his mission of rescue: "I will not take so much as a thread or a sandal strap of what is yours" (14:23).

In the previous chapter, Sodom was described as a lush and fertile place, "Like the Garden of the LORD" (13:10). Lot chose to live there because of its fertility. Yet very soon, Sodom will be utterly destroyed due to violent unkindness and lack of hospitality. This turn of events, which takes place in a later chapter (Gen. 19), is already foreshadowed here in chapter 14 by the Sodomite king's crass ingratitude and churlishness to Abram. The king of Sodom takes a lush and fertile land, a veritable Garden of Eden in the Bible's own description, and proceeds by ill will and greed to make it into hell. By contrast, the priest-king of Salem elevates bread and wine into objects of blessing.

The Melchizedek episode is actually a "Tale of Two Cities," a contrast between Salem and Sodom, between sin and grace, smallmindedness and capacious heart. We learn that goodwill, nobility, and courage have positive transformative power. God's original promise to Abram – blessing those who bless him (12:1–3) – begins to be realized in Salem (Jerusalem).

The wine and specially baked Shabbos bread, known as *ḥalla*, take us back to noble Abraham and Salem's priest-king Melchizedek. With gracious benevolence, we greet Shabbos, we greet our guests, and we greet our own inner spirits. With the help of these ancient biblical salutations, conveyers of blessing, we nourish our souls as well as our bodies.

RAISING THE CUP OF BLESSING FOR KIDDUSH

At the start of the first Shabbos meal, we proclaim Shabbos's sanctity by making a benediction over wine, referred to as Kiddush. In rabbinic tradition, this ritual is the fundamental act that fulfills the mandate of the Decalogue, "Remember the Shabbos day to sanctify it" (Ex. 20:8).

Both blessing and hallowing are relational properties of persons. We join the circle of blessing and holiness when we proclaim Shabbos as blessed and holy. God (the bestower of the day), Israel (the receiver of the day), and Shabbos (the gift of day, personified) together form a triad of mutual regard, acknowledging and ennobling each other in tightly bonded relationship.[50] The hasidic custom, based on kabbalistic symbolism, is to cradle the Kiddush cup in the palm of the hand, surrounding the cup with the five fingers held vertically (not merely grasping it between thumb and forefinger as one would a regular drinking cup). Gaze lovingly, reverently, intently at the wine's surface. This is a moment to be fully present. You are uniting your hands, eyes, and heart with your voice, intoning and declaiming the sacred serenity of creation's repose. The cup is the container of blessing and the focal point for all eyes in the room; the wine is the sacred elixir, the nectar of Eden. The words we chant – slowly, carefully, meaningfully, tunefully – are performatives. When we activate the phrases of the Kiddush, we are conjuring creative energies here and now. Do not mistake the words of Kiddush for a flat, pedestrian text, a rite to be discharged as quickly as possible. As the Talmud says, when we intone the words of *Vayekhulu* (the introductory passage of the night Kiddush), we become partners with God in the act of creation.[51]

Before beginning Kiddush, make sure that all participants are focused and truly present. Gathering around the cup celebrates the richness and diversity of individual personalities, now united for one sacred purpose.

Pronounce the words with loving attentiveness and intensity of utterance, which does not necessarily mean loudly. Caress the words gently and imbue them with grace. If you are present at the Shabbos table but not leading the Kiddush, gaze lovingly at the cup as a focal point for your sacred intention, and realize that everyone else at the table is doing the same.

Raising the Kiddush cup at the Shabbos table is to grasp and convey blessing – a shared vision of mutual beneficence and bounty for all present, and ultimately for the entire world.

---

50. See the midrash cited by *Tosafot*, Ḥagiga 3b, s.v. *umi ke'amkha Yisrael goy eḥad baaretz*.
51. Shabbat 119b.

The Three Recitations of *Vayekhulu*
Genesis 2:1–3: The Halting Problem

The passage commonly referred to as *Vayekhulu* (Gen. 2:1–3, the conclusion of the creation account) is recited three times in the course of Friday evening. The first time is in the *Amida* (called the Standing Prayer, because we are standing in reverent audience before God),[52] located in the section called *Kedushat HaYom* (the Sanctity of the Day). The second time is just after the *Amida*, and the third time is in the introductory paragraph to the Kiddush.

Why the three recitations? As noted above, it's hard to stop, to bring activities to a halt. The week has huge momentum. Without conscious effort, it continues to press forward of its own accord. Like a long passenger train entering a station, it takes tremendous energy to slow it down and eventually bring it to a safe, controlled stop. The passengers feel the momentum as they lurch forward, resisting the pressure of the brakes. The brake, as it were, is applied three times.

Furthermore, at the first encounter with this unit, each congregant recites it quietly as an individual. The second recitation, after the *Amida*, builds in intensity. Now the congregants recite the verses aloud, in unison, as a joint declamation, bearing collective witness to the purposiveness of the creation and the preciousness of Shabbos. This is the mystery of Jewish faithfulness to the seventh day; it is our continuing testimony to existence as meaningful and intentional, rather than arbitrary and random. We stand in opposition to some learned opinions that, claiming scientific warrant, see the universe as accidental and void of significance.[53] Collectively, we thank God for the beauty and wonder of creation, of which we humans are a part. Never has it been more

---

52. On the significance of the posture of standing, see Uri Erlich, *The Nonverbal Language of Prayer: A New Approach of Jewish Liturgy*, trans. Dena Ordan (Tübingen, Germany: Mohr Siebeck, 2004).

53. Nobel laureate physicist Stephen Weinberg has written that "the more the universe seems comprehensible, the more it also seems pointless." Of course, the labeling of the universe as "pointless" is not a scientific statement but a value choice. For a different perspective, see Howard Smith, "Alone in the Universe," *American Scientist* 99 (2011): 320–27; available online at www.americanscientist.org/article/alone-in-the-universe.

important to value, protect, and nurture the world for ourselves and future generations.[54] At this recitation, we stand shoulder-to-shoulder with our fellow congregants, collectively affirming Shabbos and the infinite worth Shabbos confers on our world.

Now the third recitation is at home, with family, friends, and guests gathered around the table, as prelude to the evening meal, the first of Shabbos's three sacred repasts. We have arrived; we shed the cares of the week, not out of exhaustion or lethargy, but because we know that we are recipients of God's gracious hospitality. We cast off burdens in order to freely participate in this joyous rite of welcoming. We proclaim the arrival of a higher order, inviting *berakha* and *kedusha* into our home. The performative words conjure the precious qualities of blessing and holiness into family space.

To say the words with total presence is to embody equipoise and breathe joy.

This third recitation, as introduction to the Kiddush, makes explicit the connection between the last verse of Genesis chapter 1 and the first three verses of chapter 2. The custom is to begin *Vayekhulu* with the last six words of Genesis 1:31: *Vayehi erev vayehi voker, yom hashishi,* "And it was evening and it was morning, the sixth day." These words concluding chapter 1 of Genesis are tightly connected with the first three verses of chapter 2. It is our gratitude for the week past that gives deeper meaning to the onset of Shabbos. Indeed, the commentary *Iyun Tefilla* suggests that early practice was to recite all the words of Genesis 1:31 at this point: "And God saw all that God had done, and behold, it was very good; and it was evening and it was morning, the sixth day."[55] Just

---

54. My thanks to Rabbi Everett Gendler for his insightful observations on this topic.

55. *Iyun Tefilla* in *Siddur Otzar HaTefillot*, vol. 1, 646. This is supported by *Siddur Or HaHayim*, which presents the teachings and traditions of Rabbi Hayim ben Attar, celebrated Torah commentator and kabbalist. This siddur prints the entirety of Genesis 1:31 before Genesis 2:1–3, instructing that the words be recited quietly (*belahash*). See *Siddur Or HaHayim HaKadosh*, ed. Shmuel Shayish and Elazar Moshe Gelbar (Jerusalem: 5772/2012), 421.

It is interesting that the Yemenite siddur includes the last words of Genesis 1:31 in the second recitation of *Vayekhulu* (after the *Amida*) as well. See *HaTakhlaal HaMevu'ar, Nusah Baladi* (Petah Tikva: Makhon Shetilei Zeitim LeHeker Moreshat Teiman, 5766/2006), 204.

as God admired the created world as a work of art, an opus of which to be proud (see above, chapter 2, "Shabbos in Scripture"), so do we pause in our homes at this moment to appreciate and celebrate the week that we have just brought to conclusion, setting the stage for our gracious and joyous welcoming of Shabbos.

Joining All Creation in Yearning for the Face of God

There is yet another level of depth to the recitation of *Vayekhulu*. We recall that **Stop** does not mean stasis; it is not a call to be sedentary. The dynamic qualities elicited by Shabbos as introduced by *Vayekhulu* are explored in the commentary *Or HaHayim* by Rabbi Hayim ben Attar (1696–1743), the great talmudic scholar and kabbalist from Morocco, who was deeply admired by the Hasidim, including the Baal Shem Tov himself. He takes the words to be a sublime statement of the universality of longing and yearning in God's creation.[56]

Commenting on Genesis 2:1, "And the heaven and the earth were finished, and all the host of them," the *Or HaHayim* begins by noting that in early sources, God is described as transcendent (in midrashic language, "surrounding the world") as well as immanent, the innermost essence of the world (based on Is. 6:3, "The whole earth is filled with [God's] Glory"). The *Or HaHayim* writes:

> God's light surrounds the earth as well as fills it.
>
> Why did God arrange the world this way? I have received a tradition from elder teachers of Torah that the reason God made the world round is so that all its parts should exist in a balance of forces.
>
> All creatures experience no sweeter, more cherished, more precious, more beloved, more desired, more hoped-for longing in this world than the longing to connect with God's blessed light. This is the yearning of every object endowed with vitality – when it attains some recognition of the sweetness of God's blessed light,

---

56. For more about Rabbi Hayim ben Attar and the theology of *Or HaHayim*, see Ariel Evan Mayse, "*Or HaHayim* – Creativity, Tradition, and Mysticism," *Conversations: Insights from the Sephardic Experience* 13 (Spring 2012/5772): 68–89.

its soul craves to the point of expiration "to behold the pleasantness of the LORD" (Ps. 27:4).

Everything God created in the world is imbued with awareness and discernment, each according to its level. This holds true for humans as well as for animals not endowed with the power of speech; for plants; and for minerals. Each has a faculty of awareness, recognizing its Creator according to its understanding. This explains the enduring stability of the world, why the world holds steady without shaking. [The author evidently has in mind rotational stability – NP.] "For God's mystery is revealed to those who stand in awe of God" (Amos 3:7).... By means of God's light – so sweet, so much the object of desire – the world rotates in a balance of forces. Every rotating part of the world strives with powerful flaming desire to get close to the all-inclusive Source of its desire.

Earth's rotation is perfectly balanced. This is true from the perspective of the strength of the attraction, for no part of the earth has greater desire for God than any other part. Otherwise, the part with stronger desire would tend to dominate and subvert other parts.

And the sweet divine light that surrounds the world is no closer to one part of the earth than to any other, for that would promote one part at the expense of another. Rather, everything is in balance. Every longitudinal line on earth strives to draw near, is attracted to that to which it turns. By virtue of the energy of every point of the rotating earth, the earth remains stable. Each part balances and supports the others. Thus, the world as a whole is fixed, tacked by spokes of desire for the Creator, based on utter longing to approach the Blessed Sweet One. This explains why God created the world round and why the earth doesn't shake as it spins, for shaking is a sign of imbalance of forces, a perturbation of asymmetric parts, while the world in its symmetry can never shake....

Human beings, endowed as they are with an extra measure of discernment and cognition, should take a lesson from the rest of creation. We should be inspired by the intense desire for holiness (*ḥibbat hakodesh*) that all creatures have for the Hidden Sweet One (*laNe'elam haNe'erav*). The physical world is never lax, never complacent, but always keenly seeking ever-closer beatific proximity to the Light.

Moreover, all vital creatures would never reside comfortably in their own skin but for the fact that the desired, hoped-for One is immanent in the world [and thus in each of them]. That is why spirit can make peace with corporeal existence. It is for this reason that God shined the light of Glory into the world, why God's Glory pervades the world.

To summarize: The Creator surrounds the world, so that the world is embedded within its Creator; and on the other hand, the Creator's light is immanent within the world as well. In this way, the world exists in an exquisite balance of forces, forces of yearning.

This, then, is the meaning of Genesis 2:1: *Vayekhulu hashamayim vehaaretz vekhol tzevaam*, "And the heaven and the earth entered a state of yearning (*vayekhulu*), and all the host of them." The word *vayekhulu* should be explained in accord with its usage in the verse, *Nikhsafa vegam kaleta nafshi*, "My soul yearns, craves (*kaleta*) for the courts of the LORD" (Ps. 84:3).

By means of that yearning, the world attains wholeness and stability.

The word *vayekhulu* expresses something stronger than *ḥeshek* or *teshukah* [yearning, longing]. It suggests craving to the point of expiration.... The self-assertion of this vital yearning is what sustains the world. This explains the rabbinic name for God, *Ḥei HaOlamim*, "The Life of All Worlds." This is the deep meaning of the verse *Beor penei melekh ḥayim*, "In the light of the sovereign's face is life" (Prov. 16:15).

For the *Or HaḤayim*, it is intense yearning for God – characteristic of all creation, even those parts typically viewed as inanimate or inert – that brings vitality and stability to existence. This teaching is overtly mystical, suffused with language of passionate longing. In the *Or HaḤayim*'s reading, the key word *vayekhulu* has the same root as *kaleta* in

Psalms 84:3, where the soul's yearning is intense to the point of expiration, at the edge of annihilation.[57] The divine light is felt by all creation and is sweeter than any earthly delight. The terms applied to God are notable: "The Blessed Sweet One," "the Hidden Sweet One." And the word *Vayekhulu* carries dynamic force, conveying the energetic longing for the Divine – a longing shared equally by all creation, with humans having no privileged position over other creatures. All creation feels God within and perceives the sweet divine light as encompassing, beckoning presence. The balance of forces yields equipoise and stability.

Some scientists might be aghast at the *Or HaHayim*'s framing of gravitational forces and rotational symmetry as yearning for divinity, but this is mystical biblical exegesis, not theoretical mechanics. The author is aiming his provocations at us, wanting us to better perceive the yearning that he is certain is hidden within us, a yearning intense to the point of expiration for the God he calls the Blessed Sweet One.

Gravity is God's love.

We are invited to feel yearning in Genesis 2:1–3 and to evoke it in the Shabbos evening Kiddush. When we utter the words in this spirit, we speak not only for ourselves, but for all sentient beings.

Shabbos clears space for yearning.

Yearning is manifest in the turning of the world. The turning reminds us of the apparent passage of the sun from east to west. Sunset, sunrise, and sunset are the three movements of the symphony of Shabbos. Creation's yearning and the smooth progression of the world's spin are what makes the arc of Shabbos take shape. As we bring our week to **Stop** in consonance with creation's rhythm, we are already alert to the next two stages of Shabbos's arc – **Look** and **Listen**.

Freedom to Stop Is True Freedom

The Kiddush refers to Shabbos as a "remembrance of the act of creation," as well as a "reminder of the exodus from Egypt."[58] These two phrases

---

57. This passage in *Or HaHayim* has much in common with his interpretation of the death of Nadav and Avihu, understood as a rapturous approach to the Divine. See *Or HaHayim*, Leviticus 16:1, and the essay by Ariel Evan Mayse, "'Like a Moth to the Flame': The Death of Nadav and Avihu in Hasidic Literature," in *BeRon Yahad*, 365–406.

58. *Koren Siddur*, 428–29.

allude to the two versions of the Decalogue in the Torah, first in Exodus and then in Deuteronomy. The motivating clause for Shabbos in Exodus (20:11) is theocentric, focusing on God's having made the world in six days and entering repose (*vayanaḥ*) on the seventh day. The Exodus verse invites us to join in God's rhythm and come home, to the place of **Stop**. The parallel verse in Deuteronomy (5:15) highlights freedom from slavery, enjoining householders to afford rest to all, including domestic personnel and service animals. The variation in the motivating clause between Exodus and Deuteronomy yields two complementary emphases for Shabbos – entering God's rhythm in Exodus and, for the Deuteronomic restatement, God's redemptive deliverance urging social justice and compassion for all vulnerable beings, humans and animals.

Although Shabbos in the Exodus Decalogue and its Deuteronomic recapitulation have distinctive foci, they should not be cast, as they sometimes are, as being in tension with each other, much less oppositional to one another. Exodus's concern with God's creative design surely includes a just ordering of society, and Deuteronomy's focus on rest for weary workers is not free-floating humanitarian sentiment but is grounded in a divine summons, what has been called "theocentric humanism."[59]

When examined through the lens of spiritual experience, the connection between Exodus's Shabbos and that of Deuteronomy is even deeper. It has been said that the greatest burden of slavery is not being able to govern one's own time, and the greatest boon of freedom is the ability to set one's own schedule and priorities. This is indeed another linkage between Exodus 20:8–11 and Deuteronomy 5:12–15. The call to align one's personal temporal rhythm with that of God is the mark of freedom for all, including, as Exodus 20:10 asserts, household servants, domestic animals, and sojourners. This means that Exodus's theocentric Shabbos is profoundly humanitarian in intent. Furthermore, Deuteronomy 5:15 insists that the call for sensitivity to the plight of laborers is

---

59. See Samuel E. Balentine, *The Torah's Vision of Worship* (Minneapolis, MN: Fortress Press, 1999), 177–211. The phrase "theocentric humanism" is that of S. D. McBride, Jr., "Polity of the Covenant People: The Book of Deuteronomy," *Interpretation* 41 (1987): 244 (as cited by Balentine, 184).

rooted not just in Israel's collective memory of enslavement, but also in God's redemptive power; the ethical imperative to afford free time to the powerless and vulnerable is impelled by divine example, an opportunity for *imitatio Dei*.

In line with our emphasis on place as well as time and the intimate linkage of the two, we note a location-based connection between the Exodus and Deuteronomy articulations of Shabbos. In antiquity, nearly the only way for a slave to attain freedom was to escape. (Sadly, this remains true today as well.) Before the Civil War and the Emancipation Proclamation in America, fugitive slaves found a route to freedom with a network of supportive allies and locations through the Underground Railroad. The book of Deuteronomy, thousands of years before this freedom-affording network, commands: "You shall not return to his master a slave who seeks refuge with you from his master. He shall live with you in any place he may choose, in one of your gates, wherever he pleases; you must not oppress him" (Deut. 23:17). Indeed, the drama of Israel's freedom is impelled largely by Pharaoh's attempt to reverse the exodus and return the slaves back to Egypt (Ex. 13:17–15:19). However, it was not only Pharaoh who wanted to cancel and reverse the manumission; as the Torah recounts again and again, the Israelites were mired in habits of slavery and clamored to return to Egypt at each moment of difficulty. Hasidic sources, taking up this biblical theme, teach that the worst slavery is internal, being stuck in entrenched modes of thinking, unproductive habits, self-delusions. Hasidic masters read *Mitzrayim* – the biblical word for Egypt – as *metzarim* – the straits, the tight places that afford a person no freedom of movement.

One common reaction to the awareness that one is caught in entanglements of one's own making is to try to run away, just as slaves did and do. The modes of escape are many. There are relatively innocuous entertainments and time-passing diversions, but also destructive pursuits, such as gambling. Especially troublesome activities in our day include substance abuse, addiction to shopping for unneeded and extravagant items, and overuse of electronic devices and the internet. And, of course, there is always physical escape in the geographic sense. The travel industry encourages touristic "escapes" promising surcease from the problems of everyday life, although we all know that these so-called getaways are guaranteed to end and the problems will haunt the travelers upon their return. Much of our weekday running is little more than nervous fidgeting.

The Baal Shem Tov taught that attempting to escape one's inner growth pains by running away never works; the pain travels with us and only intensifies. He invokes the metaphor of a pregnant woman about to deliver who attempts to escape labor pangs by running to another location. The path of wisdom and courage requires holding one's ground, facing the growth pangs, and bringing forth new life.

Shabbos instructs us that *freedom means not needing to escape.* On Shabbos, you are already home. There is no need to run; you are exactly where you want to be. By emulating God's cessation as articulated in the Exodus Decalogue, you enact the freedom from enslavement proclaimed by the Deuteronomy Decalogue.

The lyrics of a popular song assert that "freedom's just another word for nothing left to lose." This mordant sentiment is countered by the buoyant message of Kiddush: Freedom is the realization that, having arrived in place and on time, having everything that is truly important at hand, you are not impelled to flee from anything or anyone – especially from yourself.

Freedom and arriving home are one and the same.

This is the experiential reason why the Kiddush refers to Shabbos as a "remembrance of the act of creation," as well as a "reminder of the exodus from Egypt." The two ideas are not merely complementary; they are alternate ways of proclaiming the same dispensation of liberty, the freedom that can only be felt when one is truly at home.

SACRED EATING: SHABBOS MEALS AS SPIRITUAL PRACTICE

Over the course of a complete Shabbos, three sacred, celebratory meals are eaten. The first meal is eaten Friday night, and Kiddush (discussed above) is the opening ritual of that meal. The second meal is eaten around lunchtime the next day, again preceded by a Kiddush with a different text, appropriate for this second stage of Shabbos. The third meal is begun in the late afternoon, shortly before sunset.

In Judaism, eating is a spiritual practice, sanctified by benedictions before and after the meal, which are intended to bring mindfulness and intentionality to what might otherwise be a mere gustatory act. On Shabbos, this aim of spiritual eating is intensified and placed into sharper focus by the addition of table rituals: the already mentioned Kiddush, table hymns (*zemirot*, to be discussed shortly), elevated conversation, and sharing words of Torah wisdom.

The following comments on eating pertain to all three Shabbos meals.

In *Keter Shem Tov*, an early collection of teachings attributed to the Baal Shem Tov and his circle (1794), we find the following:

> When a person grasps a fruit or some other food and says the benediction over it, saying, "*Barukh Ata Hashem*," by mentioning the divine name, he arouses the vitality by which the food was created, for all was created by the divine name. "Like is attracted to like and awakens it" [that is, the name pronounced by the person about to eat finds the name embedded in the food, bonding with it in sympathetic attraction, thereby arousing it, bringing it to activation – NP]. The vitality thus activated is food for the soul. [This praxis raises the food] from physicality to spirituality.
>
> Rabbi Israel Baal Shem Tov thus explained the verse "Hungry and thirsty, their soul fainted within them" (Ps. 107:5)....
> Why did God create food and drink that people desire?... It is the food and drink that have the desire to attach themselves to holiness. Every time we eat and drink, we encounter holy sparks that belong to us, that we need to restore and elevate to their rightful place.[60]

The desire for food is acknowledged, experienced, and elevated by contemplation of the sacred sparks in the food, sparks that each individual can absorb and elevate in the very act of conscious eating.

Any act of eating can be the opportunity for redemptive practice, for discovering and elevating the sacred in the desire for the dish, and thereby restoring elements of one's own soul. The desire for food is one

---

60. *Keter Shem Tov*, no. 194, 520–27; cf. *Sefer Baal Shem Tov* on Deuteronomy 8:3.

example of the universal experience of longing, and longing provides the opportunity to ponder what really matters, what one really wants and why one wants it. Longing for the sacred, for ever-deeper encounters with holiness, is what Shabbos is all about. As we sit down to a table laden with culinary delights, Shabbos's **Stop** opens space for clarity and focus, for elevating eating into sacred practice.

This suggestion finds support in a teaching of Rabbi Kalonymos Shapiro, the Piaseczner Rebbe. He writes that sacred eating has little to do with special *kavanot* – that is, kabbalistic practices associated with the teachings of the great mystic Rabbi Isaac Luria of Safed (the Ari) that involve quite technical and complex combinations of divine names. Rather, sacred eating is an elevation of physical being to the domain of holiness, an act of refined embodiment that reflects a lifetime of work and that is always in process. While higher levels of this practice are surely reserved for *tzaddikim*, we can all feel reverence for the sacred quality of our food, especially on Shabbos; for the table compared to the Sanctuary altar; for the blessings associated with the wine and *halla*; for our family, friends, and guests assembled around the table; for the tradition we are privileged to partake in; for the mindful presence we are called to display in this most material of activities.

The Piaseczner Rebbe asks us to feel *haradat hakodesh* – sacred trepidation – with each morsel we chew, for each item we grasp with our fingers. This "sacred trepidation" is a state of deep awareness and presence, combining – as he goes on to say – love, awe, joy, and bonding. The bonding is a communion with the other participants in the meal; with all those in our own past and our people's history who have shown the way for us to reach this noble place; with Shabbos personified; and most of all with every aspect of our own selves – body, emotion, mind, spirit, transpersonal over-soul.[61]

Rabbi Shapiro's inclusion of "love" and "joy" in his expansion of "sacred trepidation" should make it clear that he is not calling for a stereotypic religious "fear," but rather an intense, riveting engagement that focuses all levels of one's being, the opposite of complacent indulgence or passive relaxation.

---

61. *Derekh HaMelekh*, Simhat Torah 5690/1929.

SINGING *ZEMIROT*

One further way to make your Shabbos table like the Temple altar is to sing Shabbos hymns, *zemirot*, at the table. *Zemirot* are meticulously crafted compositions marked by challenging wisdom, literary flair, and love of Shabbos. Biblical, Second Temple, and rabbinic texts speak of the choirs of Levites chanting psalms during the Temple service. Nowadays the participants at the Shabbos meal unite in sacred song, as well as in hallowed eating, Torah insights and wisdom conversation, in story and in silence to dedicate their meal to God and Shabbos. The practice of table singing is exceedingly rare in our society, where music making is generally reserved for professional musicians at the concert hall or produced in a recording studio and then accessed on demand, electronically. There are acapella choirs, to be sure, but these are generally student-based groups that hone their skills, practice for performance, and often train to enter and win competitions.

Zemirot at the Shabbos table are entirely different. All present are welcome to participate, whatever their level of musical skill. Melody emerges from harmonious spirits joining together, rather than from cultivated voices. Family members and guests have the opportunity to make sacred sound together, offering vocal cords and breath as gift to each other and to Shabbos. An ambience of collective generosity takes hold. The amazing thing is how joyous and aesthetically pleasing the result is to the ear, despite (or perhaps because of) the lack of professionalism. Of course, it does not hurt if people make an effort ahead of time, during the weekdays, to learn the melodies that will be sung at the Shabbos table. But as long as no voice attempts to dominate or control, as long as the sonic envelope is formed with grace and reverence, the result will be pleasing to God and to those present at the table.

What makes *zemirot* unique is the intentionality to form a collective sonic space by raising voices in unison, singing and breathing together. Those gathered around the table humbly offer their breath up to God, surrendering individual egos in service to the splendor of collective resonance.

The *zemirot* are love songs to Shabbos that deepen our appreciation and express our admiration for Shabbos's alluring beauty and sweet sanctity. Our collective serenade to Shabbos at the table caps the table's transformation from functional base, holding food and utensils, into sacred vessel, a resonant instrument whose fundamental tones unite those seated around it and whose harmonious overtones soar through the cosmos.

Hasidic masters would offer exegetical interpretations of the words of the *zemirot* – that is, they would "say Torah" on the texts of *zemirot* as they would on canonical texts of Scripture. The words reward such close scrutiny. While some *zemirot* are anonymous or by otherwise unknown authors, many were written by leading poets and scholars throughout the ages. For example, *Tzama Nafshi … Libi UVesari* was composed by Abraham ibn Ezra, famed twelfth-century poet and Bible commentator.[62] *Yom Shabbaton Ein Lishko'aḥ … Yona Matze'a Vo Mano'aḥ* was written by Judah HaLevi (1075–1141), another celebrated Hebrew poet and author of the *Kuzari*, the classic expression of love for the land of Israel and the personal God of Abraham, Isaac, and Jacob.[63] Kabbalistically inflected hymns in Aramaic were written by Rabbi Isaac Luria, and there is a striking hymn on the theme of yearning for Shabbos by the hasidic master Rabbi Aaron of Karlin.

ZONE OF INTIMACY

If you are blessed to have a life partner with whom you share intimacy on all levels including the physical, this is the ideal time to enact that intimacy. Your concord is deeper, more expressive, and more all-embracing on Shabbos, since Shabbos opens both partners to expansiveness and presence. The sublime alchemy of Shabbos turns silence to comprehension, darkness to radiance, surface touch to deep and tender caress.

Hasidic sources teach that true union transcends the distinction between bestower and receiver, between desire and fulfillment.[64] Your intention to bestow joy to your partner is the best way to intensify your own receptivity. Be mindful that Shabbos provides the platform for your love and is the goal of your love. With your partner, you

62. *Koren Siddur*, 440–41.
63. Ibid., 636–37.
64. See Rabbi Yaakov Leiner, *Beit Yaakov* ([Lublin, 1906] Jerusalem, 1997), *Parashat Pekudei*, 28a.

are aligning body, emotion, mind, spirit, and transpersonal levels of being, to reach the point of origins, the wellspring of blessing. Your wills have linked, joined, dovetailed, fused, become one.

Allow the joy of your love to linger and to suffuse your ongoing relationship. You are modeling Edenic existence in this world. God is within you and between you. You now understand what the Zohar means when it says that "Shabbos is the name of God."

WHEN HEAD TOUCHES PILLOW

It may come as a surprise that falling asleep has an important role in a book on Shabbos as spiritual practice. But, as we've been underscoring, Shabbos is actually a day of intense activity, and that certainly includes Friday evening. You've prayed with fervor, and your meal has been a sacred repast punctuated with melody, meaningful conversation, and thoughtful sharing. After the meal, you are likely to find yourself very tired.

Hasidic masters teach that it is a mark of spiritual greatness to fall asleep quickly, as soon as head touches pillow. But before that happens, recite the *Shema*, affirming the unity of God and the cosmos. Let go of entanglements and emotional burdens; forgive those who have slighted you, wronged you, disappointed you. Forgive your parents, your friends, your beloved. Forgive yourself.

The less you are weighed down, the quicker you will fall into sleep.

Set your intention to wake up with a pure heart and eyes open to joy. You will!

Chapter 5

Look – Shabbos Day:
How Sweet the Light

After a restorative night's sleep, we are called upon to open our eyes and see the world as for the first time. It is Shabbos morning. Our vision is not blurred by thoughts of where we need to go and to-do lists that tug at our attention. We already are precisely where we want to be, and by Friday we have called a halt to weekday projects.

Recall our discussion of Exodus 16:29 and its linkage of manna and Shabbos: "See (*re'u*) – the LORD has given you (*natan*) Shabbos; therefore, God gives for you (*noten*) on the sixth day enough food for two days; everyone should settle into their location; let no one go out of their place on the seventh day."

In the context of the manna story (Ex. 16), this episode takes place on Shabbos morning (vv. 27–29). Some people have gone outside the camp to gather manna, and in response God utters a call with great force: *Re'u*, "See!" Insofar as readers today can take the word as meant for us as well as the ancient Israelites, we can render it as, "Look!"

Nahmanides on Exodus 31:2 notes that the call *re'eh* or *re'u* is meant to highlight an extraordinary circumstance, a gift that might not be fully appreciated if not specifically pointed out. In that verse, Betzalel is designated to be the Tabernacle's supervising craftsman; God tells Moses that Betzalel is filled with the "spirit of God" and artistic talent. But, as Nahmanides points out, such proficiency is remarkable for an Israelite who grew up in Egypt as a slave. In an analogous way, Shabbos is flagged as special and remarkable in Exodus 16:29. Shabbos is singled out as God's special gift of love to Israel. Or as Benno Jacob puts it:

> [*Re'u* – Look!] presents a declaration of extraordinary importance; the character of the Sabbath was here emphasized as a *gift* of God.... [The imperative "Look!" is] limited to major disclosures.

Midrash Tehillim on Psalm 92, the psalm with the superscription *Mizmor Shir LeYom HaShabbos,* "For the Sabbath day," also refers to Exodus 16:29, "*Re'u,* Look!" and glosses: "Take note of the pearl that I have given you!"

All this means that we are called upon to open our eyes to see, to recognize Shabbos as the great gift it is, and thereby to see the entire world, and especially those near to us, as gifts of God.

HOLDING PLACE

Recall the original context of the triadic sequence that structures this book. When you are at a railroad crossing and are following the advice to **Look,** you must still hold firm to **Stop!** The same holds true for Shabbos morning. There is a temptation to lapse into habit, into weekday thoughts and patterns of interest. This is true even if (perhaps especially if) you do not need to go to work on Saturday. Finally, you have some free time, time to call your own, time to catch up on chores or to take advantage of special sales and promotional deals. There is a strong urge not to miss out.

This is nothing new. The pivotal verse in the manna narrative, "*Re'u* – See, the LORD has given you Shabbos; therefore, He gives for you on the sixth day enough food for two days; everyone should settle into their location; let no one go out of their place on the seventh day"

(Ex. 16:29) was a response to the fact that on the morning of the seventh day, some of the people went out to gather (16:27). But on the sixth day, each person had received a double portion (v. 22), enough for each member of their household. Why did some of the people go out to collect?

As we argued above, perhaps they did not really expect to find anything; they simply could not stay in place. The foray outside the camp was an expression of groundless dissatisfaction. They had what they needed and could comfortably stay where they already were. They were not foraging; they were fidgeting.

The implication is clear: Shabbos morning is the time for *re'u* – for looking and seeing, for observing with gratitude the gifts we have been given, in order to savor them, to look at them appreciatively but not possessively, to recognize them as gifts of God. Most of all, Shabbos morning is the time to confirm the previous evening's commitment to this place, to stay put, to accept that we already are where we want to be and with those we most want to be with, and that we already have everything we really need to have. The poet Wendell Berry expressed this elegantly:

> And we pray, not for new earth or heaven,
> but to be quiet in heart, and in eye, clear.
> What we need is here.

There is no greater spiritual statement than staying in place on Shabbos morning.

The following passage from the Zohar supports our understanding of the centrality of staying in place to the manna story:

> It is written: "Let no one go out from his place on the seventh day (Ex. 16:29). "From his place" – We have learned: What is *his place*? Where it is fitting to walk. The secret of the matter is as written: "Blessed be the Glory of the LORD from His place!" (Ezek. 3:12); this is *place*, and this is the secret of what is written: "For the place you are standing on" (Ex. 3:5). There is a well-known site above, which we call *place*, in which supernal Glory is revealed.

Therefore, a person who is adorned with a holy crown from above is warned not to depart from it. For by speaking of mundane matters, he leaves it and profanes the Sabbath; by his hands, as has been established; by his feet, walking beyond two thousand cubits. All these constitute profanation of Sabbath.[1]

As Matt explains in his note, "Everyone observing Sabbath is adorned with an additional soul, which he should not abandon by profaning the holiness of the day through mundane speech, manual labor, or walking too far." The metaphysical and spiritual resonances of *place* (Hebrew *makom*) augment and amplify the original locative sense; they do not replace it. For the Zohar, "staying in place" is fulfilled on three levels, entailing three interrelated modes of realization. It means not straying out of one's location, "walking too far." (Rabbinic tradition understands "too far" as going beyond two thousand cubits outside the city limits.) "Staying in place" also means preserving Sabbath sanctity by avoiding mundane, materialistic speech. And the Zohar includes "hands" – physical labor and handicrafts – in the set of activities that would run afoul of the instruction to "stay in place." Hands must be devoted to holiness. The three levels align and mutually reinforce each other. Geographical emplacement, abstaining from work, and commitment to noble, elevated speech (and the interiority associated with this higher speech register) all go together. They fulfill in unison the requirement of "staying in place."

FIRST OF THE DAY

Hasidic masters teach that the first words uttered as we awake should be words of gratitude and sweet connection to God, our near and dear ones, and the world as a whole.

It is very easy for the first period of the day – the time of awakening and rising to full consciousness – to lapse into grumbling, complaint, and fear. We are faced with the unsolved problems of yesterday, the frustrations and conflicts that accompanied us as we fell asleep, and we

---

1. Zohar 2:207a, trans. Daniel C. Matt, *The Zohar, Pritzker Edition* (Stanford, California: Stanford University Press, 2011), vol. 6, 179.

become aware of new challenges – difficult logistic hurdles occasioned by weather, health concerns, and transportation glitches. This may set in play a vortex of negative emotion.

All this is exacerbated by communication devices. Before we have come into our selves, we are deluged with "news" – that is, accounts of emergent events that are notable almost always because of their strikingly aversive character, provoking recoil, shock, fear, and outrage.

This is no way to start the day.

How wise the hasidic counsel that our first words – indeed first thoughts – must be suffused in the emotions that we want to characterize the day as a whole – love, acceptance, equanimity, gratitude, and sacred yearning.

Rabbi Kalonymos Shapiro, the Piaseczner Rebbe, writes of bringing sacred mindfulness to experience, thereby creating a new sacred self. Here is a précis of that teaching:

> This physical world is a gift from God that we must know how to use skillfully, mindfully, and effectively.
>
> Awareness precedes creation.
>
> The purpose of Torah and mitzvot is to create centers of perceptual awareness within the individual. The soul of the individual interacts with the mitzva, developing and cultivating the soul's spiritual awareness, creating a center within the self.
>
> When that holy center has a thought, it is an effective thought. This points to the importance of First of the Day. If you begin with a holy foundation, then out of that essence, holiness can grow into a robust holy being; otherwise, one's Torah thoughts have no grounding to anchor them and give them permanence.
>
> When we live consciously, with awareness and recognition, a divine personality emerges within us. That is what is meant by "creating an angel." We create our sacred selves, our angels within, according to the mindfulness (*daat*) we bring to the task.
>
> We must bring sacred mindfulness to every experience. Each experience must bring a sacred realization (*hakara tova*).

The way of Hasidism does not focus on self-mortification to remove the residue of the past. It depends on mindfulness (*shemirat hadaat*).

The path of the Baal Shem Tov, while positive, is not easy. But it is more effective, since the creation of a new self depends on the mindfulness we bring to the task.

We can then create our bodies anew. Our faces can shine with the wisdom of Torah.[2]

The first thoughts, words, and actions of the morning set us on track for the day as a whole. If we succumb to grousing and petulance, the entire day is in danger of going sour, God forbid.

In light of the importance assigned to early morning, Judaism provides practices for this crucial time of day. To be sure, the practices are intended for weekdays as well, but they are particularly appropriate for Shabbos. After the **Stop** of Friday night, we awaken with fresh eyes to a new world, to a world reborn. We look at the creation lovingly but without attachment, seeing beauty, form, color – with appreciation but without selfish desire. And we now have the inner space and time to realize our practices robustly. Here is a partial list:

Begin with *Modeh Ani*, a brief affirmation of gratitude for the gift of life and the restoration of spirit to body.[3]

Continue with *netilat yadayim*, the ritual pouring of water over the hands, thoughtfully, reverently, as an act of sanctification and dedication, as once the priests did before beginning their rites of service in the Temple.[4]

Make the blessing of *Asher Yatzar*, giving thanks for elimination.[5] The Baal Shem Tov taught that the lavatory has its own holiness, suffused with the Presence of God. (This teaching outraged many opponents of Hasidism, who considered it a serious insult to God's honor.) The process of elimination – of urination and defecation – is sacred and

---

2. Rabbi Kalonymos Shapiro, *Derekh HaMelekh*, Rosh HaShana 5686/1925.
3. *Koren Siddur*, 4–5.
4. Ibid.
5. Ibid.

deserves to be followed by a benediction. A hasidic master called this *yiḥudim,* "unifications."[6] In earlier Kabbala, *yiḥudim* meant the fusing of divine energies by contemplatively joining two names of God; here, *yiḥudim* means the realization that even that which seems unpleasant and disagreeable actually has its worthy, essential role. That which must be eliminated is also part of the divine plan; it is not lost. Awareness of the sanctity of elimination brings it under the divine canopy. Even the toilet is within the circle of blessing.

In the spirit of First of the Day practice, avoid electronic or print media before prayers, meditation, and study. This is wise even on weekdays; on Shabbos, this liberation comes naturally, organically, a seamless benefit of the ambience created by Shabbos. You want to keep your consciousness focused on the sacred, the sublime, the eternal.

Granting priority to God and one's own best self provides the grounding that enables us to face the day with confidence and clarity, and to be open to holiness.

LOOKING AT CREATION WITH EYES OF BLESSING

Rabbi Dov Ber, the Great Maggid of Mezritsh, is quoted in *Maggid Devarav LeYaakov* as reading the verse, "The person of generous eye (literally, 'good eye') shall be blessed" (Prov. 22:9) as follows:

> "The good eye": The person possessing a "good gaze" brings blessing to the object of the gaze. One can transmit blessing to the focus of one's gaze, since one brings awareness that the item is transparent to [i.e., has its origin in] the divine Nothing....[7]

The blessing is not just for the person of generous eye, but for the target of the gaze. The person brings blessing to what he or she is looking at because in that gaze the object is connected to the Divine, thus infusing the object with light.

---

6. *Tzavaat HaRivash,* ed. Jacob Immanuel Schochet (New York: Kehot Publication Society, 5751/1991), no. 22, p. 4a.

7. *Maggid Devarav LeYaakov,* ed. Rivka Shatz, no. 73; ed. *Toldos Aharon,* no. 117.

In a similar vein, Rabbi Levi Yitzḥak of Berditchev (1740–1809)[8] writes in *Kedushat Levi* of the appreciative, loving gaze that channels blessing and connects to the Source of Blessing.

Rabbi Levi Yitzḥak explains that there are two ways to look at an object: with a possessive gaze or with an appreciative gaze. The first seeks to control and has the effect of desiccating the object, emptying it of vitality and sweetness. The possessive gaze looks with desire, betrays the wish to grasp, to seize and incorporate into the self; it has the effect of visually pinching and constricting. As Levi Yitzḥak puts it, this gaze "separates the object from its supernal root in the wellspring of vitality." On the other hand, the appreciative gaze is one of blessing, seeing the object in its own intact fullness and integrity. Such a gaze imparts bounty; it enriches by strengthening the object's connection to its sources of vitality and allows for the flow of abundance to continue.[9]

Gazing with eyes of blessing is always a desirable practice, but it is particularly apt on Shabbos morning – the time of **Look**! The invitation is: See the world in a new light, without attachment, in pure appreciation, transparent to the divine Nothing that animates it, and you will see a world bathed in blessing. You will then be a source of blessing!

---

8. Disciple of the Great Maggid of Mezritsh, Rabbi Levi Yitzḥak is one of the most universally revered hasidic masters, cherished in all schools of Hasidism and beyond. Remembered for his passionate love of God, Torah, and Israel, as well as his ability to find virtue in sinners, his intercessory powers are invoked to this day in the world of Hasidism.

9. *Kedushat Levi*, Exodus 38:21–40:38. See also the excursus on "eyes of sanctity" in *Siddur Ḥelkat Yehoshua LeShabbatot UMo'adim*, 12–14. Beginning with the verse in Exodus 16:29, that essay, *inter alia*, interprets Mishna Shabbat 2:7, "Have you tithed? Have you attended to the *eruv*? Light the lamp!" in a hasidic register:

> When the light grows dim, one must tithe – understood to mean: Look for the sacred thought that stands behind all good deeds [the tithe – a tenth of the whole – is represented by the letter *yod*, the tenth letter, symbolizing thought; see Rashi on Ex. 15:1]; one must attend to the *eruv* – understood to mean: Attend to the confusing mixture of good and evil in oneself, and strive to arrive at a state of greater order and repair. Light the lamp! – understood to mean: Light the lamp of mitzva and Torah [Prov. 6:23]; come to the clarity of mind and vision that mitzva brings, so that your eyes will shine!

ON A CLEAR DAY YOU CAN SEE FOREVER

Isaiah instructs, "*Umibesarkha lo titalam,* Do not hide yourself from your own kin" (Is. 58:7), reminding us that our first responsibility is to be available to the members of our own family. Weekday mornings are inevitably taken up by the frenetic rush to get ready for school and work, making sandwiches, packing lunch boxes, arranging car pools, and the like. There is little time for calm discussion, little room for reflective engagement that might touch the souls of those you love.

But this is exactly the opportunity opened by Shabbos morning!

On Shabbos morning, there is no rush to work or school; this is the time to be available for your loved ones. Do not hide behind some object of diversion, distraction, or medium purporting to provide "news." These moments are the clearest you will have all week. Your eyes are open, freshly renewed! Use this clearing in the most meaningful way – to see those close to you as if for the first time.

When our children were young, we devoted early Shabbos morning for Torah learning. My daughters and I had special time together. With our oldest daughter, the text we studied was Maimonides's Code, "Laws of Repentance"; with our middle daughter, it was *Avot DeRabbi Natan,* a much-expanded version of the Mishna's "Ethics of the Fathers"; with our youngest daughter, it was other sections from the Code of Maimonides, as well as hasidic texts on the ten items created at twilight of the sixth day, just before the arrival of Shabbos. None of the works we chose was required reading for school; the topics and texts were inherently fascinating and generated their own motivation for joint ongoing study.

Now that the children are grown and have families of their own, Lauri and I have established a class that meets at our house early Shabbos morning before services, convening for deep and ongoing encounter with the thought of a hasidic master. We aim for meaningful engagement with the world of Hasidism in general, deepening the participants' spiritual understanding and practice, becoming better Jews and human beings, more adept seekers of closeness to God. Because Shabbos is a time to savor tasty cuisine – especially spiritual cuisine – we are at liberty to linger, to walk through a text slowly, deliberately, allowing the text to take us on a journey of its choosing.

Our text is *Derekh HaMelekh* by Rabbi Kalonymos Shapiro, the Piaseczner Rebbe. The goal of *Derekh HaMelekh* homilies is not to attain sudden flashes of illumination and exegetical epiphanies, but rather a lasting reorientation of the being that only happens over time, based on inner work grounded in deep and sustained self-scrutiny. Spiritual growth in study is only possible when one takes the time to savor, to dive deep into a text, its context, and its aspirational horizon, as well as the denotations and connotations of each word, phrase, sentence, paragraph, and the discourse as a whole.

There is a Kozienice tradition that studying Torah before prayers on a weekday morning is *Gan Eden hataḥton*, the "lower Garden of Eden"; studying Torah before prayers on Shabbos morning is *Gan Eden haElyon*, the "Higher Garden of Eden."[10]

I invite you to find your own way to lift up these golden moments early Shabbos morning. If you choose to study with family members and/or friends, choose a classic that is rich in meaning to you all, one that speaks not only to intellect but to emotion and spirit, one that

---

10. Rabbi Yerahmiel Moshe Hapstein of Kozienice, a descendent of the Maggid of Kozienice, is quoted as teaching that "one who rises at dawn on a weekday tastes the taste of the lower Garden of Eden; one who rises at dawn on Shabbos tastes the taste of the supernal Garden of Eden. But this is only true for someone who engages in Torah study and good deeds and does not turn his heart to idleness." See Malkah Shapiro, *The Rebbe's Daughter: Memoir of a Hasidic Childhood*, translated, annotated, and with an introduction by Nehemia Polen (Philadelphia: Jewish Publication Society, 2002), ch. 1.

Nahmanides, in his *Shaar HaGemul* (in *Kitvei Ramban*, ed. Charles Chavel [Jerusalem: Mossad HaRav Kook, 1966], vol. 2, 295–6), explains that there are two Edens: the physical, terrestrial one, located in an actual place on earth, and the supernal one, located in the sefirotic realm. Later kabbalists revised this notion in the direction of incremental spirituality, so that even the lower Eden is non-physical, a heavenly paradise for souls after death where they retain the personality configuration and emotional attachments they had on earth, while the upper Eden is essentially detached from any residue of earthly life; its spirituality involves intellectual apprehension of the deity. See Moshe Idel, "The Journey to Paradise," *Jerusalem Studies in Jewish Folklore* 2 (1982): 9, n. 9. Isaiah Tishby writes that for the author of the Zohar, the earthly Garden of Eden is a "staging-post or training ground for the soul in its journey." See I. Tishby, *The Wisdom of the Zohar* (Littman Library/Oxford University Press, 1989), vol. 2, 749–51 and 773, n. 17. See also Moshe Cordovero, *Pardes Rimmonim* (Jerusalem, 1962), 31:2; Rabbi Shneur Zalman of Liadi, *Tanya, Iggeret HaKodesh* 17.

demands full attention, that challenges assumptions and opens new horizons. Above all, find a work that rewards repeated visits and gives voice to multiple perspectives.

If you do this, you will discover that you are enriched in your knowledge not only of the source, but of your *ḥavruta*-partners, your co-explorers in the world of the classic text. The shared entry into the seemingly enclosed horizon of an ancient source of wisdom is the best way to get to know another person – especially those closest to your heart.

Open Your Eyes, Open Your Heart

Shabbos morning's call to **Look** includes noticing those who might otherwise escape our attention, those who, on days when the pace of life is quicker, are in danger of fading into invisibility. **Look** and see the humanity of all, consider how you might be able to lift up a broken heart, to give dignity and joy to a crushed spirit. That is truly "delight in the Lord"!

LITURGY FOR SHABBOS DAY

Weekday morning prayers begin with a selection of biblical passages designed to awaken the spirit, celebrate the wonder of creation, and express gratitude to God for the gift of life. The centerpiece of this early morning liturgy is a consecutive reading of the last six psalms in the psalter, Psalms 145–50. The Hebrew name of this section, *Pesukei DeZimra*, means "Verses of Song-Praise,"[11] though there is an alternate translation, "Verses of Pruning," pointing to the work of clearing one's inner landscape in the morning.[12] While every verse in this section is infinitely rich and worthy of study, I will focus here not on the psalms that are common to both weekdays and Shabbos, but on some of the psalms that augment *Pesukei DeZimra* on the holy day.

As noted above (in chapter 1), the transitory nature of human life is the basic theme of Psalm 90, the only psalm attributed to Moses. The psalm asserts that God is the only abiding refuge for humans; when God gives us *daat* – awareness, alertness, discernment, and perception – we

---

11. For more on *Pesukei DeZimra*, see *Koren Siddur*, notes on 70–71.
12. See Rabbi Isaac Aboab, *Menorat HaMaor* (Jerusalem: Mossad HaRav Kook, 5721/1961), 212; cited in Issachar Jacobson, *Netiv Bina*, vol. 1, 190–91.

may inhabit a "heart of wisdom." The psalm, recited during the Shabbos morning service, is in dialogue with the beginning of Genesis. Genesis chapter 1 has creation proceed through divine speech, whereas in Psalm 90 God gives birth to the world in an organic process of labor and delivery. When pondered together, the two passages suggest that security and durable meaning can be found by sheltering under the divine canopy and living in sync with God's rhythm.

Morning, *boker,* is thematized in this psalm with shifting valence. In verses 5 and 6, morning is the time of false promise, the dawn that cannot last. Plants flower at daybreak, but by evening the flowers wither and dry up. So it is with human beings; the hopes of youth are frustrated by the reversals and disappointments of aging (vv. 8–10). Yet in verse 12 there is a pivot; the psalmist realizes that if we are blessed with the awareness (*hoda/daat*) to savor each day, to count the days, one may thereby achieve a "heart of wisdom." The passage of time need not be a metric of loss; it can be the marker of growth. Life may hold new realizations, fresh insights, more expansive visions, and warmer heart-openings. In this mode of living, morning becomes the time to experience God's love/*hesed*: "Satisfy us in the morning with Your loving-kindness, that we may sing and rejoice all our days" (v. 14). Striving to see the hand of God in life, we can transmit this precious awareness to our children (v. 16). There is no greater pleasure than to feel God's Presence hovering over us, guiding us, setting in place the "work of our hands" so that all our deeds are joint achievements of heaven and earth (v. 17). To say this psalm on Shabbos morning means to have confidence that our life trajectories are meaningful and enduring, and that daybreak – especially on the holy day of cessation – brings clarity to the past, satisfaction to the present, and buoyant hope in what the future may hold.

During *Pesukei DeZimra,* we also recite Psalms 92, the "Song for the Shabbos Day," for the second of three times over the course of Shabbos. We discussed this psalm in chapter 4, the chapter focusing on Friday evening. As deployed in the evening service, it proclaims the onset of the holy day and invites us to disperse the misapprehensions of the workweek. The psalm also appears later in the morning service, as the Psalm of the Day. We will discuss how it functions in that context below. Here, in *Pesukei DeZimra,* it is part of the morning warm-up, preparing body and spirit for the main service to come. We will focus on verse 3: "To tell of Your loving-kindness in the morning and Your faithfulness at night."

We have just noted that in Psalm 90, "morning" shifts from an emblem of false hope to a time of renewal and joy. This sense of morning is now continued and amplified in Psalms 92:3, in tandem with a new sense of "evening," *erev*. Because evening ushers in darkness, it is often associated with danger and uncertainty (as in Psalms 30:6: "Weeping lingers in the evening, but in the morning there are shouts of joy"). In Psalms 92:3, however, evening becomes the time for faith, for trust that the morning will bring God's loving-kindness. *Tosafot* explains that going to sleep at night is an act of trust; we deposit our *ruaḥ*, our breath-spirit, with God, confident that we will awake in the morning refreshed, released from the previous day's weariness.[13] In a hasidic vein, the Maggid of Mezritsh understands "morning" as referring to moments of spiritual illumination, *devekut*. God's *ḥesed*, loving-kindness, is the unmerited proximity of God's warmth and the ecstasy this engenders. There will inevitably be moments of falling from this elevated state; that is what is referred to as "evening." At those moments, recitation of the verse itself gives assurance. In times of darkness, we recall the mornings we have experienced and we gain confidence that morning will come again.[14]

On Shabbos morning, when we feel the gentle caress of God's love with greater intensity, we express thanks for the cycle itself. As we luxuriate in the exuberant daybreak sunniness, we realize that the acuity of our feeling is based on the previous evening's weariness and the faith expressed then that morning would come – the morning that we now enjoy.

Nishmat: Universal Ambit of Prayers for the World

After *Pesukei DeZimra*, we recite a composition known as *Nishmat*, which expresses longing for the time when "the soul of all creatures shall bless

---

13. *Tosafot*, Berakhot 12a, s.v. *lehaggid*.
14. Israel Klapholtz, *Torat HaMaggid* (Bnei Brak: Pe'er HaSefer, 1976), 84, citing *Or Torah*. See also Rabbi Gedalya of Linitz, *Teshuot Ḥen* (Mechon Zera Avraham, 2007), 70, s.v. *vehifleti bayom hahu*.

Your name, O God."[15] In this extended benediction, we wish for a transformation of the cosmos, for a state in which "the breath of all embodied beings shall glorify and exalt the signs of Your Presence" that constantly address us if only we pay attention. While Shabbos marks the particular relationship between God and Israel, our ultimate aim is to bring the entire world, every sentient being, into the ambit of Shabbos peace. *Nishmat* picks up the universal theme already set by the last verse of Psalm 150, "Let all breathing beings praise God, *Halleluya!*"

In a famous paper, the philosopher Thomas Nagel invited his readers to try to imagine "What is it like to be a bat?" He affirms that animals do have conscious experience, but he doubts that humans could ever fully comprehend the subjective experience of bats. Be that as it may, *Nishmat* invites us to adopt, if only momentarily and in our imagination, the point of view of each and every being, bats included, and then to envisage praising God – that is, elevating each entity to higher awareness.[16] It is no surprise that *Nishmat* has evoked wonder and admiration throughout the ages.[17]

Nishmat invites us to imagine the sound of ocean waves as our voices, the radiance of sun and moon as our eyes, the span of eagle wings as our outstretched hands, and our feet as imbued with the elegant swiftness of deer, all in the service of expressing gratitude to God and celebrating the glorious wonder of existence. *Nishmat* encourages

---

15. *Koren Siddur*, 490–95. *Siddur Rashi* – an early medieval text recording authentic traditions from the great commentator – states that on Yom Kippur (and, I assume, on Shabbos) the ḥazan begins the main portion of the service from *Nishmat*. This highlights its significance.

16. Rabbi Barukh HaLevi Epstein understands the prayer in precisely this way, pointing to the closely parallel words *nishmat ruaḥ ḥayim* in Genesis 7:22, a phrase that refers to all living creatures. Rabbi Epstein provides several talmudic sources for the idea that creatures sing hymns of praise to God, and he refers to *Perek Shira*, a short midrashic-mystical work that, deploying biblical verses, scripts a cosmic hymn of praise coming from the mouths of all creatures. The origins of this work are shrouded in mystery, but it has affinities with *Heikhalot* texts as well as the aforementioned talmudic passages. See Rabbi Epstein's siddur commentary, *Barukh SheAmar* (Tel Aviv: Am Olam, 1940), 242.

17. *Nishmat* has inspired a genre of poems that frame and introduce it, such as Ibn Ezra's well-known Shabbos hymn *Tzama Nafshi*.

us to listen to the breath of all living creatures, to hear that breath not only through our ears but through *theirs*; to see the glory of the cosmos through *their* eyes, not only ours.

The expansiveness described in *Nishmat* invites us to merge our individuated consciousness and personal destiny with that of the world. To chant *Nishmat* meaningfully, we must embrace awareness of and responsibility for the earth and its fate, for all its creatures and habitats. *Nishmat* gently admonishes: Don't exploit! To intone the words with integrity, we must commit to respect the bountiful diversity of nature, to listen to the voices that make up the terrestrial and cosmic choir, to find the divine sparks that set the world ablaze with light.

As Rabbi Kalonymos Shapiro taught, the mission of the Jew is to teach the world how to sing. This is the call of *Nishmat* on Shabbos morning. *Nishmat* pleads to "arouse the sleepers and awaken the slumberers," drawing on the language of Psalms 146:7–8. The world desperately needs to be awakened, to be reminded of the sacredness of all life, of our responsibility to each other, no matter what language we speak or what faith we profess or don't profess. The fate of humanity and the planet is in our hands. This is the sweet but urgent call of *Nishmat*.

Chant each word slowly, reverently, carefully, lovingly, in community. Align your resonant frequency with that of your fellow pray-ers, and then with the cosmos and all its inhabitants.

Amida: Standing Prayer for Shabbos Morning

As mentioned, the central prayer, known as the *Amida*, differs for each Shabbos period – evening, morning, and afternoon. The morning prayer focuses on Revelation, the moment when Moses brought down the two tablets inscribed with the Decalogue, including the observance of Shabbos.[18] This Shabbos morning *Amida* prayer says, "A crown of splendor You placed upon his [Moses's] head when he stood before You on Mount Sinai."[19] This makes reference to the divine radiance glowing from Moses's face when he returned with the second set of tablets, replacing the first set he shattered in the aftermath of the Golden Calf

---

18. Exodus 20:8–11; Deuteronomy 5:12–15.
19. See *Koren Siddur*, 531.

episode (Ex. 34:29). Moses had asked to see God's Glory, and while the full vision was denied him, God does shelter him in the cleft of the rock on Sinai, shielding Moses with the palm of the divine hand and removing the hand just in time for Moses to see God's back.

This striking anthropomorphic passage has been the subject of allegorical interpretation throughout the ages and is one of the main preoccupations of Maimonides's magnum opus, *Guide for the Perplexed*. But the rabbinic Midrash and some medieval commentators were not troubled by the blatant anthropomorphism; they explained that the Godly radiance came from Moses's proximity to the divine hand that covered the cleft and pressed upon Moses's forehead.[20] However we understand these rays of splendor, this halo of divine radiance, the image evoked is a powerful aspect of the visual emphasis of this stage of Shabbos. In the words of the morning Shabbos *Amida*, we are called upon to **Look** and to see hints of the divine radiance in Torah, in the world, and in the saintly aspects of our fellow human beings.

Torah Reading

The fact that Shabbos is both local and universal is reflected in the rhythm of the weekly Torah readings. Jewish communities throughout the world, in synchronous fashion, read the austere grandeur of creation in Genesis; the Garden of Eden narrative; Noah and the flood; the call to Abraham; the great drama of Joseph and his brothers that begins with the violent fruits of envy and ends in reconciliation and forgiveness; the enslavement in Egypt; the exodus; the Revelation at Sinai; the Golden Calf; the Tabernacle; the forty-year wilderness trek; and Moses's sermonic farewell known as Deuteronomy. Layered upon this cycle is a parallel cycle of prophetic readings that amplifies, enhances, and interrogates the themes and messages of the Torah lection.[21] We know the stories so well, yet new insights and fresh perspectives are uncovered

---

20. See Exodus Rabba 47:6; Rashi, Ḥizkuni, and *Baal HaTurim* on Exodus 34:29.
21. One example of a *haftara* selection that interrogates the lesson of the Torah reading is found on *Parashat Tzav* (Lev. 6–8), which provides instructions for the sacrificial offerings and priestly investiture. The associated *haftara* is from Jeremiah 7, which calls into question the efficacy of the Israelite sacrifices and insists on the primacy and centrality of ethics.

every year. Shabbos-keepers participate richly in this annual journey. The synchronized focus on foundational narratives unites the Jewish people throughout the world on Shabbos, and it provides a perspective on reality far above the swirl of the current of events.

The public, communal Torah reading at synagogue on Shabbos morning has a different character than Torah study. It is, in part, a re-enactment of the Sinai Revelation.[22] We hear the word of God proclaimed and we receive it, thereby renewing the covenant. As stated in Exodus 19:16, the Sinai Revelation took place at morning time. In the language of the *Tur* and Franz Rosenzweig, this is the moment of Revelation. To speak experientially rather than theologically, this is the time to **Look.**

Not only do you as Shabbos-keeper enter into this worldwide synchronous community of Torah revelation, but you enter into the collective soul of all Shabbos-keeping communities of the past, of every period and circumstance. And you are laying the foundation of all Shabbos-keeping communities yet to come, until the eschaton.

Musaf Service: An Additional Dimension to Shabbos

In addition to the morning service, Shabbos features an additional prayer service, appropriately called Musaf – "added," "additional." Musaf recalls the time when the Temple in Jerusalem stood and the people of Israel had direct access to God in God's holy place, and they were able to bring offerings to God as a mark of intimacy and favor. The Musaf offerings, specified in the book of Numbers, are what I call the "supererogatory necessity." In any relationship, there are some gifts that are expected to maintain the relationship, but there are others that express an excess of devotion and faithful commitment, the desire to go beyond what is required. Musaf represents this surplus of love and intimacy. Musaf expresses the desire for embodied intimacy with God, an intimacy of

---

22. See *Tur, Oraḥ Ḥayim* 281 (end). The *Tur* cites the custom of reciting Deuteronomy 4:35, *Ata horeta ladaat,* "You have been shown in order to know that the LORD is the God; there is no other beside Him," as introduction to the Torah reading on Shabbos morning, because that verse refers to the receiving of the Torah at Sinai, which took place on Shabbos. Note the visual emphasis of the verse: "You have been shown!" See also *Taamei HaMinhagim UMekorei HaDinim,* no. 328.

Presence that goes beyond mere words and that could never be mistaken for lip service.

One feature of the Musaf service is an expanded *Kedusha*, the Sanctus that proclaims the holiness and Glory of God. Here I focus on the Sephardic rite, because this rite was adopted by the hasidic movement. The form of the *Kedusha* during Musaf, called *Kedushat Keter*, became a central marker of hasidic prayer, and it was an important reason why the early Hasidim wanted to establish their own prayer meeting spaces (*shtiblach*).

Keter means "Crown," and *Kedushat Keter* makes the audacious claim that together with the angels, the Jewish people place a crown upon God.[23] What does this bold anthropomorphic image have to tell us about the spiritual dimension of Shabbos morning, the time of **Look**?

Keter in Kabbala is the primal Nothing, the cosmic origin of origins, that which preceded and sparked what is now called the Big Bang, the dark, inscrutable core out of which all light emerges.[24] In human terms, *Keter* is the ultimate incubator of new ideas, the place where eureka moments are born. In Lurianic Kabbala, this is the dispensation called *Atika Kadisha*, The Holy Ancient One, the Divine Will, overflowing with love and compassion. Insofar as humans can approach *Keter* at all, we may comprehend *Keter* as the opportunity to re-envision the world, to see the world as it was originally meant to be – as expression of pure grace. Returning to the origin, to the Alpha point, allows us to imagine a world emerging along lines similar to the one we know but subtly shifted in the direction of love and understanding, less unyielding, more supple. This might be one reason why the hasidic masters were so insistent on introducing *Kedushat Keter* as an essential feature of their liturgy: *Keter* invites the congregation to be active participants in the re-emergence of the world, along a trajectory

---

23. See *Koren Siddur*, 592–93.
24. On the deep and mutually illuminating relationship between Lurianic Kabbala and contemporary astrophysics, see Howard Smith, *Let There Be Light: Modern Cosmology and Kabbalah* (Novato, CA: New World Library, 2006), especially 106–8, "The Sefirah of Keter."

of greater compassion and softness.[25] Contemplating *Keter* helps us to *attenuate the rigidity of being.*[26]

Psalm for the Shabbos Day

We have already discussed aspects of Psalm 92, superscripted "A Song for the Shabbos Day," in the context of *Kabbalas Shabbos,* the service of welcoming Shabbos. At that point in the service, the psalm proclaims a change in state, a phase transition to the temporal domain of sanctity. We return to this psalm now because in the morning service it has a rather different function. From the era of the Second Temple, specific psalms were assigned to be chanted on each day of the week. Psalm 24 was sung on the first day, Sunday; Psalm 48 on the second day, Monday; Psalm 82 on Tuesday; Psalm 94 on Wednesday; Psalm 81 on Thursday; and Psalm 93 on Friday. While we no longer have the Levites singing these psalms in coordination with the Temple offerings, the siddur still presents them in the daily prayer service. Recitation of these psalms marks our weekly progress toward the goal of Shabbos, helping to give the week its texture and directionality toward the seventh day. Equally

---

25. See Rabbi Jacob Joseph of Polonoye, *Toledot Yaakov Yosef* (Koretz, 1780 [photographic reproduction of first edition: Jerusalem, 1986]), p. 201b, addenda section at end of volume, labeled "These are the things I heard from my master [the Baal Shem Tov]": "One should contemplate the 'Crown of all Crowns' (*Keter Kol HaKetarim*), as this practice has talismanic power to elevate fallen souls." *Idem, Ketonet Pasim* 38b, in the name of the Baal Shem Tov. See *Keter Shem Tov,* part 2 (20a), cited in *Sefer Baal Shem Tov, Yitro,* no. 44: "In Shabbos Musaf during *Kedushat Keter,* we raise the world of Speech to the world of Thought. There the light is so great that divisions are transcended, and we channel love down to our world, which we effect when we say *Ayeh mekom kevodo.*" See also Rabbi Yisrael ben Shabbetai, the Maggid of Kozienice, *Or Yisrael: Be'urei HaTikkunei Zohar* (Chernowitz, 1862), 29, column b: "God's name is K-K-H, *Keter Kol HaKetarim,* the Crown of All Crowns; therefore, everything is possible for God [every transformation to good is within the divine power]." *Idem, Ner Yisrael al Tikkunim,* 37b: "*Keter* is the place of unity, the identity that transcends distinctions. Therefore, the Baal Shem Tov said, we should contemplate K-K-H, *Keter Kol HaKetarim,* and our entire redemption depends on this." These texts on the power of *Keter* have been collected and are conveniently available in *Sefer Baal Shem Tov,* 205–8, *Parashat Lekh Lekha,* no. 11, and n. 10.

26. I owe this wonderful phrase to Professor Menachem Lorberbaum of Tel Aviv University.

important, the psalm assignments enhance each day's identity, giving each a unique scriptural voice that distinguishes it from the other week-days and that remains stable through the succession of weeks arranged in the calendrical grid (see above, chapter 2, "Shabbos in Scripture"). These assignments are listed in Mishna Tamid, and some of them are noted in the Septuagint, the Greek translation of the Bible.[27] But only one psalm bears a superscription in the biblical text itself announcing its relationship to a specific day: Psalm 92, which joyously proclaims its intimate connection to Shabbos.

As noted above, the psalm celebrates the wisdom and profundity of the creation, called God's "handiwork." The seven-fold occurrence of the tetragrammaton makes a subtle gesture to the heptadic pattern of the creation story in Genesis, culminating in Shabbos. Here as elsewhere in Scripture, Shabbos's ethical aspect is highlighted: Those who are willing to take unethical action seem to thrive, but their achievements wither quickly, while those who live lives of uprightness are assured that they will partake of God's stability and enduring vitality (vv. 7 and following). Rooted in holy ground, they continue flourishing, producing fruit even in old age, "full of sap and freshness" (v. 15).

The Gerer Rebbe, in his Psalms commentary (called *Sefat Emet*, like his Torah teachings), offers a hasidic insight into the idea of temporality that pervades Psalm 92, linking it with the theme of song and music (vv. 2–4). The Midrash Numbers Rabba states that the Levites in the Temple played on a seven-string harp. In the messianic era, the midrash continues, the restored Temple service will feature a harp with eight strings; and in eschaton, *le'atid lavo*, the harp will have ten strings.[28]

The *Sefat Emet* comments:

---

27. For details, see Peter L. Trudinger, *The Psalms of the Tamid Service: A Liturgical Text from the Second Temple* (Leiden and Boston: Brill, 2004), 41–51. Trudinger does a careful analysis of our knowledge of the Septuagint Psalter on the basis of manuscript evidence and concludes that "the daily psalms in the late Second Temple period were Ps. 24, 48, 82, 94, 81, 93, and 92, as given in Tamid 7:4" (47, 51). This means that the Mishna's historical memory in this instance is confirmed by an external source that antedates it by about three hundred fifty years, if not longer.

28. Numbers Rabba 15:11, on Numbers 8:6.

Melody is inherently connected with time. Every day has its own song; each day's innovative vitality (*hithadshut*) imparts the new melody.... Each day has its own illumination; as Rabbi Isaac Luria (the Ari) is quoted as saying, no two days have ever been alike since the creation....

All individuals are responsible to repair their personal place and time, by mending their own soul. The Levites had a more global responsibility to elevate the time dimension, so they were assigned to offer music in the Temple.

Changes in time imply changes in music, so in the messianic era, and still later in the eschaton, musical modes will change. This explains why Psalms 92:4, the psalm for Shabbos, refers to singing praises with a "ten-stringed harp." Shabbos is a foretaste of the World to Come. On Shabbos, we already live in redeemed time, and we can enter the musical mode of the eschaton.

[This new musical dispensation does not erase or suppress what preceded it. To the contrary,] Shabbos is also characterized as the "Song of Songs." Shabbos embraces and uplifts all the weekday songs that came before.

Time-consciousness is key to the *Sefat Emet*. His writings often discuss the spiritual danger of lapsing into routine or staleness. But this danger can be defeated by touching the sacred source of renewal, divinity's "inner point," which in this teaching is linked to the qualities of music. The wondrous surprise and satisfaction of a melodic line hovers between inevitability and unpredictability. The notes dance into one's heart, seize it lovingly, and move it to pulsate with expressive vitality. To grasp a melody is to perceive discrete temporal moments unfolding serially yet in unison. One must hold the early notes firmly even as one reaches a cadence and experiences that deep sense of arrival. The sequence moves graciously, but the succession is a yielding, not a displacement. A true arrival means that the early notes are honored and cherished, not forgotten. The sequence of notes and moments is experienced phenomenally as passage of time. But while time passes, it does not pass away. Music both captures and releases time.

It is not only individual musical compositions that connect time awareness and melody. Consider also the shifts in musical taste from one era to the next. Our parents' music may seem lovely but outdated to us, while our children's often seems brash and cacophonous. It was always so. There is mystery in the way one musical style eventually plays itself out and is followed by the next.

This is the promise of the final lines of Psalm 92. The person "planted in God's courtyards," understood both spatially and temporally, never stagnates, but remains fresh and vital, in tune with the music of the time yet not forgetting anything that came before. The God of the Bible is not frozen in a static eternity, but rather alive with suppleness, alert to the rhythms and tonalities of each new generation. The eschaton is the fulfillment of historical time, not its erasure. In just that way, Shabbos lifts up the days of the week, giving them dignity and identity. When we sing the song of Shabbos, we enter this domain of divine alertness to the new while giving fresh meaning to the old. This is indeed the Song of Songs!

THE GREAT KIDDUSH

The daytime Kiddush over wine is called *Kiddusha Rabba*, the "Great Kiddush." This is generally taken as a euphemism, since according to the Talmud, the daytime Kiddush has lesser standing than the evening Kiddush that preceded it on Friday night.[29] But it is possible to see the designation "Great Kiddush" straightforwardly, as meaning exactly what it says.

Recall that Friday night is the **Stop**, when we bring the week to a halt. By morning, that stage has already been accomplished. We have cleared our ground from the thicket of the week. The morning and daylight hours pose another challenge: With what shall we fill this gentle clearing?

The text of the daytime Kiddush as presented in many prayer books begins with verses in Isaiah (58:13–14).[30] Isaiah invites us to shift our focus from self-enclosure to self-transcendence, from

---

29. Pesaḥim 106b.
30. *Koren Siddur*, 628–29.

business and busyness to being present for others, from frenetic rushing to taking pleasure in gifts of God, thereby giving honor to God. The Kiddush text continues with Exodus 31:16–17, highlighting Shabbos as visual sign (*ot*) of the covenant between God and Israel,[31] and concludes with the Shabbos commandment from the Exodus Decalogue (Ex. 20:8–11), inviting us to join in the divine rhythmic rest established at creation.

The daytime provides the opportunity for greater social interaction, for people from different communities to visit and exchange greetings. Unlike the prior evening's Kiddush, the recitation of the daytime Kiddush does not need to be immediately followed by a formal meal, but by a modest spread whose main purpose is the opportunity to share Torah, sacred melodies, and camaraderie. You do not need to set a guest list; your home or synagogue *kiddush* is open for unplanned encounters, for new faces and voices to share the Shabbos spirit. This is indeed *Kiddusha Rabba*, the Great Kiddush!

SECOND MEAL:
SACRED SPEECH AT THE SHABBOS TABLE

The Shabbos table is a place for *leshon kodesh*, sacred speech. The phrase *leshon kodesh* is typically understood to mean the Hebrew language, and it is true that some pious Jews throughout history had the practice of speaking only Hebrew on Shabbos. But the early hasidic masters taught that *leshon kodesh* is not only about language. Sadly, even Hebrew can be debased; on the other hand, one can elevate one's level of discourse in any tongue. Yiddish was a sacred language for many Eastern European Jews, and English can be one as well. It is all a matter of focus and intention. What is most important is the content, not the dialect. For example, political discussions are not appropriate for the Shabbos table. Partisan wrangling and point-scoring are inimical to Shabbos spirit. And Shabbos is no time to critique or criticize anyone – no invidious comparisons.

---

31. Shabbos-keepers are clearly visible to the eye. They are not engaged in commerce or travel, and their stoves are not being used for cooking. Shabbos's striking visual impression is intensified when the cessation is kept by an entire community.

Conversations should focus on the experience of Shabbos, on the *parasha*, on Torah, prayer, and other aspects of the sacred. And don't be afraid of silence; embrace its resonance and eloquence.

You are cultivating a way of speaking, a discourse of holiness. Avoid weekday discussions, especially business matters. Avoid bitterness, grievance, rectitude, and indignation. Jokes at someone's expense, cynical comments, and deflationary remarks are not in the spirit of the Shabbos table.

Speech is sacred. Go deep and aim high! Draw on the well of ancestral wisdom.

In his vision of redemption, Isaiah says, "Enlarge the site of your tent" (Is. 54:2). This expansive vision means having an inclusive tent. Remember that people with whom you might initially feel incompatible may one day become your closest friends, may be the ones whose voice you most need to hear.

Share stories about yourself and others that are consistent with the buoyant spirit of Shabbos. Share what you are grateful for.

Make sure the stories you tell reflect the world you wish to see.

It is customary to share *divrei Torah*, wisdom teachings and insights related to the day's Torah reading. When sharing your insights, keep in mind the core dispositions of inclusion, benevolence, love, respect, and compassion. Listen more than you speak.

The *Sefat Emet* writes that the skin affliction called *tzaraat* (often mistranslated as "leprosy") indicated a closing of the skin's natural porosity, the thickening and calcification of the body's interface between itself and the world.[32] This suggests that the remedy for *tzaraat* cannot be reduced to a formulaic set of rules about which speech-acts are permitted and which are prohibited. While rules may provide basic guidance and orientation, ultimately we are called upon to become more sensitive and open human beings. The strictures against *lashon hara*, "gossip," should serve as an invitation to exfoliate the hard boundaries that we think are necessary to guard the individual and collective self. Ultimately, the *Sefat Emet* teaches, the problem with gossip is that it is talk that remains on the surface, and the antidote is the endless quest for deeper

---

32. *Sefat Emet, Parashat Tazria* 5635/1875, s.v. *adam ki yihyeh beor besaro.*

layers of meaning in ourselves and in others. As the *Sefat Emet* assures us, the deeper we dive, the higher we soar.

It is easier to stay on the surface than to dive deep – so avoid the shallows!

SHABBOS REST, SHABBOS WALK

Napping on Shabbos is sacred practice! You have permission to give yourself a well-deserved rest. Shabbos is indeed described as a day of rest from exertion in the second version of the Decalogue in Deuteronomy (5:11–14). The spiritual dimension of this slumber is assured, since you have not been occupied with mere indulgence, but rather with truly ennobling activities. And there is more to come; you are preparing for the deep **Listen** of the late afternoon (see below). So take the time. Your rest will be more refreshing and restorative with the awareness that you are not missing out on anything or anyone. When you sleep on Shabbos afternoon, you are doing precisely what you ought to be doing, and your bed is cradling a person who even while asleep is focused and filled with purpose.

Our family always takes a Shabbos walk after waking up from the afternoon nap. We are fortunate to live close to a scenic reservoir, and we often stroll around it. But there were times when we lived in less picturesque locations. The main point is always the opportunity to look at the world at a slower pace, to observe, to sense, to appreciate, and, most of all, to share leisurely, agendaless conversation with those we love.

Chapter 6

Listen – The Gift of Stillness

The three stages of Shabbos – **Stop, Look, Listen** – impart a directionality to the day, a momentum with incremental intensity. By late afternoon, we reach the pinnacle, the capstone. This is the time of coming into ourselves in the most balanced way, integrating and aligning all aspects of our being.

At the afternoon service, we recite a verse from Psalm 69, "As for me, may my prayer to you, O LORD, be at a time of grace; O God, in Your abundant kindness, answer me with the truth of Your salvation" (Ps. 69:14).

The afternoon is the time of *raava deraavin* – deepest favor, deepest grace.[1] This time is ripe for listening, because we have finally come to genuine repose, to stillness.

---

1. The phrase *raava deraavin* is from Zohar, *Yitro* 2:88b; 3:136b. For discussion, see Yehuda Liebes, "Zemirot LeSeudot Shabbat SheYised HaAri HaKadosh," *Molad* 4 (1972): 540–55.

In our discussion of Friday evening, the stage of **Stop**, we talked about the glow of the candles that were lit on Friday afternoon, before the onset of Shabbos. Those candles provided the opportunity for meditative reflection, for gazing upon the transmutation of matter into energy and light.

In the phase of **Look**, the rising sun brought the dawn and new illumination, bestowing compassionate gaze, eyes gifted to see the world and its inhabitants with benevolence.

We have finally arrived at the time of **Listen**. The sun slowly sets, darkness settles in with the most gradual gentleness, and in our attunement we feel less need to visually sweep our environs. We have no desire to judge those in our field of vision or uncover that which teases us with supposed allure. We are exactly where we want to be, and we have everything we need to have.

The **Stop** of Friday evening is a hard stop; we bring our quotidian week to an end with the setting of the sun, a sunset that asks us to find place and settle down. Now, nearly twenty-four hours later, we have indeed found our place, and the sun's setting is subjectively more gradual, with a soft, gentle feel – a soft landing for the "Great Light"[2] that mirrors the depth of the repose we have achieved. With our full-day stillness, we have aligned our resonant frequency to that of the sun. The arching cosmic interval of solar setting-rising-setting has become our own; together with the sun, our spirits offer quiet praise to God (see Psalm 19).

The gradual dimming of the light signals the opportunity to awaken our acoustic sense more intensely.

COMPLETE TRANQUILITY

The liturgical text of the Shabbos afternoon Minḥa service, the final service of the day, rises to a poetic crescendo beyond anything seen in the prior Shabbos services.

The central passage (*Ata Eḥad*) may be rendered in English as:

You are One and Your name is One,
and who is like Your people Israel,

---

2. The sun is called the "Great Light" in Genesis 1:16.

a singular nation on earth?
Magnificence of greatness and crown of salvation,
You have given your people a day of tranquility (*menuha*) and
holiness (*kedusha*).
Abraham rejoices, Isaac exults,
Jacob and his children will find tranquility in it.
Tranquility of love and generosity,
tranquility of truth and faith,
tranquility of peace and serenity,
stillness and trust;
a complete tranquility that You accept favorably (*sheAta rotzeh
bah*).
May Your children recognize and know
that their tranquility comes from You,
and that by their tranquility they sanctify Your name.[3]

The seven-fold deployment of the noun *menuha*, "tranquility" (eight if
we include the verb-form *yanuhu*, "will find tranquility") confirms the
view I have been advancing throughout this book – that Shabbos is best
understood as a day of heightened awareness and keen attention, not a
day of sedate inactivity. I translate *menuha* as "tranquility," rather than
"rest." Tranquility suggests a realignment of the being, a repositioning
of the self toward inner stability, equilibrium, balance, and coherence.
There is physical, mental, and spiritual alertness at the same time. This
prayer-poem makes explicit that the ultimate aim of Shabbos is to refine
and ennoble our inner dispositions, our orientation to the world, to
other human beings, to God, and to ourselves.

The anaphoric insistence on ever more profound levels of *menuha*
yields a rapturous appreciation for the spiritual gifts that only Shabbos
can give.

Furthermore, the words that modify "tranquility" are relational words, pointing to a state of reciprocal relationship with Shabbos and with God. The "love and generosity" (*ahava unedava*), for
example, describe how God gave Shabbos to us. We reciprocate the

---

3. See *Koren Siddur*, 664–65.

love and generosity by displaying love and generosity to all God's creatures, to our families and ourselves. This becomes our gift to God. The other terms work much the same way. The word I translate as "stillness," *hashket*, is what makes deep listening possible; it is a *substantial* stillness, not merely an absence of noise. It frames the call to **Listen** at this time. We receive stillness as a gift and attempt to savor and deepen it. The way we enter and hold the stillness is our gift to Shabbos and to God. We are not throttling the urge to speak, not muzzling ourselves. We have entered a dispensation of grace that is too rich for words.

When we accept the *menuḥa* in this manner, with deep appreciation and reverence, then we are sure that God accepts our Shabbos as a reciprocal gift. That is, our Shabbos becomes an offering, and as we come closer to the end of the day, our tranquility ripens into *menuḥa shelema*, a complete tranquility, a tranquility that is worthy to present to God as gift and that we can be sure God will accept.

Acceptance of a gift or offering is never to be taken for granted. This concern is what stands behind the occurrence of R-TZ-H in the book of Leviticus (for example, Lev. 1:3, 4, and elsewhere). This is the hope expressed as the last stage of the Passover Seder, *Nirtza*. *Nirtza* affirms our trust that our Seder has been welcomed by God with love and grace. This is the meaning of, "*Retzeh... beyom haShabbos hazeh,*" the paragraph inserted on Shabbos in the Grace after Meals;[4] we ask God to accept our Shabbos as gift.

GIFT-EXCHANGE RELATIONSHIP WITH GOD

All this means that Shabbos enables us to be in a gift-exchange relationship with God.

I am drawing upon an understanding of gift-giving as an essential element in relationships, an area of study first described rigorously by the sociologist-anthropologist Marcel Mauss. Here I quote from a recent thinker in this tradition, the philosopher and anthropologist Marcel Hénaff, who writes:

---

4. *Koren Siddur*, 1022–23.

The purpose of ceremonial gift exchange is not to transmit goods as a quantum of wealth or to transfer property but to honor a partner...and, above all, to express reciprocal attachment. The primary value of those offerings is symbolic: On behalf of the giver, whether group or individual, they are a pledge of oneself – or even of the self as such.... Therein lies the incalculable value of the thing given.[5]

This is the significance of the last lines of the prayer: "May Your children recognize and know that their tranquility comes from You, and that by their tranquility they sanctify Your name."[6] That is, may we realize that the *menuha* is not simply rest, but rather a sacred gift from God that we savor, appreciate, and offer back to God in grateful reciprocity.

Another writer, the poet Lewis Hyde, says the following about gift: "Something comes to us unbidden, alters our lives, and leaves us with a sense of gratitude."[7] Hyde explains gratitude as "a labor the soul undertakes to effect the transformation after a gift has been received. We work, sometimes for years, until the gift has truly ripened inside of us and can be passed along."[8] The experience of the Jewish people over millennia with respect to Shabbos can be described in precisely this way. Jews have endeavored to realize the transformation that Shabbos effects on the soul, to cultivate and ripen their appreciation of the gift each week, and to pass on their practices and their realizations to coming generations with openness to ever deeper insight to appear in the future.

Shabbos is what bonds us to God in gift-exchange relationship. This understanding goes back to what has become our pivotal verse, Exodus 16:29: "See – the LORD has given you Shabbos [as a gift]." We endeavor to grasp and appreciate this more deeply every Shabbos, especially as the day approaches completion, the time of Minḥa and the third Shabbos meal, *Seuda Shelishit*.

---

5. Marcel Hénaff, *The Price of Truth: Gift, Money, and Philosophy* (Stanford, CA: Stanford University Press, 2010), 386–87.
6. *Koren Siddur*, 665.
7. Lewis Hyde, "The Gift Must Always Move," *CoEvolution Quarterly* (Fall 1982): 10.
8. Ibid., 11.

WHERE ARE YOU?

Rabbi Shneur Zalman of Liadi (1745–1812), the founder of Chabad Hasidism, was arrested on false charges instigated by opponents of the hasidic movement. He was incarcerated and interrogated in St. Petersburg. One of his jailors, evidently a devout Christian, was deeply impressed with the rabbi's wisdom and piety, and he began asking him questions on biblical topics. The jailor pointed to Genesis 3:9. At this point in the narrative, Adam and Eve are in the Garden of Eden, attempting to hide from God after having eaten from the Tree of Knowledge. God calls out and asks the first direct question ever posed in the Bible, "Where are you?" The Hebrew captures the question in a single word, "*Ayekah?*" The jailor was puzzled by God's question, in light of the fact that God knows everything.

The rabbi responded that God was probing Adam about his existential situation, his inner state, his attainments and shortcomings set in relief of the horizon that was originally granted him. Then the rabbi gazed directly at his interlocutor and said, "God said something like this: You are now forty-six years old. Where are you?" The rabbi's apparently casual choice of a number turned out to be the jailor's precise age, which shook the jailor and opened his heart.

The story's main point is not the rabbi's paranormal knowledge or clairvoyance, his guessing the questioner's age exactly; rather, like many prison narratives, the story is about the meaning of freedom and incarceration. It was the rabbi who was truly free, liberated in spirit and available to be present to his interlocutor.

The story's topic brings the message home with particular forcefulness. The biblical passage brought up by the jailor is one of the most powerful in all Scripture, posing the ultimate question that all humans must face: Where are you? The question is relevant wherever one may think one is located, but it resonates with special intensity in a prison. In effect, the rabbi was located in the Garden of Eden itself. And that confident emplacement enabled him to respond with transformative insight to the jailor's earnest question, deepening it in a way that the jailor, reading the textual surface, could not have anticipated.

In this way, the hasidic story casts new light on the Garden of Eden narrative, placing the theme of location and emplacement front and center. Adam was emplaced in the Garden by none other than God (Gen. 2:8, 15). In that location, Adam was at home with God, with his life partner Eve, with himself. After the sin, Adam and Eve were exiled from the Garden, tantamount to an estrangement from their own inner selves. This interpretation was advanced with great eloquence by Rabbi Abraham Isaac Kook (1865–1935),[9] who wrote that the root of Adam's sin was self-estrangement. Listening to the serpent meant the loss of access to one's inner voice, the loss of self.

Adam could give no clear answer to the question "Where are you?" because he no longer knew his own soul, because he had lost touch with his own identity as a consequence of bowing to falsehood. Rabbi Kook writes:

> [As a result of grasping after inconsequential, peripheral matters,] the self, the "I" is forgotten by stages.
> And since there is no "I" – no first-person subject – there is no third-person, no "he/she."
> And – even more crucially – there is no "you."[10]

That is, exile from the Garden means losing access to one's own truest self, losing touch with one's inner voice. Estranged from oneself, it is impossible to have meaningful relationships with others, to address someone else as person, as You. One is detached, disconnected.

That is indeed exile.

Shabbos is a foretaste of the World to Come, a return to the Garden, but with the benefit of experience. If so, the deep meaning of Shabbos must be a reversal of exile, reversal of self-estrangement, a reattachment to one's own being, a reconnection to location, to place, to time, to the rich resonance of one's innermost voice and to the voices of others. It is that reconnection that Shabbos as spiritual practice aims to achieve. It is that return to oneself that has the

---

9. First Ashkenazic chief rabbi of modern Palestine, later the State of Israel, Rabbi Kook was a major mystic, religious thinker, and inspirational communal leader of enormous influence to this day.
10. *Orot HaKodesh* 3:140, cited from Rabbi Re'em HaKohen, *Makom*, 7.

capacity to banish addiction to falsehood and superficiality and to restore genuine presence.

THE THIRD SHABBOS MEAL: *SEUDA SHELISHIT*

Until well into the twentieth century, most small towns and villages in Eastern Europe had no electricity. As *Seuda Shelishit* – the third Shabbos meal – continued, the sun proceeded to set, and those present began to hear each other more than see each other. In this tradition, the *zemirot* were the most immersive of all three meals because of the poignancy and holiness of the moment. The melodies are plangent, enchanting, incantatory – an aperture to interior spaces never before reached or imagined.

The sweet depth of the Torah teachings reach an unparalleled intensity. We can share the softest, most delicate truth of the soul.

Mizmor LeDavid: Psalm 23

While many recite the twenty-third psalm Friday evening as well as at the second meal during the day, this psalm is particularly associated with the third Shabbos meal. The psalm's themes of trust in God and gentle repose are especially fitting for late Shabbos afternoon, when we have most fully settled into place and wish to linger in *menuḥa,* tranquility. Consistent with the spirit of this most gentle time of **Listen**, we are led to the "still waters," *mei menuḥot,* in a mood at once buoyant and serene. We open our ears and our hearts, taking in soft melodies and eloquent whispers.

The last words of verse 4, "I will fear no evil, for You are with me," have given comfort and assurance to innumerable people in times of distress and danger. Hasidic master Rabbi Tzadok HaKohen of Lublin notes the pivot here. In the first three verses, the psalmist has spoken of God in the third person; God is the benevolent shepherd but is not addressed directly. However, in verse 4, the psalmist fears no evil "for You are with me." Now God is directly addressed, as You (*Ata*). Rabbi Yisrael the Maggid of Kozienice taught that the very fact that humans are able to utter the pronoun "you" in prayer, addressing God directly, is an expression of divine love. God is the *Ein Sof,* the Infinite One, of whom nothing can be said or comprehended. What a gift that the

Absolute desires to enter into relationship, to be open to entreaty in prayer![11] We address God as "You," and the resultant sense of Presence, at once unfathomably powerful and infinitely caring and protective, is the source of our confidence and fearlessness. Wherever we are, whatever we face, we are never alone.

The awareness of God's Presence continues in verse 5, where we experience ourselves as honored guests at God's table. This expresses not smug self-satisfaction, but rather humility and thankfulness for God's grace. Oil on the head is a mark of distinction and nobility; the overflowing cup is a symbol of abundance. In response to these gifts, our hearts open wider with generosity; we seek not the comeuppance of haters, but the transformation of hatred into friendship. This is due to God's hospitality, never more felt than on late Shabbos afternoon, at the third meal. We are truly at God's table!

The psalm's final verse is translated, "May goodness and kindness follow me all the days of my life, and may I live in the House of the LORD for evermore."[12] The Hebrew *yirdefuni*, "follow me," is more literally rendered "pursue me," and this is the basis of a teaching of the Baal Shem Tov. What does it mean to ask for goodness and kindness to *pursue* us? The Baal Shem Tov explains that we sometimes close our hearts and our minds to a gift even if we really desire it, even if we have been waiting for it all our lives. Misperceiving its nature, we may be unprepared to receive it. When the doorbell rings, as it were, we may assume that we are being pestered by an unwanted interruption. Out of pique and irritation, we may be tempted to refuse to open the door. As transmitted by disciples, the Baal Shem Tov says:

> God in compassion may cause beneficence to actively pursue us, so that we might receive the light of salvation and success. Nevertheless, we may still turn our backs and flee from that which

---

11. See *Avodat Yisrael* (Bnei Brak: Peer Mikdoshim, 5773/2013), *Parashat Lekh Lekha*, s.v. *uMalkitzedek melekh shalem*, 19; *Parashat Devarim*, s.v. *ki Hashem*, 247–48; *Parashat Va'ethanan*, s.v. *Ata haḥilota*, 249–50; in this last citation, the teaching is attributed to Rabbi Dov Ber, the Great Maggid of Mezritsh.

12. *Koren Siddur*, 740.

is truly good. So David prayed, "When I wish God to bestow goodness and kindness upon me but I don't have the sense to receive them, and I may even be actively running away, then, I ask of You, God: Make the goodness pursue me in such a way that I cannot escape, till finally I realize that I must accept the gift, and the blessing makes its way into my house."[13]

We often do not know what is best for us; we may not perceive an opportunity as the boon it can be. There are times when God wants to bestow a beneficence, but we may be too suspicious, too rigid, too harried to receive the blessing. Preoccupied with our patterns of thought, we are disinclined to pause, and it may not be easy for God to capture our attention. The last line of Psalm 23 is a humble recognition of our limited understanding and self-awareness. As we linger in the Edenic atmosphere of the third meal, we find space and time to cherish the blessings we already have, and we pray for openheartedness to accept the new gifts that God wants to place upon us.

The psalm's capstone is the last phrase, "May I live in the House of the LORD forevermore." The House of the LORD is the Temple, at once a physical locale in Jerusalem as well as an Edenic space of beauty, grace, and moral perfection. The *Sefat Emet* writes that the goal of the Tabernacle (precursor to the Temple) was to model a perfect cosmos, and thereby to invite the movement toward that perfection, to sustain the impulse to improve the world, to nurture the ongoing hope that such constructive activity is possible.[14] As a model of the perfected universe, the Tabernacle/Temple evokes the desire to realize that perfection in wider circles and more modalities ÷ interpersonal, societal, aesthetic, moral, spiritual. This is the "House," the mode of being in the world, in which the psalmist wishes to live and where we are invited to make our home. This is the climax of the psalm, and the culminating mood

---

13. *Sefer Baal Shem Tov*, 262, *Parashat Vayishlaḥ*, no. 3 on Genesis 32:8.

14. *Sefat Emet, Parashot Vayak'hel-Pekudei* 5637/1877, s.v. *bapasuk marbim haam... ish va'isha al yaasu od... vayikalei haam mehavi*. On the intimate connection between cosmos and the Tabernacle, see above, chapter 2, section "*Melakha*: 'Work' or Creative Activity?"

of Shabbos, when our small minds melt away and everyone and everything is perceived under the expansive dispensation of grace.

Dibbuk Ḥaverim – Camaraderie and Friendship

This is the time for *dibbuk ḥaverim* – the camaraderie and friendship of peers that ideally characterizes the hasidic community. The third Shabbos meal provides an opportunity to learn from and listen to fellow seekers on the path. "The gathering of Hasidim in friendship causes a divine revelation of absolute compassion."[15]

Saying Torah, Listening to Torah

The Baal Shem Tov is quoted by his disciple Rabbi Jacob Joseph of Polonoye as teaching that every word of Torah can sustain two opposing interpretations, one pointing in the direction of severity and one pointing toward compassion, and "the righteous transform the sense of severity to that of compassion."[16]

For the Baal Shem Tov, since every word of Torah can be taken in an expansive or restrictive mode, the true teacher is charged with the mandate of bringing the words to the side of bounty and blessing, comprehending the text in the most beneficent way. The active interpreter's understanding shapes the sense of the text, transforming the world itself.

Beginning with the Baal Shem Tov, hasidic interpreters are intentionally responding to what they perceive as a mandate to express meaning that conveys blessed, joyous possibility.

The charismatic hasidic interpreter embraces Scripture in a dynamic personal relationship, believing that fresh understanding of verses changes reality itself, moving all in the direction of compassion and beneficence.

Here is a way to think about hasidic interpretations of Scripture: When you tune a stringed instrument such as guitar or violin, you turn the tuning peg to increase the tension on the string so as to release a sweet sound. You are applying force, but you are not forcing the string.

---

15. Rabbi Kalonymos Kalman Epstein of Krakow, *Maor VaShemesh, Parashat Devarim,* s.v. *vaatzaveh et shoftekhem* (Deut. 1:16).
16. *Keter Shem Tov,* no. 21, from *Ben Porat Yosef, Parashat Noah.*

Rather, your effort is to enable the string to release what it is inside, to do what it was made to do – vibrate at a crisp, sweet, pleasing frequency. At some point, the tension seems right. In an analogous way, the stretch of the verse is not arbitrary, but rather tuneful. Your aim must not be to impose your will, to make it do your bidding, but to allow it to find the voice it wants to have in this time and this place, to reveal its inner beauty, to release a sound and resonate harmoniously. If you have tuned each string successfully, each will resonate with others in pleasing harmony, in a way that seems not arbitrary but inevitable. Successful tuning differs from forcing in that it involves listening more than applying pressure. You are cultivating habits of the heart and mind, habits of holiness that will percolate into the week and will transform your entire life and the lives of your *haverim*.

There is a gradual diminishing of the light, a natural orchestration of mood so that the visual element slowly recedes and the auditory takes primacy. The mood is so soft, so gentle. You want to savor the difference between late Shabbos afternoon and the two stages that preceded it.

The Doorknob Moment

This is what I refer to as the "doorknob moment." My research on hasidic history has involved conducting interviews with individuals with memories of life in Eastern Europe before the Second World War and the Holocaust. It has been my experience that such interviews tend to follow a pattern. The meeting begins by establishing common ground and building trust. My interviewees have been gracious with their time and generous in sharing their recollections. Yet there were frequently memories, insights, and feelings that they were reluctant to share. I have often found that just as I put away my notebook, pen, and recording device, put on my coat, get up from the chair, offer my thanks, say goodbye, and reach for the doorknob, my interviewee will say, "Wait! I have one more thing to tell you." And this turns out to be the insight I've been waiting for, the disclosure that makes the entire meeting memorable.

The third meal is the "doorknob moment" of Shabbos – the moment we realize that the access to the deepest, most intimate places is about to close, and this sparks a burst of revelation and disclosure.

The Piaseczner Rebbe on *Shalosh Seudos*

Rabbi Kalonymos Shapiro writes that the task of a Hasid is to know how to contemplate (*lehistakel*). By "contemplation" (*histaklut*) he means the ability to perceive both internal and external phenomena with greater awareness and sensitivity, and to develop a full-fledged perception that gives definition to inchoate feeling. He is referring in particular to inchoate sensations of holiness that would be indistinguishable, unidentifiable, without actively contemplating their origins and envisioning their growth possibilities. He gives the example of sacred times: It is essential to be able to distinguish between the elevation one feels at the Passover Seder, for instance, from that felt on Rosh HaShana or Yom Kippur. Each time affords entry into an internal and external reality of holiness, but only active contemplation will enable one to develop the sensitivity to be aware of the difference, and eventually to articulate the distinction. For the Piaseczner Rebbe, it is not enough to be open to spirituality; you must sharpen your soul's palate, so to speak, to be able to taste with discerning awareness, so that the clarity of your perception may make a difference in your spiritual life. In his view, this is equivalent to "finding the hidden God" within the self and in one's environs. The process of discernment is crucially dependent on being unhurried. Haste militates against sensitivity and awareness.

The Piaseczner Rebbe's prime example of measured, deliberate cultivation of interiority is the third Shabbos meal, *Seuda Shelishit*, which is also known as *Shalosh Seudos* ("three meals") because it captures the essence of all the Shabbos meals in that it is not about food or drink. Rather, it is the opportunity to seek "the God concealed in beautiful secrecy"[17] and to be nourished by divine radiance rather than by culinary delicacies. The hasidic *Shalosh Seudos* is a social gathering. As the Piaseczner Rebbe describes the meal, "You are in the company of fellow God-seekers." He continues:

> You are sitting in the dark. This is a hallowed custom that brings your physical body into alignment with your soul's situation at

---

17. See the poem *El Mistater BeShafrir Ḥevyon* by Rabbi Abraham Maimin (1522–1570).

that moment. There are different types of darkness. Scripture writes that God "made darkness His hiding-place" (Ps. 18:12). That place, then, is true light; it is only dark with respect to the things of this world. Neither this world nor the things of this world are visible now. Since for an entire period of twenty-four hours you have distanced yourself from worldly matters, and, step by step, you have drawn close to the place of ultimate grace, the place of Supernal Will,[18] in mind, heart, and bodily sensation – it follows that your body must enact this higher darkness physically, palpably. God is hiding in this darkness. All Shabbos, you have searched for and entered "the thick cloud where God is" (Ex. 20:18). You have searched for and found your soul's love (cf. Song. 3:1). Your soul is approaching God, melting in divine holiness.[19]

But, the Piaseczner Rebbe reminds his readers, this state of bliss will soon end, moving from *arfillei tohar* – the "nimbus of dark but clear radiance" – into the genuine opaque darkness of the workaday world, its cares and burdens.

You tremble at the thought, and the only consolation is from verses such as "even though I walk through the valley of the shadow of death, I will fear no harm, for You are with me" (Ps. 23:4), chanted in the course of reciting the twenty-third psalm at *Shalosh Seudos*. Rabbi Shapiro asserts that experiencing *Shalosh Seudos* with these thoughts in mind and in this state of contemplative awareness is sufficient to leave an impression throughout the entire week and to transform the individual into a "person of spirit and pure mind."

SPIRIT ARRIVES MOST FULLY AT THE MOMENT OF DEPARTURE

The Talmud speaks of the *neshama yetera*, the "supplemental spirit" that God gives Israel as the most delicate and sublime aspect of Shabbos,

---

18. Hebrew *ratzon ha'elyon*; in the terminology of the *sefirot*, *Keter*.
19. Rabbi Kalonymos Shapiro, *Bnei Maḥashava Tova* (Tel Aviv: Vaad Hasidei Piaseczna, 1973), section 11, 28–30.

a feature that is inexpressible, incapable of full description. Rashi explains *neshama yetera* in a straightforward manner as "expanded capacity for tranquility and joy, for openness and spaciousness; a state in which one may eat and drink without dulling the senses."[20] This state of sensory alertness, buoyant spirit, and convivial mood opens the being to the blessing and hallowing that the Bible promises again and again as features of Shabbos. These features are wondrous, mysterious, and ineffable, a sweet bonus of observance that comes unawares and unexpected, a mark of transcendence felt deep in the body. The contours of *neshama yetera* can be sketched, but its content cannot be put into words.

This fullness of Shabbos is realized only at the moment of departure. Shabbos is only achieved as Shabbos is about to conclude. Ripening awareness of *neshama yetera* is the experiential high point of the day, and the fullness of this awareness at *Shalosh Seudos,* coupled with the imminence of the supplemental spirit's departure, makes this time sacredly, achingly poignant. Rabbenu Ḥananel (on Beitza 16a) speaks of a surplus of significance and satisfaction that is revealed over the course of Shabbos. He writes:

> Creation was intended *ab initio* to be revealed in its full glory on Shabbos; all aspects of creation deploy their glory with greater amplitude, expanding and growing during the course of Shabbos. Once a person has fully accomplished the cessation of Shabbos [which only happens as Shabbos ends], one senses the imminent departure of the surplus of spirit; one feels the incipient return to diminished spirit.

The Hebrew word *shavat* in Exodus 31:17, typically translated as "[God] rested/ceased," is understood by Rabbenu Ḥananel as a pluperfect, therefore translated as "had ceased." The focus of the verse is not on the start of the day but on its conclusion. As the holy day came to an end, God *had ceased*; it became clear that God had held the cessation for a full day, from setting sun to setting sun. This is the model for us to emulate. Shabbos is only achieved, only accomplished, in retrospect.

---

20. Beitza 16a; Rashi ad loc., s.v. *neshama yetera.*

You can only genuinely say that you have rested, come to repose, when you have held your cessation and repose for a complete cycle of sunset-sunrise-sunset, and you can look back with joy and satisfaction at the fullness of the day that is now closing.[21]

---

21. These thoughts are based on Rabbenu Ḥananel on Beitza 16a. See also Taanit 27b and Rashi ad loc., s.v. *keivan sheshavat*. Note Rashi's comment: *shenaḥ veshamar et haShabbat*, "once the person has rested and has kept the Shabbos" – that is, it can only be said that one has kept Shabbos, held to Shabbos, at the moment of Shabbos's conclusion, but just at that moment one feels the poignancy of Shabbos's departure. Like all great visitors, Shabbos's elevating presence is felt most powerfully at the moment of leave-taking. This is the sense of the talmudic wordplay: *Vayinafash – Vay avda nefesh*! "Woe! The supplemental spirit is now gone!"

Chapter 7

Savoring Darkness's Return

The signal that the time has arrived to bring Shabbos to closure is the arrival of darkness. We go beyond sunset, waiting for three stars to appear in the night sky. This is one aspect of traditional Shabbos observance that is now beclouded, quite literally, for most people in urban areas. Because of the ubiquity of electrification and the intensity of artificial illumination, most of us never get to see the heavens in their true splendor. Many Shabbos observers now rely on internet websites for the end-time of Shabbos that translate the "three stars" requirement into astronomical calculations executed by algorithm. What is gained in exactitude is lost in awareness of the natural movements of the heavenly bodies. Reminding ourselves that Shabbos day is meant to come to closure not by the dictate of a computer program but by visual observation is one way that we can restore Shabbos's intimate connection with the natural world. And the loss of the night sky in urban areas should remind us of the challenge of light pollution. Darkness is a precious resource that needs to be safeguarded and cultivated. Only when we savor the darkness will we truly appreciate the light.

HAVDALA – SHABBOS AFTERGLOW

Havdala is the liturgy that marks the end of Shabbos. The word Havdala means "separation," and we draw Shabbos to a close with boundary-markers akin to the ones deployed when Shabbos began. Just as Shabbos was ushered in with the lighting of candles, a candle is lit now as well. At the start of Shabbos, just before sunset, candle-lighting was our final act of preparation, assuring that once Shabbos arrived we would be able to maintain the mandate of Exodus 35:3, "You shall kindle no fire throughout your habitations on the day of Shabbos." Now, after nightfall a full sun-cycle later, lighting the flame becomes a performative enactment, a statement that Shabbos has concluded and our *now* is no longer governed by Exodus 35:3. Refraining from kindling fires on Shabbos gives substance and materiality to the candle-lighting at Havdala; conversely, Havdala testifies to our having held the Shabbos-place for a complete sun-cycle. Havdala is no mere decorative ceremony, but rather a tangible demonstration of our having journeyed into a deeper place, the Edenic locale that has now been surrendered and offered up as gift to God, whole and complete. The texture of time is marked by flame, a source of illumination that simultaneously banishes and honors the darkness that has descended upon the world with sun's plunge into the horizon.

A cup of wine – the biblical elixir of blessing – is raised, just as during the Kiddush, now to mark a transit from sacred time to ordinary time (though, as we shall see in a moment, the concept of "ordinary time" is refined as a result of our Shabbos observance). The biblical passages recited are verses that bespeak confidence that with God's help we will be able to navigate the challenges and opportunities of the week and that our efforts will be marked with success.[1]

But with all the focus on separation and movement to the quotidian, there is an emphasis on continuity as well. As we take leave of Shabbos, we want to retain Shabbos's blessings and apply them to the week. There is a practice that enacts this in a very material way. At the end of Havdala the custom is to extinguish the candle flame in wine that has overflowed from the wine cup. Some have the further practice of dipping their fingers in the wine that is now mixed with candle wax

---

1. See *Koren Siddur*, 246–49.

and gently applying a few drops to their eyelashes. We wish to take the spirit of Shabbos with us into the week, to see the events of the week with the eyes of Shabbos. It is a tangible reminder, enacted in our bodies, that God's blessings are permanent and their impress never leaves us. The practice further imparts a truth about holiness. While holiness is often taken to mean separation, the separation is pro-visional, with a gracious aperture that shines lovingly on the not-yet-holy.

Each Shabbos deposits a baseline of preparedness for further growth. Every Shabbos enriches – blesses – the following weekdays, to enable them to be days of preparedness for the Shabbos to come.

Remember that Shabbos is called God's gift to Israel. The *Sefat Emet* notes that a gracious gift-giver will provide instructions on how best to use the gift. In our terms, this might be compared to giving someone a musical instrument as a gift, and then giving music lessons for learning how to play the instrument. In just that way, when God gave Israel the gift of Shabbos, God enabled the weekdays to be days of preparation to make the most of the gift of Shabbos. We access Shabbos through the efforts we make during the week. This is a cumulative, endlessly recursive process.[2]

The *Sefat Emet* invokes the rabbinic exegetical maxim: *Kol hayotzei min haklal… lelamed al haklal kulo yatza,* "Whatever has been taken out of a general category has been taken to teach about the category as a whole." This is a technical hermeneutical rule, but the *Sefat Emet* deploys it as an overarching theological principle: That which has been separated – designated as "holy" – has been set aside for the benefit of the not-yet holy, to enable a new view of what is perceived to be the non-sacred, the common.[3] Shabbos is for the benefit of the week, to transform the week. Conversely, each weekday is an opportunity to savor the reverberations of the previous Shabbos and to prepare for the Shabbos to come.

Havdala does not enact detachment. It is not a severance of weekday from Shabbos. Havdala invokes categories that are distinct but also interdependent; the domains are never estranged from each other.

---

2. *Sefat Emet, Parashat Toledot* 5649/1889, s.v. *bapasuk veyiten lekha haElokim.*

3. Ibid., *Parashat Mishpatim* 5663/1903, s.v. *ve'eleh hamishpatim.*

ELIJAH MOMENTS: "EUREKA" REVELATIONS

This is the time when we welcome Elijah the prophet. In the Bible, Elijah has a fiery personality, zealously fighting pagan worship and defending the honor of the God of Israel. The mystery of his miraculous power is intensified by the scene at the end of his earthly life, when he does not die but is transported bodily into heaven by a whirlwind in a chariot of fire (II Kings 2:1–11). The last book of the Prophets in the Hebrew Bible concludes on a note of Elijah returning as a harbinger of the end-time, the Day of the Lord. Elijah will restore the hearts of parents to their children, and children to their parents (Mal. 3:23) – that is, he will restore family harmony and intergenerational understanding. In later Jewish folklore, Elijah appears at life cycle celebrations, at the Passover Seder, and at moments of distress, often in disguise, defending and intervening on behalf of beleaguered Jewish communities.

One particularly powerful application of the Elijah motif is found in the classic hasidic work *Meor Einayim* by Rabbi Menahem Nahum (Twersky) of Chernobyl. Rabbi Menahem Nahum links the eschatological promise of Malachi with that of Isaiah 11:9: "[They shall not hurt nor destroy in all My holy mountain;] for the earth shall be full of the knowledge (*de'ah*) of the LORD [as the waters cover the sea]." Rabbi Menahem Nahum's understanding of the Hebrew word *de'ah* is better captured by the English word "awareness" – that is, intimate and direct experience of the Divine, rather than primarily intellectual knowledge. He writes that in preparation for the messianic era, there will be an expanded awareness of divinity in the entire world. And we need not wait for the final eschaton for this to happen. A glimpse of this experience, which he calls the "Elijah-moment," is available at all times and places.

Rabbi Menahem Nahum describes a situation in which a student of Talmud is stuck on a problem and, despite having given it a best effort, arrives at an impasse. Suddenly, there is a burst of awareness. In the rabbi's words:

> There enters into the individual something like an annunciation (*besora*) – a feeling in the mind of a single focal point. This is the Elijah-moment. Afterward, "the earth is filled with awareness," meaning that the person experiences an expansion of

consciousness and an infusion of energy that reaches all parts of the body, including the feet.

Individuals bearing good tidings are invested with the spirit of the prophet Elijah. Elijah-illuminations are part of the fabric of creation that manifest in varied garb and in different individuals in each generation. That is why people are so eager to tell good news – their souls feel the presence of Elijah and they wish to realize that spirit in their own being. And it is the same for the recipients of good news; the Elijah-spirit enters them, and they experience an expansion of awareness, which can then be channeled to holy purpose, raising and uniting all parts of their being. This is what Malachi intended by the words, "The coming of the great day of the LORD" (Mal. 3:23).[4]

Rabbi Menahem Nahum anticipated by two hundred years the description of a psychological phenomenon known today as the Eureka or Aha! moment, involving a conceptual breakthrough accompanied by positive, buoyant affect. It should be noted that, in Rabbi Menahem Nahum's careful description, this single-pointed burst of illumination is not identical with intellectual comprehension, but rather precedes it, phenomenologically and temporally. It is the annunciatory awareness that a breakthrough has arrived, details to follow. Thus, the rabbi precisely tracks the sense of Malachi chapter 3, wherein Elijah anticipates and announces the arrival of redemption. The Elijah-moment is the illumination one receives at the realization that new understanding has arrived, even before that understanding has percolated into the conscious mind.

In good hasidic fashion, the eschaton as an anticipated epoch in history can be realized at all times, in all places, with all people. The Elijah-moment refers to a conceptual breakthrough, but perhaps even more importantly, it points to the opportunity to be bearers of good tidings, to give courage and buoyancy to ourselves and others in heartening ways, thereby expanding awareness and unity – what Rabbi Menahem Nahum (following the biblical prophets) calls the "knowledge of God."

---

4. Rabbi Menahem Nahum of Chernobyl, *Meor Einayim, Parashat Vayetzeh*, s.v. *vayisa Yaakov et raglav vayelekh artza benei kedem.*

Every harbinger of good news has a spark of Elijah. And Elijah-moments have the potential to unite disparate elements of being, to bring God-consciousness to individuals and the world.

This is the time of *melaveh malka*, "escorting the Queen." When we say goodbye to an honored guest – and every guest in one's home is an honored guest! – courtesy requires that we accompany the guest beyond the threshold, that we walk with them a good distance, continuing the conversation, promising to stay in touch and to see them again, and finally taking leave reluctantly with warmest words of blessing and, if appropriate, hugs. In this spirit, the custom is to have one final meal in honor of Shabbos, after nightfall and following Havdala, escorting our guest with song and words of Torah.

In the liturgy for *melaveh malka*, praise of Elijah has a prominent position. In light of the hasidic teaching just presented, the affirmation implied here is that we will keep Shabbos-consciousness with us during the week, that we commit ourselves to be Elijah-people, bearers of good tidings, being open to heartening and buoyant illuminations that not only enliven the life of the mind, but also lift up hearts and send positive energy in all directions. This indeed is realized eschatology.

Because Elijah-realizations are breakthroughs, they must be fervently desired and worked for but at the same time remain unexpected; they must arrive unawares. The classic narrative for scientific breakthroughs is that of a researcher puzzling over a problem, often for many years, and then, perhaps at a moment of seeming inattention or even during sleep, coming up with the solution "out of the blue." While intense effort at solving a problem is indispensable, one must also learn to let go, to allow for peripheral as well as focal awareness, to open space for possibilities unenvisioned and unimagined, for what is now called "out-of-the-box thinking."

Hasidic masters would apply this wisdom to the realm of human interaction. Elijah may come in a guise we are not expecting, embodied as a person whom we might not recognize. Don't expect Elijah to look like a prophet in calendar art or to appear as a learned sage or pious wisdom teacher. The redemptive message I've been waiting for may come from the shabbily dressed stranger, the refugee, the panhandler, even the thief. Don't exclude anyone from the circle of humanity, concern, worthiness. The person who we are tempted to disregard may just be Elijah the prophet; he or she may just have the insight I so desperately need, that I've been so fervently waiting for. When put into practice, this means giving respect and honor to all persons, to every individual without exception.

GOTT FUN AVRAHAM

In addition to Havdala, there is another leave-taking prayer that deserves mention, the Yiddish paragraph known as *Gott fun Avraham*, "God of Abraham." Its genre is that of a *techineh*, a prayer composed in Yiddish rather than Hebrew, asking God for assistance, usually in domestic matters, such as health, livelihood, peaceful relations between spouses and family members, children's happiness, spiritual growth, and the like. These deeply emotional prayers, expressing intimate personal concerns, were generally composed for, and in some cases by, women. Versions of *Gott fun Avraham* had circulated in Eastern Europe for centuries, but with the rise of Hasidism, it was augmented with hasidic motifs and came to be associated with the name of one of the greatest and most popular masters, Rabbi Levi Yitzhak of Berditchev, who, according to folk tradition, stated that those who recite the prayer would be assured a week filled with success.

As long as my mother was alive, it was a high point of our end-of-Shabbos activities to recite *Gott fun Avraham* together – three times. My mother embodied the folk traditions of the old country, and she was eager to recite the *techineh* for the sake of a good week for her family. She passed away a decade ago, but we continue to recite *Gott fun Avraham* in her memory and with her spirit.

I offer a translation of *Gott fun Avraham* as my family recites it:

> God of Abraham, of Isaac, and of Jacob, guard Your people Israel from all harm – in your praise! As the beloved, holy Shabbos departs, may the week bring us to complete faith, to faith in sages, to love for and bonding with good friends, to bond with the blessed Creator, believing in your Thirteen Principles, and in the complete and near redemption, speedily in our days, and in the resurrection of the dead, and in the prophecy of our teacher Moses, peace be upon him.

Master of the universe, You are one who gives strength to the weary. Give Your beloved Jewish children strength to praise You, and to serve You and no one else.

May this week come to us for kindness, and for good fortune, and for blessing, and for success, and for health, and for wealth and honor, and for children, life, and adequate nutrition – for us and for all Israel. Amen.

Matters crucial for family survival – especially health and prosperity – are foregrounded in this prayer. But we also discern the influence of hasidic spiritual values, especially in the phrases about bonding (*devekut*) with good friends and with God.

Gott fun Avraham figures prominently in the Holocaust recollections of Bertha Ferderber-Salz, who wrote a memoir in Yiddish titled *Un di Zun hot Gesheint*, a story of her survival and eventual reuniting with her two daughters in hiding. In January 1945, Ferderber-Salz was in Bergen-Belsen; she describes hearing a voice chanting *Gott fun Avraham*. Ferderber-Salz was overwhelmed with emotion on catching the words, since it brought her back to her earliest memories of childhood, when her mother would chant the prayer as twilight would descend at the end of the Sabbath. While there are minor variations in the wording, the version Ferderber-Salz recalls hearing ended with the words: "May we receive a healthy week, a week of prosperity, a week of good fortune: for me, my family, and all Israel. Amen!" The woman intoning the words in such a tender and affecting manner was skeletal, at the verge of death, with sunken eyes that nevertheless were focused on a patch of sky, gazing at the stars signaling nightfall.

Ferderber-Salz addressed her: "You recited *Gott fun Avraham* so beautifully!"

She replied, "God must be praised – no matter where we find ourselves. And if it's already too late for us here, there are still Jews elsewhere in the world, and they need a good week...."

The memoir continues (translation mine):

I expressed my gratitude and told her that thanks to her, I found out that today is Shabbos, and that the next week I intended to come to her, so that I could say *Gott fun Avraham* at least one more time with her.

I asked her, "How did you know that today is Shabbos?" She responded that she comes from Hungary and arrived just a few weeks ago, and she is very devout. She keeps track of the days by making a sign – a knot in her ragged clothes.

I returned the next Shabbos at the end of the day, but someone else was already in her place. No longer was her voice to be heard; the recitation of *Gott fun Avraham* was silenced. But it yet lives within me, and I want it never to be stilled.[5]

It is revealing that the memoirist is grateful to have learned that the day was Shabbos and remarked with admiration and wonder that the pious woman (whose name we never learn) has kept track of the days of the week. This is a striking example of how difficult it was to hold on to the most basic elements of the calendar that we take for granted, and how the loss of time's rhythm was itself an aspect of demoralization and dehumanization in the camps.[6] Second, the Sabbath-observer knows that she is about to die and declares that she was praying not for herself but for others, who still had an opportunity to live. The story is thus one of solidarity and concern with the fate of fellow Jews, even at the point of death. Finally, Ferderber-Salz is reminded of a religious practice from her childhood that she had presumably allowed to lapse. The last sentence of this section – beginning with the word *ober*, "but" – signals a decision to honor not just the memory of the expired woman, but to lift up her practice, perhaps to take it on and restore it to its place in her life, and at minimum to cherish it in her heart. The gaunt woman's chanting was a gift, a treasure recovered unexpectedly from the past, an offering from the near-dead to the living, bestowed in the darkness, touching heaven.

---

5. *Un di Zun hot Gesheint* (Tel Aviv, 1965), 134–35 The memoir was translated into English as *And the Sun Kept Shining* (New York: Holocaust Library, 1980). My translation follows the original Yiddish version; the Holocaust Library translation inexplicably omits the last sentence.

6. For more on this and related topics, see Alan Rosen, "Tracking Jewish Time in Auschwitz," *Yad Vashem Studies* 42 (2014): esp. n. 50; *idem, The Holocaust's Jewish Calendars: Keeping Time Sacred, Making Time Holy* (Indiana University Press, 2019).

Since we do not know this saintly figure's proper name, perhaps we should call her the lady of *Gott fun Avraham*.

Or the woman who at the edge of death continued to pray for others.

Who, when everything was taken away, continued to count the days to Shabbos.

Who tracked Shabbos with the frayed edges of her garment – the true Shabbos-keeper.

Or should we remember her as Elijah the prophet at Bergen-Belsen?

CLEARING, LINGERING

On Saturday night, the Shabbos dishes and tableware are washed, dried, and arranged reverently in their boxes and shelves in preparation for the coming Shabbos; the tablecloth is washed, folded, and set in place to be ready for use next Friday. These Saturday night activities bear witness that our hearts and our home are already attuned to the next rendezvous with Shabbos. It is a privilege to clean up, to be reminded by the visible remainders, by the resonances of the songs, the camaraderie, the joy. Leftovers may no longer be usable, but they are still treated with respect for what they remind us of, for what they still embody. "Residue" is connected to "reside." The act of cleaning is transformed from a chore into a holy deed that connects us to the Shabbos we have just experienced and the Shabbos that we eagerly anticipate.

Later in the evening, or, preferably, the following morning, you may retrieve the articles of weekday empowerment that, from a weekday perspective, seem to be so essential to functioning in the world and even one's identity – driver's license, communication device, vehicular keys, and so on. You are now able to place these items into better perspective. They are useful but not essential. You have inhabited a richer, full, more vibrant place, a sacred place and time, and you take that embodied knowledge with you wherever your weekday travels may lead you.

This is the time I commit to writing the insights that have arrived over Shabbos – wisdom teachings, thoughtful reflections, the fruits of *ḥavruta* learning, memorable points from a synagogue sermon, stories shared by family and friends conveying life lessons. I have an old file cabinet made of solid wood (oak, I believe) with shelves sized to fit four-by-six file cards, which I purchased many years ago at a used-furniture store. I've arranged the cards by rubrics keyed to my interests, largely biblical passages and holy days, but also topics of broader interest – "parents and children," "stages of life," "friendship," "literary anecdotes," "paradoxes of self-referentiality," "scientific and non-scientific knowledge," "the virtues of unclarity," "varieties of human personality." It is a quirky, idiosyncratic grab bag reflecting my interests and passions, sometimes called a "commonplace book," though in my case not a book but an array of file cards written over decades. The committing of thoughts to writing is an important part of my post-Shabbos debriefing. I find that even the most impressive, seemingly unforgettable insights and experiences tend to fade or are forgotten over time. Part of the joy of the file-card system is the discovery of old ideas, with the opportunity to revisit them and notice how my perspective may have shifted and changed. All this is part of the joy and sweetness of the post-Shabbos time.

You will find your own way of gently transitioning from Shabbos to week. The important point is not to see Saturday night as a time of escape, as if you've been holding your breath for twenty-four hours and are finally coming up for air. If your Shabbos has been an immersion in holiness, you will be reluctant to leave. Even after Havdala, you will feel Shabbos's breath and caress. Allow yourself to linger in the impress of Shabbos, in Shabbos's slipstream, as long as possible.

Chapter 8

Your Call Is Important to Us

The meaning of Shabbos unfolds slowly. The three stages **Stop, Look, Listen** are cumulative, deploying over the course of each individual Shabbos, then week by week, over one's lifetime, through many lifetimes in an intergenerational conversation – always unfinished, always open, forever ampliative.

As you move through the week, be a *shomer Shabbos* – that is, someone who holds dear and safeguards the gifts of Shabbos, someone who lives each weekday in preparation for the Shabbos to come. Weekday winds may blow with intensity and vehemence, but if you maintain Shabbos awareness throughout the week, your serenity will be rippled but not ruffled.[1]

The preparatory work for Shabbos enables us to be worthy of Shabbos. The opportunity to prepare is part of the gift, transforming

---

1. This lovely phrase is borrowed from Thoreau, *Walden*, deployed there in a somewhat different context.

weekdays into times of preparation, pathways that lead to Shabbos, the Shabbos to come.

When we make Shabbos a priority in our lives, when we put Shabbos first, when we invite Shabbos to shape the contours of our week, we say to God, "Your call is important to us. We will not put You on hold; we will be present. We will **Stop, Look, Listen**, turn our being toward You, surrender our time to You."

As you enter the workaday week, you will return to your projects. You will be called upon to explain yourself, to convey your motives, methods, and presuppositions. People will ask, "Where are you coming from?" Whatever else you may choose to say, you can honestly and confidently reply, "I am coming from Shabbos."

As your week proceeds, you will be challenged to defend a line of argument, a mode of reasoning. You might be asked, "What's your point? Where are you going?" Whatever else comes to mind, you can reply honestly, "I am going toward Shabbos."[2]

God responds to our attentiveness by giving us Shabbos as gift, as holy heritage. One day a week, we inhabit the domain of freedom, returning to Paradise. On that day we are locals, entirely at home wherever we are in the world. Allow each Shabbos that you keep to open your heart incrementally. Become increasingly aware of a gentle, restful, enveloping Presence in your life that is tangible, as real and comforting as the caress of a lover or the safe hug of a parent. The mystics call this Presence *Shekhina,* but you do not need to consider yourself a mystic to sense the Presence's warm closeness and inhale the Presence's sweetly fragrant breath.

ASYMPTOTIC FREEDOM

Once Shabbos-consciousness has entered your life, no time is ordinary time. Shabbos-keeping gives definition to the week. The awareness of the coming full stop Friday at sunset shapes the week's contours in blessed ways. Anticipation frames weekday work, affording a vantage point to

---

2. The existential significance of the positional questions "Where are you coming from?" and "Where are you going?" was suggested by Greg Milner, *Pinpoint: How GPS Is Changing Technology, Culture, and Our Minds,* 89, citing Edward Tuck.

assess it even as one engages in it. You are not chained to or defined by your work. You espy it from the place of freedom you are preparing and, in some sense, already inhabiting.

As one learns to speak Shabbos language as mother tongue, one reaches a state of asymptotic freedom, to borrow a term from physics. You are bonded to Shabbos, captivated by Shabbos's allure and fascination. On Shabbos, you are entirely enthralled by Shabbos's beauty and grandeur. But here is the paradox: The greater your bonding and the more your heart is captured, the more you feel that you are inhabiting a region of freedom and expansiveness. You are centered and secure, confident and radiant. Rather than feeling oppressed by restrictions and restrained by rules, you feel liberated, possessed of a newly expressive language with words that ordinary place and time do not provide. You hold a passport affording safe passage to deep and varied terrain of unlimited range.

To become fluent in the language of Shabbos, a Shabbos local, you must have both feet within Shabbos's domain. When Shabbos comes, you must be fully present; you cannot have one eye on Shabbos and the other on weekday concerns, no matter how alluring or pressing. Both ears and your whole heart must attend to words of wisdom, the whispers of prayer, the hum of *niggun*, the yearnings of family and friends. Your hands must be devoted to the loving touch and the reverent cradling of the *ḥalla*, the Kiddush cup, the siddur and sacred books, the Torah. Your wrists are free of electronic handcuffs.

You are hospitable to all, welcoming to all. This requires you to deepen your own practice, your own immersion in Shabbos. Keep in mind that it is the fragrance of *your* Shabbos that attracts your guests. They have come to taste your home's ambrosia and feel your repose, and you can only share the sweetness that is within you. Shabbos helps us restore the lost parts of ourselves, and one reason why we welcome guests is that *they carry the lost parts of ourselves.*

Shabbos communities are both spatial and temporal sanctuaries. By committing to one place – your place, at a personal yet collective time, in community – you have made yourself available to your family, your friends, your own deepest self, in a powerful and transformative way. Your steadfastness and embeddedness enable you to tap energies that would otherwise seem to be antithetical – stillness and suppleness, inwardness and outward-facing openness, satisfaction and yearning.

Being in one place on Shabbos is an act of trust and faith; it means trusting that your work of preparation is adequate, that everyone and everything you need is already here.

The prophets speak of *kelei gola*, travel or exile utensils (see Jer. 46:19; Ez. 12:3). In a sense, all the tools of technology are *kelei gola*, designed to shift focus from one physical location to another. The shift of focus leads to estrangement from place, alienation from self, so that one is neither here nor there.

By contrast, Shabbos invites us to prepare tools of homecoming. Since every Shabbos is a homecoming, weekdays engage us with the project of outfitting the trip home – the most meaningful journey we can take. The Mishna's categories of prohibited activity, the *melakhot*, may be thought of as a weekday to-do list, helpful reminders of what we need to provide, the supplies we should prepare, for the great journey home.[3]

THE SHABBOS SENSORIUM

The Shabbos sensorium is unlike any earthy pleasure. The main gifts of Shabbos are spiritual, not utilitarian. Shabbos gives release from the tyranny of technology, yes, but the deepest rewards of Shabbos go beyond direct utility and practicality. They are in the social, interpersonal, and spiritual realms – family bonding, community formation, opening the heart to grace, nobility of character, orientation in place and time, rediscovery of the self, liberation of voice and spirit, personal relationship with God, the love that inhabits an open heart. *Shabbos enables us to experience what the word "God" can mean in our day and age.*[4]

---

3. The idea that the thirty-nine *melakhot* represent weekday opportunities for sacred action and preparation for Shabbos was suggested by the early hasidic text *Oneg Shabbat* by Rabbi Aaron of Zelichov ([Lemberg, 1793] Jerusalem: Machon Sod Yesharim, 2008); see also *Siddur Ḥelkat Yehoshua LeShabbatot UMo'adim*, 16.
4. Recall the Zoharic teaching that "Shabbos is the name of God"; Zohar, *Yitro* 2:88b. The convergence of Shabbos and divinity is evident in the poem *Yah Ekhsof No'am Shabbos* ("God, I long for the sweetness of Shabbos") by Rabbi Aaron of Karlin (1736–1772), disciple of Rabbi Dov Ber, the Maggid of Mezritsh, and one of the foremost early hasidic masters. This *zemer* remains popular to this day and is widely

These gifts overwhelm and humble us and move the soul to infinite gratitude. They are gifts that emerge effortlessly from the nature of Shabbos. They are part and parcel of Shabbos's essence, and they come authentically, naturally, as our rightful legacy and heritage. We need not be shy about accepting these gifts and celebrating them.

A Day Entire

Throughout this book, we have treated the three stages of Shabbos **Stop, Look, Listen** as a unit, an indivisible triptych bestowed and accepted as one gift, whole and complete. This temporal integration is another aspect of Shabbos that is not obvious until it is lived and experienced. We all know that modernity has accentuated the rush of time, its pace and relentless momentum, but our contemporary post-industrial society, with its ubiquitous artificial illumination, has also divorced us from

---

sung in many hasidic and neo-hasidic circles. The last stanza contains the words, "Holy Shabbos! The souls of Israel find refuge in the shadow of Your wings / They are sated from the abundance of Your house." The poet takes lines from Scripture that refer to God (Ps. 36:7; 36:9) and addresses them to Shabbos.

The divinity of Shabbos is already intimated in classic rabbinic literature. The Talmud (Shabbat 12a–b) records a range of opinions about how, on Shabbos, to express one's concern for the sick while avoiding conveying anxiety or a mood of alarm inconsistent with the spirit of the day. Several *Tanna'im* suggest variations on the phrase, "May God (*HaMakom*) have mercy upon you ...." Another formula offered is: *Shabbos hi milezok urefua kerova lavo*, "It is Shabbos – a time to refrain from crying out [to God] in distress – but [don't worry] healing is sure to come soon." As Rashi explains, our goal should be to comfort and reassure the patient, evoking possibilities of healing and restoration to well-being. This last formulation has been incorporated into the synagogue liturgy as the standard prayer for the sick that is offered on Shabbos.

R. Meir (second-century *Tanna*; disciple of R. Akiva and central figure in Mishna) offers the following three-word formula: *Yekhola hi sheterahem*, "She has the ability to be merciful." As Rashi explains, honoring Shabbos by refraining from expressing distress creates a bond of reciprocity; in response to the respect accorded Her, Shabbos is moved to special compassion and focuses Her healing powers upon the patient in need. While standard theological language – evident in the rest of the passage – locates healing in the hands of God, this formula has healing performed by Shabbos. R. Meir's formulation encapsulates a view of Shabbos as divine being, with the power to heal and – equally important – with full personality and capacity to enter into benevolent, reciprocal relationships with humans.

the most natural rhythm of all – the diurnal cycle orchestrated by the movement of the sun. It is not just that Shabbos-keepers receive the gift of time; they receive *the fullness of the day*, a single parcel with clear beginning, middle, and end, rather than a mere aggregation of disconnected, isolated segments. As Emmanuel Levinas once put it in a related context, "The dispersion of time is brought back together and retied into a permanence."[5] The ever-increasing accuracy and precision of chronographic devices, coupled with their ubiquity, convenience, and the control we afford them over our lives, leads to fragmentation in our subjective temporal experience. Not only does the modern world disconnect us from place, it shatters the continuity of time, carving it into disjointed units that sit in cold, barricaded isolation from each other. We may mark twenty-four-hour periods, but these devolve into episodic intervals, neighbors that abut but do not talk to each other. When we have mindfully entered and held Shabbos space-time for an entire solar cycle, we are rewarded with a sense of arrival and attainment. We grasp a day and hold its fullness in heart and mind. All parts have reached their destination; all stages fit together. We know this because we have guided their docking and encouraged their rapport.

With Shabbos, we need not search for lost time. Shabbos time is not remembered as a thing past. Shabbos days are achieved. Shabbos transcends mere duration, rising to occasion, to palpability, to personality. The uniqueness of each Shabbos is never lost. Shabbos observance gives the seventh day a compelling narrative arc, and the story told is one of safe arrival and sacred accomplishment.

---

5. Emmanuel Levinas, "Model of the West (Tractate Menahoth 99b–100a)," in *Beyond the Verse: Talmudic Readings and Lectures*, trans. Gary D. Mole (London and New York: Continuum, 2007), 13–33; quote on 25. The talmudic passage that is the focus of Levinas's exposition discusses the *leḥem hapanim*, the Bread of the Presence or Bread of the Face, arranged on the Tabernacle's gold Table every Shabbos. In Levinas's exposition, the "Face" is not only the Presence of God, but the face-to-face communion between different priestly cohorts. "The bread exposed before God's eyes" is removed and refreshed in interpersonal relation. "The continuity is ensured by a movement of collaboration…between collaborators who know and look at each other" (p. 22). The rite of continual emplacement and replacement of the sacred bread takes place on Shabbos; see Exodus 25:23–30 and Leviticus 24:5–9.

For the Shabbos-keeper, the seventh day becomes an *entity*. Shabbos rises to the level of personhood. Shabbos will smile at you, and you will smile back.

The astronomical facts of sunset on Saturday afternoon are nearly identical with those of the preceding Friday afternoon, but the internal feelings for the Shabbos observer could not be more different. Friday's sunset has the character of a deadline, an inexorable curtain-down prodding the being into action, urging the observer home, directing all energy and attention to one aim: arrival at the destination, the Shabbos locale. A full day later, the sunset and ensuing twilight on Shabbos after Minḥa have the opposite quality. They invite lingering in the great repose, in the canopy of peace that has been spread and within which we have stretched body, spirit, and soul. The pace is now not hurried but measured, the mood lingering, the ambience enchanted, the beat *ritardando*. One is peripherally aware of the week to come, the challenges that will soon arrive, and one wishes to tarry in the presence of sacred silence, to luxuriate a bit longer in the stillness of one's soul and in the presence of beloved company, divine and human, to feel the equipoise and inhabit it just a bit more deeply. This inner landscape, this richly saturated spectrum of temporal hues, is the phenomenology of experience that Shabbos observance yields as gift. Nothing is more satisfying than to be able to savor a day in its fullness, to contemplate its entirety, admire its timbres.

We come to the gifts of Shabbos honestly when we offer the most precious thing we have, the only irreplaceable element of life – time. We do so in confidence that every gift to God is accepted and then restored to us, immediately, with overflowing love, from a dispensation beyond infinity.

Going Beyond the Self

Shabbos moves individuals and communities from self-cultivation to self-transcendence.

Moving from self-absorption to self-improvement and then to self-transcendence is release from bondage. When you resolve to curtail a habit such as overuse of social media by vowing to unplug one day a week, you may chafe against the imposed constraint and eventually feel compelled to break your commitment. But when you cherish Shabbos as a gift from a place beyond this world and observe Shabbos as an offering of sweetness and grace, you grasp something beyond yourself. You grow in ways that self-cultivation alone cannot imagine.

Of course, Shabbos has enormous material benefits, but overemphasizing these may cause the pivotal spiritual core to be muffled. To draw a rough analogy, it may or may not be the case that having young children listen to Mozart will raise their IQ (I doubt it), but be that as it may, such utilitarian motivations are unlikely to foster a sustained love of music, to inspire a life of concert-going or a vocation in performance. To give another example, it may be true that married people live longer on average than unmarrieds, but a clergyperson officiating at a wedding would be ill-advised to tout this information while conducting the ceremony, where the focus needs to be love, sacred commitment, and mutual devotion. What must be foregrounded is an aspirational horizon of noble purpose beyond the immediately functional and flatly pragmatic. What you achieve in marriage is committed love with your covenanted partner. What you get from music is … music. The deeper your engagement, the more your heart will open, the more you will hear, the more your soul will flower.

What you receive from Shabbos is – Shabbos. This is a gift beyond measure.[6]

---

6. In an essay published shortly before his death, famed neurologist Oliver Sacks reminisced about his childhood in London, with special focus on his family's observance of Shabbos, permeated with religious reverence and warmth. A painful rupture with his mother led to his rejection of religion in general and his abandonment of Shabbos in particular. Sacks recalls the inner emptiness and lack of meaning that ensued, partially ameliorated by his healing vocation and his craft of narrative medical writing. It took six decades for a rapprochement with his family to occur, brought about by his cousin, the eminent economist Robert John Aumann. Sacks was deeply moved when the strictly observant Aumann welcomed him and his partner in Jerusalem for a Shabbos meal. Sacks experienced this as a homecoming after an estrangement of sixty years, not only to his family, but to Shabbos, to Shabbos's peace, "to a stopped world." Sacks quotes Aumann as saying, "The observance of the Sabbath is extremely beautiful, and is impossible without being religious." Aumann's commitment to Shabbos was absolute, not subordinate to personal interest or advancement. This was manifest when Aumann was awarded the Nobel Prize and special arrangements

TO LINGER INTENTLY

The Russian literary critic Mikhail Bakhtin writes:

> Lovelessness, indifference, will never be able to generate sufficient power to slow down and *linger intently* over an object, to hold and sculpt every detail and particular in it, however minute. Only love is capable of being aesthetically productive; only in correlation with the loved is fullness of the manifold possible.[7]

To the Shabbos-keeper, it is love of God, love of Shabbos, and the reciprocity that we feel – God's love for us, Shabbos's caressing presence in our lives – that makes for what Bakhtin calls "the fullness of the manifold," the totally expansive yet utterly focused wonder of being.

To frame Shabbos as mere leisure time, to mistake Shabbos for weekend or day off, is to make a category error. Rephrasing Bakhtin, we may say that fitful, desultory periods of relaxation and diversion will never be able to generate sufficient power to enable us to slow down and linger intently over our time and place in the world, to hold and sculpt every detail and particular. Time earnestly cleared will quickly fill with the week's detritus if not centered in sacred purpose. Only *bless* and *hallow*, only *remember* and *safeguard*, can hold the place reserved as a day unencumbered by distraction. Only covenantal commitment and collective intentionality will join individual households into a convivial community. This is the Jewish inheritance of Shabbos, unique in all the world.

---

were made so that his trip to the ceremony would be fully in accord with halakha. Sacks notes with evident admiration that had the trip involved violation of Shabbos, Aumann would have refused the prize. "His commitment to the Sabbath, its utter peacefulness and remoteness from worldly concerns, would have trumped even a Nobel." The essay – titled "Sabbath," published in the *New York Times*, August 14, 2015, and included in the collection *Gratitude* (Knopf) – was Sacks's last published writing.

7. Mikhail M. Bakhtin, *Toward a Philosophy of the Act*, trans. and notes by Vadim Liapunov, ed. Michael Holquist and Vadim Liapunov (Austin: University of Texas Press, 1993), 64. I am grateful to Rabbi Jordan Shuster for pointing me to this wonderful passage.

Chapter 9

Shabbos for the Whole World – The Fate of the Earth: Aspirational Thoughts

War is the ultimate stain on the human condition. Famine and epidemics cause death on a massive scale, and they are often the direct consequence of war and the ensuing collapse of governance and social order. As a totalizing event, war consumes all in its path and knows no boundaries. Throughout history, wars have begun with the idea that they would be short and limited, only to grind on for years or even decades. Moral constraints are swept away as each side becomes more enraged by the brutality of the other side, more convinced of its own rectitude, more desperate to "win." Weapons and tactics that were shunned as unconventional and immoral are reclassified as necessary and quickly become conventional and routine.

Universal Shabbos observance would entail the cessation of war. This is the vision of the Hebrew prophets, articulated most vividly in the final chapters of Isaiah. This vision may seem utopian, unrealizable in the world as presently constituted, but we need not wait for the eschaton to begin to implement this prophetic vision. Keeping Shabbos calls for bracketing the world of competitiveness in all its forms. If everyone felt secure and calm in their own place, there would be no need to seize the place of another.[1] Hasidic masters teach that allowing anger to inflame one's emotions to the point of losing control is a form of violating Exodus 35:3, "You shall kindle no fire throughout your habitations on the Shabbos day."[2]

If my Shabbos repose requires me to maintain congeniality and friendship with all in my ambit, this must hold not only for Shabbos itself, but for weekdays as well. Spousal spats, family feuds, and neighborhood rows would be self-limiting. Firebreaks are set in place with the awareness that Shabbos is coming, and all will need to make peace with their erstwhile antagonists.

The penultimate verse of Song of Songs reads: "O you who dwell in the gardens, companions are attentive to your voice; let me hear it" (Song. 8:13). The Midrash in Song of Songs Rabba understands this verse as alluding to Shabbos, when the people Israel gathers for prayer and communal Torah reading. God takes pride in the people's vocal offerings and says to them, "Raise your voices so that the companions may hear." According to one view in the midrash, the "companions" are the angels, who hover above the people and bear witness to their pious devotion. Another view is more earth-centered: The "companions" are the members of the community themselves. They are enjoined to be respectfully attentive to one another and to avoid hatred, jealousy, quarreling, and shaming. As the commentary of Rabbi David Luria (early nineteenth century, Lithuania) on this passage puts it, the members of

---

1. See Rabbi Mordecai Yosef Elazar Leiner (Izbica-Radzin), *Tiferet Yosef* (Bnei Brak, 1997), 132, *Haftarat Mahar Hodesh*.

2. See Rabbi Itamar ben Yisrael of Konskivalli, *Mishmeret Itamar* (Jerusalem, 2007), *Parashat Vayak'hel*, 317; Rabbi Yaakov Leiner of Izbica, *Beit Yaakov* ([Lublin, 1906] Brooklyn, 1976), 53, based on *Shelah* and *Tikkunei Zohar*, *Tikkun* no. 48.

a Shabbos community must be devoted friends, genuinely listening to one another, so that each may lovingly fulfill the wishes of his or her companions. Then the voices raised are truly angelic, and the communal garden within which they reside is indeed paradisic. Similarly, another midrashic text avers that Shabbos is the time when breadwinners who may be distant from their families during the week are reconciled with and favorably received by their children and households on Shabbos.[3]

What is true for families and communities is true for nations. Early on during the Maccabean revolt, the Jews allowed themselves to be killed rather than fight on Shabbos (I Maccabees 2:31–38). In the aftermath of this catastrophe, Mattathias and his friends mourned the martyrs deeply and decided to fight in self-defense if attacked on Shabbos, so as not to be "destroyed from the earth" (2:40–41). The text preserves the initial shock of the Jews that the enemy did not respect the Jews' religious commitment by displaying deference to the holiness of Shabbos. The thousand men, women, and children who were massacred on Shabbos without offering any defense are quoted as saying, "Let us all die in our innocence; heaven and earth are testifying for us that you are killing us unjustly" (2:37). The Maccabees were finally compelled to fight on Shabbos because their enemy left them no choice. However, if two Shabbos-abiding nations were tempted to engage in conflict, their shared Shabbos observance would be a natural check against the fateful decision to go to war. Since the only sure way to limit a war is to refrain from starting it in the first place, Shabbos-consciousness would effectively rule out the first shots.

What is true of nations certainly holds for neighborhoods and families. The knowledge that I will be spending Shabbos with someone persuades me to come to terms with that person during the week. Isaiah's ideal of world peace and worship of the God of Israel at the Jerusalem Sanctuary is linked by the prophet with universal reverence for Shabbos. It is easy to dismiss this as the musings of a naïve visionary, but those who have tasted the serene enchantment wrought as Shabbos settles into their homes and hearts know that Shabbos rapture is utterly compelling yet totally gentle. Peace and Shabbos go together.

---

3. *Tanna DeVei Eliyahu*, 1.

They are two words that say the same thing. As the adage advises, we should become the change we wish to see. Shabbos is the best hope for individuals and for nations.

The first chapter of Genesis suggests that humanity's link to Shabbos holds the key to the fate of the earth. On day six of creation we read, "And God said, 'Let us make the human in our image, in our likeness'" (Gen. 1:26). Classic rabbinic sources develop this verse's suggestion that creation was a consultative process. The Talmud states that all creatures gave their consent before being created.[4] This is a rabbinic way of saying that existence is considered advantageous in and of itself. Rabbinic thought, so deeply rooted in the Bible, sees the very fact of being as the ultimate bestowal, the greatest gift. The eagerness to exist is manifest in every creature. The Rabbis perceived an essential, inescapable joy-of-being residing in every organism.

Taking up this theme, the hasidic master Rabbi Yaakov Leiner (1828–1878) writes that God asked creatures if they wanted to be brought into existence. Apparently, they all responded affirmatively, at least those that are now part of our cosmos. However, while all beings were consulted before being made, no individual creature was asked to give consent to the making of any other creature. Since the abundance and diversity of the world is of manifest benefit to all, mutual agreement was a foregone conclusion.[5] That is to say that all creatures are tacitly in a state of concord with all others; the plenitude of creation benefits each one individually as well as collectively.

A corollary of this is that no single organism can imperil the entirety of creation. There is one exception: the human being. Because humans are endowed with freedom of will, they have the capacity to damage all other life forms; indeed they can imperil the entire world. God therefore solicited the advice and consent of creation as a whole before making humans; each life form contributed an aspect of its energy and potential as a component of human endowment.[6] While

---

4. Rosh HaShana 11a.
5. Rabbi Yaakov Leiner, *Beit Yaakov al HaTorah, Sefer Bereshit* ([Warsaw: Hayim Kelter, 1890] Jerusalem, 1998), s.v. *vayomer Elohim naaseh adam*, p. 26, no. 41, on Genesis 1:26.
6. Ibid.

this inclusivity is no guarantee against human overreach and malfeasance, it provides a hopeful sensitization against complete disregard of other creatures. Inter-inclusion serves to heighten awareness that human flourishing depends on protecting the earth in its plenitude and that the destiny of humanity is inseparable from the destiny of all other creatures.

This is precisely how to understand the sabbatical principle. Shabbos establishes limits and halts the impulse to expansion (Gen. 2:1–3). Shabbos summons to respect all creatures, non-human as well as human. Shabbos's invitation to steadfastness and staying in place confers dignity, power, and grace on everyone and everything. Indeed, nothing is merely a "thing" on Shabbos; sparks of holiness and blessing rise to the surface and make just claim upon us to be humbly appreciative instead of extractive. Shabbos is not only the capstone of creation, Shabbos is creation's ultimate protector and sentinel.

SHABBOS APPRECIATION FOR ALL

The promise of Shabbos is meant for all people, not only for Jews.[7] Yet Jews heard the sweet and noble call of Shabbos first, as biblical and early historical sources attest. The Shabbos liturgy repeatedly refers to Shabbos as the Jewish heritage, our most treasured heirloom (*ḥemdat yamim*). While the seven-day cycle has been adopted by all humanity, Jews have inherited Shabbos in its most robust form, comprising a full palette of sacred states and realizations – ritual, liturgy, celebration, social filiation, family bonding, hospitality, community building, table melodies, worldwide shared cycle of scriptural readings, and, as this book has emphasized, commitment to one place for a full period of evening-morning-evening. If Jews do not devote themselves to cultivating this heritage of panoramic, all-embracing practice, no one will. The more that Jews commit to Shabbos, the more blessing will redound not only to themselves but to the world.

The British philosopher Adrian William Moore has written about a circumstance of fully "embracing" or being fully engaged with a concept. By this he means going beyond merely understanding the concept as an insightful observer. According to Moore, fully embracing a concept

---

7. See Isaiah 56:3, 7; 66:23.

involves applying it "in how one thinks about the world and in how one conducts one's affairs. What this requires, roughly, is sharing whatever beliefs, concerns, and values give application of the concept its point." He illustrates his idea with Shabbos, which he refers to as the Sabbath. He writes that while the concept of the Sabbath may readily be grasped, "only a Jewish person recognizing an obligation to keep the Sabbath can grasp the concept in an engaged way. We might say that such a person *lives by* the concept."[8]

In recent years, it has become popular to motivate Shabbos observance by stressing the need to decouple from technology, and this is indeed a pressing concern, as we have noted throughout this book. However, pragmatic arguments unrooted in the deep and fertile soil of religious tradition are unlikely to bear long-lasting fruit. Contemporary scholar Ellen Davis, addressing the temptation to promote Shabbos merely as a hedge against overwork and burnout, notes that "Exodus enjoins Sabbath observance on theological, not pastoral, grounds." She writes that keeping the day holy enables us to "consider what it is to be the creatures of God, living among other creatures in a world that God has made. We are not our own, and we are not in charge."[9] "Sabbath is designed for one purpose only, to bring humans into intimate contact with God."[10] This intimacy will bring blessing on all levels, including the material, but our aspirational gaze must always be directed toward the sacred.

Davis's readings of biblical texts are deeply congenial to Jewish practices and perspectives. Regarding Shabbos, she writes that "the blessing of Sabbath is a striking indication of God's desire for a non-utilitarian relationship with the human creature."[11] Like a parent who simply wants to be close to their child for no particular reason, on Shabbos God takes pure delight in our company.

---

8. Adrian Moore, "Maxims and Thick Ethical Concepts," *Ratio* (New Series) 19 (2006): 129–47, at 137. Moore draws upon the work of Bernard Williams. My quotes are from Peter Goldie, "Thick Concepts and Emotion," in *Reading Bernard Williams*, ed. Daniel Callcut (London and New York: Routledge, 2009), 96–97.
9. Ellen Davis, *Opening Israel's Scriptures* (New York: Oxford University Press, 2019), 56.
10. Ibid., 12.
11. Ibid., 13.

The blessings of Shabbos are intended for the entire world, but Jews would do well to be particularly mindful of them, cherishing their ancestral legacy with care and dedication. As Davis writes, the Israelites and Judeans who would eventually come to be known as Jews "are the only peoples of the biblical world to retain their religious identity, despite losing their national territory and independent monarchy, the religious apparatus of the temple, and a functioning priesthood. This is something of a historical miracle."[12] This miracle is surely related to the enduring memory and ongoing vitality of the biblical covenant with God, a trace of which may be discerned in even nominally secular Jewish persons. More than anything else, this vitality is grounded on, and nourished by, Shabbos observance.

As mentioned above, the two versions of the Decalogue – in Exodus and in Deuteronomy – have different presentations of the Shabbos commandment. Exodus 20:8 tells us to "Remember (*zakhor*) the Shabbos day, to hallow it," whereas Deuteronomy 5:12 has, "Safeguard/ observe (*shamor*) the Shabbos day, to hallow it." The Midrash *Pesikta Rabbati* parses the distinction between the two versions in several ways, but the one attributed to R. Yudan (fourth-century *Amora* of the Land of Israel) is particularly relevant for our discussion: "*Zakhor* is for non-Jews; *shamor* is for the people Israel." That is, all peoples are asked to remember Shabbos, to bring Shabbos-consciousness into their lives, honoring the Godly time signature inscribed in creation (Gen. 2:1–3), but the full complement of observances is the distinctive calling of Israel. Indeed, the ongoing maintenance and flourishing of Shabbos-awareness in the entire world, with all the blessing this entails, is grounded in Jewish faithfulness to the crown jewel of their covenant with God.[13]

---

12. Ibid., 126.

13. Some readers will be familiar with rabbinic dicta that restrict Shabbos to Jews; see, for example, Reish Lakish's statement in Sanhedrin 58a severely sanctioning Shabbos observance by non-Jews. Deuteronomy Rabba 1:18 compares a non-Jew who observes Shabbos without converting to Judaism to someone who interposes himself between a king and queen while they are sitting and having a private conversation. Shabbos is the intimate conversation between God and Israel; this is the import of Exodus 31:17, "Between Me and the children of Israel, it [Shabbos] is an eternal sign."

HOLINESS IS CONTAGIOUS!

In the prophetic view, Jews are charged with bringing knowledge of God to all creation, connecting all creatures with God.

An early midrash records the following story:

> Our teacher R. Judah the Patriarch made a meal for Antoninus on Shabbos. Cold dishes were set before him; he ate them, and he found them delicious. [On another occasion] he made a meal for him during the week, when hot dishes were set before him. Antoninus said to R. Judah, "I enjoyed those others more." R. Judah replied, "These lack a certain condiment." Antoninus exclaimed, "Does the royal pantry lack anything?" R. Judah replied, "They lack Shabbos. Do you possess Shabbos?"[14]

Yet there is more to the story. Beitza 16a suggests that the entire world is expected to observe Shabbos. Rashi, Yevamot 48b, s.v. *ger toshav,* asserts that a *ger toshav* – a non-Jew committed to monotheism and ethical conduct – is expected to observe Shabbos. Rashi explains that the commitment to monotheism means foreswearing idolatry, and, Rashi continues, "Shabbos violation is tantamount to idolatry."

The tannaitic Midrash *Mekhilta DeRabbi Ishmael, Tractate Kaspa* on Exodus 23:12 (ed. Lauterbach, vol. 3, 178) states that a *ger toshav* observes Shabbos in the same manner that Jews observe holy days – that is, refraining from weekday *melakha* with the exception of food preparation and similar immediate needs. See also Keritot 9a, quoting R. Akiva with the same view – the *ger toshav* keeps Shabbos like Israelites with the exception of those activities permitted on Yom Tov. As for the meaning of *ger toshav,* the *Tanna* R. Meir says this involves a formal acceptance of monotheism; other Sages say that in addition, the *ger toshav* accepts the basic ethical commitments called the Noahide laws. Rashi throughout his corpus explains *ger toshav* as referring to any person who foreswears idolatry. See *Talmudic Encyclopedia,* vol. 6, 289–90, especially n. 7. All this indicates that the Rabbis see Shabbos in some aspect as essentially universal, not limited to Jews. To be sure, the full complement of Shabbos celebratory rites, observances, and practices is seen as the unique expression of covenantal relationship between Israel and God.

Transitioning from the classic rabbinic period to the teachings of Hasidism, it is clear that Shabbos-consciousness is meant to percolate from the Jewish people to the entire world.

14. Genesis Rabba 11:4 on Genesis 2:3. There may be a subtle pun at play here. R. Judah may be playing gently with his guest's question. As *Arukh* points out, SH-B-T is actually the name of a spice, a condiment. The Lublin 1922 edition suggests this is anise; Jastrow translates "dill."

The Roman guest Antoninus assumes that the savory delight he experiences is a condiment, a secret ingredient. But R. Judah wishes to disabuse him – that is, us the readers – of the idea that a particular ingredient by itself imparts the special taste of Shabbos.

The *Pesikta Rabbati* has a variant of the story:

> When R. Judah the Patriarch entertained the emperor Antoninus, he would serve him cold dishes on Shabbos and hot dishes on weekdays. Antoninus used to say, "I find the cold dishes tastier than the hot ones." R. Judah would reply, "The hot dishes lack a certain ingredient." Antoninus said, "Can there be anything at all lacking in the king's pantry?" R. Judah responded, "But how am I to put into weekday dishes the ingredients of 'blessing' and 'hallowing,' as indicated in the verse, 'And God blessed the seventh day, and hallowed it' (Gen. 2:3)"?

A similar story appears in the Talmud, where the ending is, "[The seasoning] is only effective for someone who keeps Shabbos, but it does not work for those who do not keep Shabbos."[15]

The story in its several versions gently refutes the idea that the savor of Shabbos can be reduced to a formula, to an ingredient or procedure that can be isolated from its sacred context and decanted with the same beneficial effect. It was because Emperor Antoninus was immersed in the ambience of R. Judah's Shabbos that he was able to savor the taste and aroma of Shabbos. The taste that Antoninus noticed was not mere gustatory sensation; it was the taste of life itself. With Shabbos, life has meaning, buoyancy, direction, telos. An inner smile radiates from the heart and is met by warmth reflected from the world.

Furthermore, the story of R. Judah and Emperor Antoninus teaches us that all guests are most welcome at the Shabbos table, even or perhaps especially those who are not Shabbos-keepers. This gives them the opportunity to perceive the beauty and nobility of Shabbos and to experience the sensual aura Shabbos imparts. There will likely be a desire on the part of the guests to learn the secret of this palpable

---

15. Shabbat 119a.

richness and make it available in other times and places. The guest's search for the condiment represents the search for a tangible object that might be secured, a potion to magically reproduce Shabbos's inner serenity and delight. But, as the story concludes, only immersion in the totality of Shabbos with blessing and holiness can produce the desired effects. The sweet delight is not reducible to an extractable formula; it cannot be captured in a bottle. To receive the blessing and the sanctity, one must align oneself with the verse, "And God blessed the seventh day and hallowed it." As the version in the Talmud puts it, the special Shabbos condiment only works for Shabbos-keepers.[16]

You can speak the language of Shabbos with fluency and confidence. This requires entering the practice with discipline and commitment, in humble relationship with the community that has kept Shabbos from inception. The more fluidly you speak the language of Shabbos, the more sweetly you sing Shabbos's melody, the more you will find your voice. You will join with other voices in Shabbos community, and your collective chorus will be heard by all.

Shabbos is the Jewish heirloom practice. Nothing reveals wisdom and noble purpose more than reclaiming one's heritage. When anchored

---

16. In a recent essay, Seventh-Day Adventist theologian Jacques B. Doukhan urges his co-religionists, who mark the biblical Sabbath on the seventh day of the week, to continue to learn from Jewish practice. He writes: "The Jewish testimony about the Sabbath sounds much louder in the world than the one by [Adventists]." Doukhan notes five aspects of Jewish observance that, he asserts, Adventists would do well to consider: (1) Beauty (honoring Shabbos with one's finest objects and with all one's senses); (2) Food (sacred eating: "eat the day itself!"); (3) Relationship (with God, with community); (4) Grace (slowing down, expanding time for study, prayer, reflection); (5) Hope (Shabbos as foretaste of the World to Come, pointing to "another order"). Doukhan quotes from Heschel, as well as from Rabbi Nahman of Bratslav: "When we experience the holiness of Shabbat, we attain the highest levels of *daat*, of knowing God. And the highest level of this *daat*-consciousness that we can achieve is the realization that God is altogether incomprehensible" (*Likutei Moharan* II, 83). Doukhan's essay, "What Can Adventism Learn from the Jews About the Sabbath," *Spectrum* 39.1 (2011): 15–20, illustrates the ongoing power of robust Jewish Shabbos observance to inspire non-Jews. If Jews are to fulfill their calling to share Shabbos with the world, they need to deepen their own Shabbos practice and enhance their commitment to it.

in blessing and holiness, Shabbos produces the ultimate contact high, a domain of peace for which the world hungers.

HOLY COVETING

The last utterance of the Decalogue directs: *Lo taḥmod*, "Do not covet" (Ex. 20:14). But the Talmud qualifies this with the observation that envying a sage's knowledge is a good thing; it acts as a spur to the growth of wisdom. In a similar way, we might consider what in our practice of Shabbos inspires noble desire, admirable coveting. How might a spiritual seeker, who heard of Shabbos as "day of rest" in a functional sense, discover the sublime horizons that Shabbos affords? How might we make Shabbos even more radiant, more beautiful, more transformative? The answer surely has little to do with elegance of table settings or sumptuousness of cuisine, and everything to do with palpable blessing and sanctity, with welcoming smiles, with sweet melodies, with wise speech and even wiser silence.

In this spirit, I propose what might be called holy coveting for the unrealized potential in Judaism, in particular with regard to Shabbos. In the phrase of the siddur, Shabbos is *hemdat yamim*, "most cherished of days" or "most desirable of days."[17] There is an ancient tradition cited by Rashi, *Baal HaTurim,* and *Or HaḤayim* that the phrase should be understood as, "most coveted of days/most envied of days."[18] This is grounded in a provocative reading of Genesis 2:1, "*Vayekhal Elohim bayom hashevi'i,*" as "God introduced [holy] envy on the seventh day."[19] I understand this to mean: By creating the seventh

---

17. The first translation is from *Koren Siddur*, 532; the second is from ibid., 598.
18. See the impressive range of sources collected by Rabbi Menahem Mendel Kasher in *Torah Shelema* (Jerusalem: Torah Shelema Institute, 5752/1992), vol. 1, 183, no. 11; and 186, no. 26. The earliest version is a no longer extant Targum Yerushalmi quoted by the medieval authorities: *Vehamad Hashem bayom hashevi'i,* "God coveted on the seventh day." The formulation in Numbers Rabba is that "God had yearning (*nishtokek*) to create the world," whose beauty emerged most splendidly on Shabbos: *Ein vayekhulu ela lashon taava,* "The word *vayekhulu* means nothing other than intense desire, craving." God has an intense desire for Shabbos!
19. To buttress this reading, the sources cite Psalms 84:3: *Nikhsefa vegam kaleta nafshi leḥatzerot Hashem,* "My soul yearns, indeed it expires in longing for the courtyards of the LORD."

day with its ampliative, alluringly unfolding blessing and holiness, God introduced the principle of holy coveting into the world. We are permitted, indeed invited, to covet a Shabbos yet-to-be: a Shabbos more alive with a spirit of generosity and openheartedness; a Shabbos more abounding with blessing, tranquility, repose; a Shabbos of richer *niggun, zemirot*, listening, and learning, of eloquently resonant silences and of joyously buoyant words; a Shabbos on which more and more co-religionists surrender the automobile and electronics for a full day; a Shabbos of interpersonal availability; a Shabbos of presence; a Shabbos *uninterrupted*.

This is possible without censorious admonition. My model here is Yom Kippur in Israel. Out of respect for the sanctity of the day, all motorized traffic stops. There are no cars, busses, or trucks on the streets, even in large, predominantly secular cities such as Tel Aviv. The mood of solemnity and introspection is pervasive, palpable even for those who do not think of themselves as religious in the conventional sense. What is most remarkable is that the cessation is achieved by universal consent, not by official mandate. No Knesset law, no municipal regulation, no ruling from the office of the Chief Rabbinate makes a demand that motor traffic cease. The stillness that ensues – the absence of shifting gears, of tires against asphalt, of screeching brakes, of impatient drivers leaning on horns – arises naturally, by consensus.

I learned about Tel Aviv on Yom Kippur from a former Bostonian who made aliya and now lives in the Neve Tzedek neighborhood in that metropolis, who writes vivid letters of her experiences to her friends back in the States. Speaking of the mood of serenity that prevails, she writes: "Ben-Gurion Airport is closed on Yom Kippur, so we didn't hear the usual roar of the commercial flights over Tel Aviv on their final approach to the airport. Of course, all businesses are closed, too. I also noticed there was no loud music coming from private homes. It was surreally quiet!"[20]

What an impact it would make if this serenity were to be achieved, by mutual concord, not only on Yom Kippur, but every Shabbos!

---

20. Anne Dubitsky, letter dated October 5, 2014.

THE GRACES OF SURRENDER

Like all coveted states such as happiness, Shabbos endowments are best attained by not striving to possess them. The Shabbos graces are bestowed upon those who seek Shabbos out of love and hear the call of holiness, rather than those who seek reward, whether material or spiritual.

Now at the end of our journey, it is worthwhile revisiting Michael Polanyi's work *Personal Knowledge*. Polanyi speaks of the energies of mental companionship released by sharing "a convivial passion for others greater than themselves, within a like-minded community – the partners must belong to each other by participating in a reverence for a common superior knowledge."

Polanyi speaks of a "family of things which exist only for those committed to them" and the recognition that arises from submission to excellence and respect for it. Polanyi is referring to scientific knowledge and cultural excellence. His ideas on tacit knowledge address philosophy of science, but they hover at the edge of the religious spirit. Like many Jews of Hungarian origin at his time, he grew up almost entirely devoid of knowledge of the sources of Judaism,[21] but his ideas find resonance here.[22] The awareness that Shabbos creates is a tacit knowledge, one that we should not be shy to call the inhabitation of the Divine Presence. As Rabbi Menahem Nahum of Chernobyl writes in *Meor Einayim*, in order to prepare for Shabbos, we must leave every trace of small-mindedness behind, filling our hearts with expansive awareness and acceptance. When we do so, the turbulence and distractions of mundane existence fall away and we are able to internalize Shabbos sanctity, which is effectively to "bring the Creator into one's heart and commune with God."[23]

---

21. See Paul Knepper, "Michael Polanyi and Jewish Identity," *Philosophy of the Social Sciences* 35, no. 3 (2005): 263–93.

22. For some of the religious implications of Polanyi's thought, see Douglas Adams and Phil Mullins, "Conscience, Tacit Knowledge, and the Art of Judgement: Implications of Polanyi's Thought for Moral Reflection," *Soundings: An Interdisciplinary Journal* 66, no. 1 (1983): 33–45.

23. Hebrew: *Makhnis haBorei belevavo umityahed im Bore'o*. See *Meor Einayim, Parashat Vayak'hel*, s.v. *kol hame'aneg et haShabbat notenim lo mishalot libo*, p. 345.

It is the palpability of this Presence that transforms the person from within, that banishes psychological habituation and somatic addiction.

This, I believe, explains at least in part the transformation I witnessed in my father, from someone chained to tobacco into a person whose lungs and body were free and clear one day a week. Submission to the sacred elevates and frees both body and soul.

Coda

Full Stop. Full Day. Full Embrace.

T he time has come to summarize the main points of our journey to Shabbos, share some closing thoughts, and make a few suggestions. Back in the preface I posed questions that this book might help answer. I reprise them here for convenience:

> What is the core of Shabbos experience? How can it be cultivated, sustained, enhanced? What is the most effective way to introduce Shabbos to those not familiar with it? What is the best way to explain Shabbos to newcomers as well as to those who have grown up with it, who consider themselves veterans but may be in danger of lapsing into habit and taking Shabbos for granted?

For newcomers to the Shabbos modality presented here, I suspect the main innovation – actually an ancient practice waiting to be revived – is Shabbos as *destination*, involving arrival at a location on Friday afternoon before sunset, settling in, and remaining at that location until nightfall the following day. When done in concert with a like-minded group, you become an ensemble of co-celebrants who join to form a Shabbos environment, a habitat of repose, a sanctuary domain. This changes everything. Nothing sculpts weekdays more powerfully than the awareness that you and others – family and friends – are physically in transit to a destination that you have collectively committed to.

Those who have grown up with Shabbos and consider themselves totally familiar with the laws and customs may be surprised to hear that they might have much to learn. There is a danger of lapsing into habit and taking Shabbos for granted. As the hasidic master Rabbi Menahem Nahum of Chernobyl emphasizes, one's internal state is as important as external observances. The goal of Shabbos is mindful awareness that aligns with bodily repose. One must speak differently on Shabbos, with graciousness and kindness, with understanding of people whom one is tempted to dismiss as different. On Shabbos, we avoid language that disparages or belittles. Our elevated speech should reflect the benevolence that has settled in our hearts. We arrive to a place of greater nobility, to a disposition of hospitality, acceptance, and embrace.

REFUGE

Both veterans and newcomers need to make sure that business concerns and traces of commercial entanglement are entirely absent. Shabbos space is robust, powerful, and transformative, but also delicate and vulnerable. There is a lesson to be learned here from another biblical institution, the "city of refuge." Discussed at least six times throughout the Bible,[1] the cities of refuge were sanctuary cities in the land of Israel where certain individuals in danger of violent retribution could find safety from their pursuers. Rabbinic exegesis, elaborating on the already rich biblical material, emphasizes that these cities were to be places of culture and learning, urban centers of wisdom and ethical life. One further point, of particular relevance to Shabbos, is made in *Sifrei Zuta*, an early rabbinic Midrash. Noting the insistent repetition of the word *tihiyena* ("let them be") in Numbers 35 (vv. 11, 13, 14, 15 – a total of

---

1. Exodus 21:13; Numbers 35:9–34; Deuteronomy 4:41–43; 19:1–10; Joshua 20:1–9; I Chronicles 6:42.

four times), the midrash glosses: "Fight for them"; "support them"; "If destroyed, rebuild them." In addition, the midrash mandates that factories must not be located in cities of refuge. The suggestion is that there is a temptation to co-opt these special places for some utilitarian purpose. This temptation must be resisted. We must fight to preserve the cities of refuge from encroachment, misuse, or neglect. Precisely because the city of refuge has a preferred status as an asylum and is so attractive in its quiet nature, there will be temptation to site it for a commercial center that would change its character and erode its purpose. We must fight to preserve the character of these special places.

In our world, we can think of cities of refuge as resources and institutions where we can retire for spiritual sustenance, stillness, and refreshment. One example is the United States system of National Parks, considered the "crown jewels" of America. These protected areas are places of great natural beauty, unique ecosystems richly endowed with flora, fauna, and minerals. Precisely for that reason, there have been attempts throughout the history of the parks to exploit them for various commercial purposes, to turn them over to developers or extract their resources for profit-oriented industries. Fortunately, the parks are considered public trusts and have inspired a network of advocates who defend them against exploitation, by means of legal representation, legislative initiatives, and educational activities. Nothing can be taken for granted; the threats are constant and ongoing, and those who love the parks and the wilderness must remain vigilant.

The greatest "city of refuge" we have is Shabbos. As the midrash suggests, precisely because Shabbos presents such an attractive, uncluttered space of buoyant openness, temptation will arise to co-opt it. The Shabbos observer must be a vigilant defender of Shabbos space as a sacred trust from the primordial past and unique legacy for the future. You have worked hard to clear this paradisic domain. Safeguard it from encroachment; avoid the temptation to pave your paradise and put up a parking lot.

THE PALPABILITY OF EMPTINESS

The delicacy and fragility of Shabbos are associated with Shabbos's core feature: *desisting*. It is true that we celebrate the arrival of Shabbos with our finest food, clothing, and décor. Shabbos is greeted as royalty, serenaded and saluted with poems, prayers, and praises. Still, the essence of our welcoming Shabbos is not what we do, but what we don't do. We arrive at our destination and we stop. We desist. This, after all, is the meaning of the Hebrew SH-B-T.

This can be compared to the way that the Bible, especially the book of Leviticus, makes the Presence of God, the Glory (*Kavod*), palpable to readers. God is never graphically portrayed (the prohibition against iconic images applies to depictions of the God of Israel), but rather circumscribed, afforded a welcoming location. The partitioning of space and the sacred gradient marked by curtains and veils of the Tabernacle (and later, the walls of the Temple) comprise the arena where the sacred drama unfolds and wherein the unseen Glory can reside. The Tabernacle and its elements are an encirclement of the Presence; they do not capture, define, or delimit, but cradle the space where the Glory settles. In the Torah's description of the Tabernacle and its furnishings (starting at Ex. 25), the Glory is surrounded by physical objects: altars, Menora, Table with "Bread of the Presence," fragrant incense. The Holy of Holies holds the Ark of the Covenant, containing stone tablets with the words of the Decalogue in God's own handwriting; atop the Ark is the gold plate, *Kapporet*, from which emerge Cherubim and toward which all Yom Kippur sacraments are directed (see Lev. 16). Together they form an envelope that shapes perception of what is beyond perception. In the Second Temple, the Ark was absent, and the Holy of Holies was entirely empty.

Just as the Tabernacle's architecture and furnishings encompass the Divine Presence in space, while the space so defined is left unfilled by anything humans might supply, so do material items (candles, ḥalla, Kiddush cup with wine, fragrant spices, etc.), together with the rites that make use of them, help to define Shabbos space and mark it off as distinct and special, but the essence of Shabbos is entirely intangible. More fundamentally still, Shabbos is circumscribed by all the maker-activities that fill our six-day workaday lives, from which we mindfully desist as the sun sets Friday. The act of desisting is the compass that creates the blessed Shabbos circle in time. The circle is festooned with tangible objects as attractive and beautiful as we can make them, but its core is emptiness, which is not empty at all, but rather the inhabitation of the Absolute. Absence both hides and reveals Plenitude, and this awareness dawns slowly, gradually, calling for the most exquisite attentiveness on the part of those who wish to embrace Shabbos.

Such is the deep nature of Shabbos's vulnerability. It is said that nature abhors a vacuum, and Shabbos is the vacuum that must not be cluttered with the detritus of the week if we are to discern the plenitude of Presence. Every Shabbos arrives with the label: "Fragile: Handle with Care."

This, I believe, is the meaning of Exodus 31:17, with the first-person voice of God speaking: "Between Me and the children of Israel it [Shabbos] is an eternal sign, that in a six-day period God made the heavens and the earth, and on the seventh day desisted and was refreshed." The word "sign" in Hebrew is *ot*, usually meaning a visible indicator, such as a written letter or other graphic mark. But what is this mark that makes Shabbos visible to the eye? The weekday activities that come to a halt when Shabbos arrives are what make Shabbos manifest, just as God's desisting from maker-activity of creation brought the original Shabbos into the world (Gen. 2:1–3).[2] By desisting from weekday activity, you are realizing the Maker's mark in time; you are re-inscribing the *ot*. Shabbos is the temporal mark of aniconic Presence, visible in seeming absence. No wonder Shabbos is so delicate!

Shabbos observance is challenging, perhaps especially for those who have grown up with it. It is not just that it is easy to lapse into routine; more fundamentally, one may forget (or may never have learned) that the essence of Shabbos is a figure/ground relationship in which the desired shape stands out in salient relief precisely by not applying pressure to it. This is a stillness that can only be discerned with the greatest care and delicacy, in the innermost recesses of one's being. While *oneg* (delight/pleasure) is a core feature of Shabbos, going back to the Bible – "if you proclaim Shabbos as delight" (Is. 58:13) – our sacred texts make it clear that the pleasure is not primarily gustatory but spiritual, derived

---

2. We may think of this "sign" as writing by relief – that is, the creation of a contoured form by etching the surrounding material and allowing the desired shape to emerge by contrasting projection.

from the practices – song, study, joyous prayer, family and communal bonding, walking unhurriedly, looking appreciatively without judging, a posture of openness, humility, and attentive listening to the resonances of silence.[3] When it comes to enjoyment of physical delights, think of others more than yourself. Seek ways to provide for others who may not have the material resources or social network to celebrate Shabbos fully.[4]

Shabbos can transform the world, but first Shabbos must transform you. The deeper your Shabbos, the more standing you will have to effect the change you want to see. Others will notice your conviction, your commitment, your gentle buoyancy. Your Shabbos will truly be inspirational and desirable, and you will have the voice and the vision to make a positive contribution to the world – during the six workdays as well as on Shabbos.

One never arrives at the ultimate Shabbos; if you are doing Shabbos at all, you realize that each one is a preparation for the next, in a never-ending quest for more gentle, subtle, delicate places of the heart and soul. The Absolute – the sacred Nothing from which Plenitude emerges – can never be possessed, only desired and sensed in the softest whisper.

If you are new to Shabbos, the novelty is surely an advantage. The true connoisseur of music will be rightly envious of the person hearing Beethoven's Fifth Symphony for the first time – yearning for those freshly opened ears. In just that way, Shabbos newcomers bring much-needed sensory and spiritual keenness to possibly jaded Shabbos tables and formulaic recitations.

While Shabbos is the quintessential Jewish practice, the redemptive Shabbos vision embraces the entire world. Shabbos wishes to include all people in its blessing, sanctity, and six/one rhythm. Shabbos calls the whole world to ethical action, noble speech, benevolent thoughts, horizons beyond the self, care for the earth. Most of all,

---

3. See Radak on Isaiah 58:14: *Vehataanug al Hashem hu taanug hanefesh*, "The 'pleasure' is spiritual pleasure."

4. For the intimate connection between social justice and Shabbos, see Isaiah 56:1–2; 58:6–14. Following this tradition, later sources underscore the primacy of inclusiveness and ethical sensitivity in the celebration of festive days. See Maimonides, *Mishneh Torah, Hilkhot Yom Tov* 6:18; *Hilkhot Megilla* 2:17.

Shabbos calls gently and urgently for *shalom*. This is the message we all need to hear and take to heart, now more than ever.

CLOSING THOUGHTS: SHABBOS-CONSCIOUSNESS

- The highest goal deserves top priority. When choosing a place to live, think of Shabbos first.

- Sacred time is not contingent. Call a halt to business as usual.

- Go beyond "day of rest." Overcome restlessness, check the urge to accumulate, allow Shabbos to let you *rest assured*.

- Join the circle of blessing and sanctity. Move beyond self-cultivation to self-transcendence.

- Drop your burden. Rejoice in free hands and open heart.

- Cultivate a different way of inhabiting the world: *appreciation without grasping, perceiving without attempting to incorporate into the self.*

- Find place and linger intently.

- Arrive in time for Shabbos!

- Come for Shabbos!

Acknowledgments

In writing this book I consulted with family, friends, and colleagues on matters large and small. Pride of place goes to my wife, Lauri, my confidant, advisor, and first reader. Lauri, I cannot thank you enough for your assistance in finding the right direction at crucial moments. My daughters and sons-in-law gave essential guidance at a delicate early stage. Adina and Ariel, with great wisdom, clarity, and gentle persistence, explained why the book needed to have the voice it now has, my voice. Sara Henna and David, Esti and Elisha, read major sections and helped me make crucial decisions.

As the book progressed, I shared early drafts with trusted friends. Amy Bernstein sat with me patiently for many long editing sessions and illumined fine points of grammar as well as matters of overall structure; Amy's writerly skills were essential. Efraim Krug was equally devoted and perceptive, asking what I wanted to say and pushing me to say it better.

Rabbi Arthur Green read the entire manuscript and, with his enormous fund of knowledge and wisdom, as well as open-heartedness, gave essential advice on bringing major themes into sharper focus. Rabbi Joseph Polak grasped the significance of the book in a deep way and wrote a warm and gracious appreciation. Other family members, friends, and colleagues who read the manuscript in whole or in part and/or discussed and clarified issues with me include Rabbi Alon Goshen Gottstein, Rabbi Yaakov Halberstam, Dr. Jesse

Hefter, Jim Nuzzo, Dr. Joel Rosenberg, Rabbi Meir Sendor, Rabbi Jordan Shuster, Avinoam Stillman, and Janet Zimmern.

The early stages of my writing were supported by Congregation Kehilath Jacob in Manhattan, the Carlebach shul. I wish to thank Rabbi Naftali Citron, Shy Yellin, Dr. Leon and Dr. Karen Sutton (Leon also read the entire manuscript in an early draft and offered valuable suggestions), and Libby Dreisinger.

Special thanks go to my dear friend Dr. Marc Winer, who facilitated a publishing subvention from Congregation Ahabat Shalom of Lynn, Massachusetts. I am grateful to Congregation Ahabat Shalom for providing me with this opportunity. Rabbi Samuel Zaitchik, Ahabat Shalom's rabbi for fifty years, mentored me with his noble wisdom and generosity of spirit, serving as a model of compassion and sacred reverence.

The staff at Koren Publishers Jerusalem is blessed with a rare combination of professionalism, wise discernment, and commitment to the highest Torah values. My gratitude goes to Rabbi Reuven Ziegler, Ita Olesker, Aryeh Grossman, Meira Mintz, Debbie Ismailoff, and Tani Bayer for bringing this work to fruition.

Maggid Books
The best of contemporary Jewish thought from
Koren Publishers Jerusalem Ltd.